EMBODYINGHEBREWCULTURE

EMBODYING
HEBREW

Wayne State University Press | *Detroit*

CULTURE

AESTHETICS, ATHLETICS,
AND DANCE
IN THE JEWISH COMMUNITY
OF MANDATE PALESTINE

Nina S. Spiegel

ISBN 978-0-8143-4803-1 (paperback)

The Library of Congress has cataloged the cloth edition as follows:
Spiegel, Nina S.
Embodying Hebrew culture : aesthetics, athletics, and dance in the Jewish community of mandate Palestine / Nina S. Spiegel.
pages cm
Includes bibliographical references and index.
ISBN 978-0-8143-3636-6 (cloth : alk. paper) — ISBN 978-0-8143-3637-3 (ebook)
 1. Jewish athletes—Palestine—History—20th century. 2. Jewish dance—Palestine—History—20th century. 3. Jews—Palestine—Social life and customs—20th century. 4. Great Britain. Palestine Royal Commission—History—20th century. 5. Palestine—History—1918–1948. I. Title.
GV709.6.S73 2013
796.089'924—dc23
2012047996

Publication of this book was made possible through the generosity of the Bertha M. and Hyman Herman Endowed Memorial Fund.

Parts of chapter 3 were first published in *Jewish Folklore and Ethnology Review* (2000) and in *Seeing Israeli and Jewish Dance,* edited by Judith Brin Ingber and published by Wayne State University Press (Detroit, 2011).

Parts of chapter 4 were first published in *Jewish Cultural Studies,* v. 3, *Revisioning Ritual: Jewish Traditions in Transition,* edited by Simon J. Bronner and published for the American Folklore Society by the Littman Library of Jewish Civilization (Oxford, 2011).

Cover photographs: Folk dancing during the 1947 Dalia Festival. By Zoltan Kluger.
(Israeli Government Press Office)
Cover and interior design by Charlie Sharp, Sharp Des!gns
Typeset by Maya Whelan
Composed in Culluna and Scout

To my parents,
Fredelle and Steven

Contents

ix Acknowledgments

1 INTRODUCTION: Embodying Hebrew Culture

21 **1** Searching for Hebrew Beauty: The Queen Esther Competitions, 1926–1929

57 **2** Promoting Sport: The First Maccabiah Games, 1932

97 **3** Producing Theatrical Dance: The National Dance Competition, 1937

133 **4** Creating National Folk Dance: The Dalia Dance Festivals, 1944 and 1947

175 CONCLUSION: The Enduring Legacy

187 Notes

223 Bibliography

245 Index

Acknowledgments

I have researched and developed this book over many years and a variety of locations and am grateful to numerous people and institutions.

The seeds of this project were planted while I was an undergraduate at Brown University. I owe a great debt to Calvin Goldscheider, who first encouraged me to embark on this path and has remained a trusted adviser ever since. He recommended that I pursue graduate studies on this topic and has steadfastly supported my work and offered mentorship and guidance at every juncture along the way. I am also deeply grateful to my other professors at Brown, especially Vicki Caron, Susan Slyomovics, and Julie Strandberg. The generous support of a Dorot Fellowship enabled me to travel to Israel for research. Fusion Dance Company, Brown's student-run performing dance troupe, where I was first a member and later a co-director, taught me experientially, through the diverse dance genres and backgrounds of company members, the connections between movement, the body, and culture. These perspectives have profoundly shaped my research.

The early stages of the book developed during my doctoral training in history at Stanford University. My advisers, Steven J. Zipperstein, Aron Rodrigue, Janice Ross, and Mary Louise Roberts, offered a rich environment and intellectual rigor in which to pursue interdisciplinary work. I am grateful that Steven Zipperstein was ready to take on an unconventional topic in the field and that Janice Ross was prepared to serve as my dance history adviser outside the history department; they provided instrumental approaches and analyses. I also owe a great debt to another of my professors, Hanna Berman, who offered essential advice, guidance, and friendship.

My peers at Stanford fostered a collegial and stimulating environment, and I especially benefited from conversations with Michelle Campos, Cecile Kuznitz, Elizabeth Lazaroff, and Tony Michaels. Zachary M. Baker, Reinhard Family Curator of Judaica and Hebraica Collections at Stanford, has been particularly helpful over the years. While at Stanford, I received generous support from the Department of History, the Andrew W. Mellon Foundation, the Program in Jewish Studies Newhouse Foundation Grant, and the Reinhard Graduate Fellowship in Jewish Studies.

When I was conducting research in Israel, I received valuable advice from Eli Shaltiel and Carmit Gai-Shaltiel, Nili Aryeh-Sapir, Yosef Ginat, Aliza Shenhar, and Shifra Shonman. Shmuel Regulant was particularly helpful and introduced me to Zila Agadati, who gave me access to her personal collection. Shmulik Shtick facilitated a meeting with Devorah Bertonov and connected me to Israeli folk dancers. I am deeply appreciative of the hospitality of Sharon Ashley, the Klein family, and the Zelniker family. Carolin Aronis kindly accessed documents for me at an important moment when I was out of the country.

I appreciate the assistance from all the archivists at the multitude of collections and sites I investigated in Israel. I especially thank Nellie Varzarevsky at the Tel Aviv–Jaffa Municipality Archives; Victoria Khodorkovsky, Head Librarian of the Dance Library of Israel; the late Radu Klaper, former director of the Dance Library of Israel; Rony Dror, Archive Director of the Joseph Yekutieli Maccabi Sports Archive; and Hillel Tryster, former director of the Steven Spielberg Jewish Film Archive.

I am grateful to all those who granted me interviews. Yardena Cohen graciously spent extensive time with me, guiding me through her experiences, philosophy, and choreography. Ayalah Goren-Kadman has served as an invaluable resource, offering ongoing interviews, Israeli folk dance instruction, insightful comments, and treasured advice.

Along the way, I received invaluable support from a variety of institutions. The Lucius N. Littauer Foundation offered assistance in the initial stages of writing. The Schusterman Teaching Fellowship at American University provided an important time to develop my ideas. I greatly appreciate the mentorship and astute advice I received from Pamela S. Nadell. I am also deeply grateful to the Foundation for Jewish Culture, especially Elise Bernhardt, Director, and Paul Zakrzewski, Program Officer and Director of the Jewish Studies Expansion Program, who have offered important guidance and served as significant advocates of my work. The Jewish Studies Expansion Program provided an outstanding supportive and collegial environment and served as an invaluable resource. I am also indebted to the Hadassah-Brandeis Institute and Shulamit Reinharz for my fellowship as Scholar-in-Residence. I am thankful to my research seminar colleagues there, Tamar Barzel and Michelle Gewurtz, for their insights, analytical perspectives, and friendship.

Over the years, many scholars have offered important advice. I have valued conversations with Carolin Aronis, Adriana Brodsky, and Judah Cohen. Yael Warshel gave especially significant and perceptive suggestions. My colleagues at the University of Maryland provided valuable critiques, especially Marsha Rozenblit and Eric Zakim. Baruch Link kindly offered important suggestions at an essential moment. Grace Cohen Grossman introduced me to the discipline of Jewish art history and mentored me in curatorial practices, all of which proved essential in working with visual materials for this book.

I have benefited immensely from the support and advice of Michael Berenbaum, Linda J. Borish, David N. Myers, and Kenneth W. Stein, who have all offered treasured guidance and generously given their time and insights. Judith Brin Ingber has provided indispensable critiques and continues to serve as a dedicated resource and mentor. Barbara Kirshenblatt-Gimblett has been a long-time supporter of my work and a beacon to the field. I am tremendously grateful for her ongoing sage advice, especially at several critical junctures.

My colleagues in the Harold Schnitzer Family Program in Judaic Studies at Portland State University, Natan Meir, Loren Spielman, and Michael Weingrad, have provided astute counsel in the final stages of the completion of the manuscript. I appreciate the generosity of the Program for a subvention grant from the Lorry I. Lokey Endowed Fund for Israel Scholarship toward the cost of printing the images in the volume.

I thank all of the archives and personal collections that allowed me to use images from their collections. I am especially grateful to Gaby Aldor; Rony Dror, Archive Director of the Joseph Yekutieli Maccabi Archive; Ayalah Goren-Kadman; Vivienne Silver-Brody; Ruth Eshel; Judith Brin Ingber; Irit Magal-Meltzer and Noam Ordan, daughter and grandson, respectively, of Yardena Cohen; Victoria Khodorkovsky, Head Librarian of the Dance Library of Israel; Diana Berner and Tali Lanir, daughter and granddaughter, respectively, of Riquetta Chelouche Gobernik; Violet Radnofsky, Littauer Hebraica Librarian at Harvard University; Robin Zalben, Cataloger and Librarian, and Deborah Steinmetz, Director, of the Steven Spielberg Jewish Film Archive; Einat Anker, of the Israeli Government Press Office; and Jamie Nathans and Rachel Misrati, of the Jewish National and University Library. Rebecca DeWolf assisted in the early stages of photo research. Michelle Gewurtz served as a valuable adviser, offering her insightful curatorial lens on the photo selection.

I appreciate the care that Wayne State University Press has provided for the manuscript. Kathryn Wildfong, editor-in-chief at the Press, has been a major source of support and encouragement. I also thank Kristin Harpster, Kristina Stonehill, Maya Whelan, and Emily Nowak at the Press, as well as freelance copyeditor Mimi Braverman. The manuscript benefited from the insightful comments of the anonymous reviewers. I also thank one of them for the second half of the book's title.

I am blessed with wonderful friends and family to whom I am tremendously grateful. A heartfelt thanks to Mira, Ariella, Talia, and Rami Cohen; Adina Batnitzky, Avi and Lilia Spiegel. My grandmother, Claire Spiegel, of blessed memory, loved history and encouraged my intellectual pursuits. To my parents, Fredelle and Steven, I dedicate the book with love and gratitude.

INTRODUCTION

Embodying Hebrew Culture

When soon to be prime minister David Ben-Gurion proclaimed the establishment of the State of Israel on May 14, 1948, the Jewish community there spontaneously flocked to the streets en masse and celebrated by dancing the hora, a fast-paced communal circle dance that had become a quintessential marker of a new Jewish society. This image, in photographs and film footage, became an iconic symbol of that moment and has remained a significant component of Independence Day celebrations in contemporary Israel (Figure 1).[1]

The mass hora dancing in the streets in May 1948 was the culmination of a process of inculcating an embodied Hebrew public culture. How was the public, collective robust dancing in the streets related to the process of forming a political state?

In this book I tell the story of how an embodied public culture developed, revealing how the Jewish community in Palestine, known as the Yishuv (settlement), created a national public culture during the British Mandate era.[2] In the process I uncover how that culture was intentionally and distinctively physical.

In this study I also demonstrate that a Hebrew national public culture crystallized during the British Mandate era.[3] After some 400 years of Ottoman rule, Palestine shifted to British control in the aftermath of World War I. From their conquest in 1917 during World War I until the establishment of the State of Israel in 1948, the British controlled the territory of Palestine; they were granted a mandate, ratified in 1922, by the newly formed League of Nations. During the Mandate era, the Jewish community generated the base for what would later become the State of Israel. The

Figure 1. Crowds dancing the hora in the streets of Jerusalem in celebration of the declaration of the establishment of the State of Israel, 1948. Photo courtesy of Ayalah Goren-Kadman.

social, political, religious, and cultural forms that developed in this period served as the underpinnings of the Zionist state.

Emerging as a movement at the end of the nineteenth century, Zionism, one form of Jewish nationalism, aimed to create a revolution in modern Jewish life. Jews who moved to Palestine to fashion a novel society sought to construct a new culture and to develop innovative forms of expression in a multitude of arenas, such as language, literature, and the visual and performing arts. All these creations were deemed Hebrew culture, in order to link the new society to the ancient Hebrews and to separate itself from Diaspora Jewish life—communities living outside the ancient Land of Israel, which were referred to as *galut*, *golah*, or the Diaspora, denoting an exilic existence. In Mandate Palestine the Jews modernized the Hebrew language and developed Hebrew literature, Hebrew music, Hebrew dance, Hebrew theater, and Hebrew art.

One central arena of cultural creation in the Mandate era—and one of the pivotal innovations of Zionism—was the building of a Hebrew national public culture. The development of a public culture is significant because Jews had arrived in Palestine from all parts of the world, with different languages and cultural backgrounds and a range of attitudes toward and approaches to Judaism, the religion of the Jews. Many discovered that they had little in common with one another. A Jewish national public culture, one that would satisfy a variety of Jewish interpretations, was deemed necessary to unify the Jews of Palestine into a national community.[4]

As with many nationalist projects of the time, the public arena and public events, such as festivals, performances, and celebrations, played a significant role. Theodor Herzl, the leader of political Zionism, understood the importance of festivals from a secular and national vantage point rather than from a religious view and maintained an emphasis on the public display of Zionism.[5] Cultural displays were already prevalent at the Zionist Congresses held in Europe.[6] The Yishuv adopted notions of festivals from Western and Central European nationalism, where, as George Mosse has shown, they formed critical components of nationalist endeavors, fulfilling the function of both consolidating a national community and producing an "aestheticization of politics."[7] They also implemented concepts from Russia, where festivals served an important purpose, especially during the great changes in the 1920s and 1930s.[8]

Central to the Zionist concept was the notion of transformation: Zionists aspired to create a "new Jew," aiming to alter how Jews acted, thought, spoke—and looked. Although the emphasis or the path to revitalization was different for various Zionist strains, the groups agreed on the importance of building a new Jewish physique; they sought to change the image of the Jewish people from a "people of the book" to an image that valued the corporeal.

Some scholars have considered how the Hebrew national public culture developed and emerged, but the centrality of the culture's corporeal character has been either overlooked or underestimated.[9]

As demonstrated in several studies of Zionist discourse in Europe, creating a "new Jewish body" was a central goal of the Zionist endeavor.[10] Yet the process through which this goal was attained in the Jewish community in Palestine has been largely disregarded. Zionist theorists developed their ideologies and Zionist Congresses held in Europe debated these views, but Jews who moved to Palestine to start a new life applied these ideas in their daily lives and practices.[11]

Building a Hebrew national public culture that was to be physical was a fundamental goal and characteristic of the emerging society. It was also one of the key innovations of Zionism: embedding a new value—the importance of the corporeal—into national Jewish life. This physical character of the national public culture remains a significant feature of contemporary Israeli culture.

As with many national projects, the public arena was an important site for gathering together and "negotiating shared meaning."[12] By showing the ways in which Hebrew national public culture was invented and embodied, in this book I demonstrate how political and social issues were embedded in the new society. The process of instilling the value of the corporeal thus served as a canvas for viewing national concerns, debates, and dilemmas, because the public arena was a place to reflect, wrestle with, and at times resolve social and political concerns.

Moreover, in this book I uncover central tensions and their outcomes in the Mandate era, presenting a Hebrew cultural aesthetics. These aesthetics, solidified in the British Mandate period, have had a lasting effect on contemporary Israeli society and provide a dynamic framework for interpreting present-day Israeli culture. Indeed, the examination of the embodiment of Hebrew culture serves as a window into the defining characteristics and tensions of the new Hebrew ethos and the sense of being Hebrew—and later Israeli—that has continued to the present day.

Consciously Creating Culture: National Events and Their Legacy

Four significant events in the development of a national public culture during the Mandate era form the basis of this study: (1) the beauty competitions for Queen Esther in conjunction with the Purim carnivals in Tel Aviv from 1926 to 1929; (2) the first Maccabiah Games or "Jewish Olympics" in Tel Aviv in 1932; (3) the National Dance Competition for theatrical dance in Tel Aviv in 1937; and (4) the Dalia Folk Dance Festivals at Kibbutz Dalia in 1944 and 1947.

Each of these events was pivotal in framing and solidifying a Hebrew national public culture during the Mandate era, and each one demonstrates how the value of the corporeal was inscribed. They also all connect to the development of specific forms: the creation of new holiday celebrations stemming from Judaism, the fostering of beauty contests, the importance of sports, and the development of theatrical and folk dance. The emphasis on fostering agility, grace, beauty, strength, and fitness is a central innovation of Zionism that has remained underexplored.

Although a variety of festivals took place during this period, these four events, from the first in 1926 to the last in 1947, span the full range of the British Mandate. Together they demonstrate the nexus between nationalism and gender, sports, dance, and beauty. Several of the activities were important attractions for tourists from around the world. Many of them—or the forms they consolidated—were exported to the Jewish Diaspora as markers of Hebrew culture, and, fulfilling one aspect of Zionist cultural ideologist Ahad Ha'am's vision, they asserted the Yishuv as the center of Jewish culture around the world. The festivities have had a lasting effect on contemporary Israeli society not only through the events themselves but also through the forms they fostered and developed.

By joining these events, which took place in both the urban and rural arenas, I show how the built environment, both urban and rural, formed a stage for cultural production. The first three events took place in Tel Aviv, demonstrating how the urban arena developed, how culture and the city grew side by side, and how the city served as an arena for cultural creation.[13] Established as a garden suburb of Jaffa in 1909, Tel Aviv became the dynamic cultural and economic center of the Yishuv during the Mandate period. The last example in this book took place on a kibbutz, a collective agricultural settlement, where all aspects of life were shared, including work, finances, eating, and child rearing. The kibbutz is the best known institution of socialist Zionism,[14] an ideology that emphasized the collective and called for an ascetic and simple lifestyle.[15] It also promoted a myth of gender equality, proclaiming that women and men were to be treated alike in the new society, although that was not the reality.[16] By looking at the city and the kibbutz together, I show that public culture—and the body—was fostered in both locations. Moreover, because the Yishuv was small, an interrelationship in cultural development between city and kibbutz often arose; several urban dwellers created events and activities on kibbutzim, and some had spent time living in agricultural settlements. At the same time, several kibbutz members and leaders participated in cultural activities in Tel Aviv.[17]

Each of the events is an interesting and important story of the building of Hebrew public culture. Most of the activities discussed here have not been extensively examined: They have either been left out of the scholarly conversation entirely or have been addressed only briefly in other works.[18] Thus writing about these events, which have stood at the margins of Yishuv history, and how they developed, materialized, and shaped Hebrew culture, is significant in itself. Yet precisely by analyzing these diverse activities together in one study and showing how the culture came to be embodied, I uncover the process, product, and aesthetics of Hebrew culture.

The beauty competitions for Queen Esther in Tel Aviv were an important component of the Zionist transformation of the Purim holiday, a minor and joyous festival in the traditional Jewish calendar. From 1926 to 1929 an elite evening gala in Tel Aviv was the scene of a beauty competition held about one month before the Purim holiday. The winner of this competition was crowned Queen Esther, the heroine of the Purim story, and she appeared at the annual Purim ball and, beginning in 1928, led the carnival procession. The Purim carnivals, and Queen Esther's participation in them, were a central activity in Yishuv life. Tourists traveled from all over Palestine as well as from all over the world to participate in the festivities.

Although the competitions themselves were short-lived, the role of Queen Esther had a lasting effect on the Yishuv and the Diaspora. Because the Purim carnivals promoted tourism from within and outside Palestine,[19] the chosen Queen Esther became a symbol of the budding society. And the custom spread: Queen Esthers were selected all over the world, and they traveled to Tel Aviv to appear in the Purim parades. In fact, the custom lasted longer in the Diaspora than in Palestine.[20] Thus, already in the 1920s, the Yishuv had developed an important new cultural symbol that was exported and became widespread.

In contemporary Tel Aviv annual Purim celebrations still take place, but they have not retained as large and central a role as in the Mandate period, with the exception perhaps of the 1950s, when they gained the greatest prevalence in the statehood era. Although beauty competitions take place in present-day Israel, they are not connected to Jewish tradition. The Miss Israel or Beauty Queen contest has been held annually since 1950, but it is not associated with Purim or Queen Esther.[21] Nevertheless, the valorization of beauty plays a significant role in contemporary Israeli society through the media and fashion industry.

The first Maccabiah Games, a nine-day sports festival in Tel Aviv held from March 29 to April 6, 1932, was a Jewish Olympics. Directly influenced by European culture, the games were modeled after the modern Olympics first staged in Athens in 1896. They included the usual diversity of Olympic sports competitions for men and women, and Jewish athletes from twenty-seven nations participated in the first Jewish international athletic games. The event aimed to exhibit the achievements of the Jewish community in Palestine and to promote and solidify the Yishuv as the center of Hebrew culture. The Maccabiah Games linked Jewish communities around the world through sports while establishing the Yishuv as the center and promoting Zionism. Like the Purim carnivals, the Maccabiah Games also promoted tourism.

The Maccabiah Games still take place in present-day Israel. As of 2009, eighteen Maccabiah Games have been held. They continue to serve as an important symbol of Jewish unity and strength through athletics. Unlike the Olympic Games, all Maccabiah Games take place in Israel, continuing the tradition established during the Yishuv era.

The National Dance Competition of 1937, a contest between trained choreographers, sought to identify the most original Hebrew theatrical or concert dance. Convening at Mugrabi Hall in Tel Aviv, the competition aimed to foster the creation and dissemination of this high art form. Several dancers presented their works, and the audience selected the winners. This event solidified a space for concert dance in the Yishuv; the victors were seen as representatives of the new Hebrew dance. Following the event the prizewinners performed in Europe, becoming symbols of Hebrew concert dance.

Although the 1937 National Dance Competition was a one-time event, the aim of fostering Israeli theatrical dance was achieved. Contemporary Israeli society features numerous large dance companies, especially for a small country, as well as a growing number of independent choreographers. In 2009 the Choreographers Association, established in the 1990s, had fifty-four members, a vast growth from its initial four constituents.²² In 1988 the Suzanne Dellal Center for Dance and Theater in Tel Aviv arose to promote performances and to serve as a home for contemporary dance. It houses the renowned Batsheva Dance Company, founded in 1964, and the Inbal Dance Company, established in 1949.

The final events in this book took place at Kibbutz Dalia in the Jezreel Valley. The Dalia Festivals in 1944 and 1947 aspired to develop and foster a national folk dance. At the first festival dancers and onlookers arrived from all over the Yishuv to participate in the celebration and to share in what would prove to be a defining moment in the creation of Israeli folk dance.²³ By nationalizing and institutionalizing the Israeli folk dance movement, the festival was a watershed event that solidified a space for folk dance in the Yishuv. Three years later, after extensive dance activity, another festival took place at the kibbutz.

The Dalia Festivals continued after statehood with three additional folk dance festivals at the kibbutz in 1951, 1958, and 1968. These events were succeeded by the annual Karmiel Dance Festival. Held in the Galilee development town of Karmiel, this event began in 1988 in celebration of the fortieth anniversary of the establishment of the state.²⁴ In addition, the Dalia Festival concept spread to the Diaspora; many Jewish summer camps in the United States host "Dalia Dance evenings" and sports associations in Argentina also present "Dalia" programs.

Not only did the festival itself have a lasting impact, but the goal to develop an Israeli folk dance form was also achieved and became widespread. Folk dance, especially the hora, came to be linked to tourism to Palestine and was often a noted feature of visitors' experiences during their stay.²⁵ Already by the 1940s Israeli folk dances were exported and viewed as significant markers of the new Jew.²⁶ They became an important link between Diaspora Jewish communities and Jewish life in the Yishuv and later Israel.

In contemporary Israel the repertoire of Israeli folk dances is vast and still growing, and this form appears around the world at workshops, camps, weekly dance sessions, festivals, and celebrations. Folk dance has become an important symbol of Israeli identity and one of the most significant and successful exports of Israeli culture around the world.²⁷

A Culture of Debate: Societal Tensions and Hebrew Aesthetics

An analysis of these four events—the Queen Esther beauty competitions, the first Maccabiah Games, the 1937 National Dance Competition, and the Dalia Festivals—uncovers the process of creating a public culture in the Yishuv. Every aspect of the new public culture was self-consciously examined and viewed as critical, pressing, and urgent. Members of the Yishuv believed that building a national public culture was central to developing a modern nation, and thus they viewed all cultural developments with meaning.

Indeed, the British Mandate era was a period in which ideology inculcated daily life.[28] Reflecting on her childhood in British Mandate Palestine, the journalist Ruth Jordan said in her memoirs, "Most of the people I knew as a child were not involved with politics; yet, because their very being in Palestine was a fulfillment of an ideal, everything they did or said transcended the personal and took on a national significance."[29] Jordan's words attest to the way in which all aspects of daily life in this period were considered important, ideological, and national.

Cutting across a range of diverse arenas, disciplines, and conversations, the public events discussed in this book were not specifically related. Yet by placing these disparate activities together and drawing from the discipline of performance studies,[30] I show how different arenas actually were interconnected and demonstrate how the Jewish community generated a culture of debate. Contestation was a significant component of each of these activities and a central quality of Yishuv life. Nearly every aspect of these proceedings was openly discussed and disputed; nothing was taken for granted or left unexamined. Indeed, not only was debate a defining characteristic of Hebrew culture in the Mandate period, but it has also remained a central feature of contemporary Israeli society.

Through analyzing the nature and content of the debates over these activities, I uncover that they each grappled with parallel and overlapping issues, illustrating how the Yishuv wrestled with national dilemmas and how it attempted to resolve them. In showing how, through the project of embodiment, the same questions appeared and were repeatedly addressed in events as different as sports, dance, and beauty contests, I present vital goals and tensions. Some tensions remained; others were resolved to varying degrees, resulting in the formation of cultural aesthetics.

An Undisputed Goal: The Renaissance of the Body and the Aesthetic of Toughness

The importance placed on recreating the Jewish body stemmed from European circles and was espoused in particular by the ideologist Max Nordau.[31] In 1898, when Nordau called for the formation of a *Muskeljudentum*, a muscle Jewry, at the Second Zionist Congress in Basel, he proclaimed:

> We must again create a strong, muscular Judaism. . . .
> We shall renew our youth in our old age, and with broad chest, strong limbs and

valiant gaze—we shall be warriors. For us Jews sport has a great educational significance. It needs to bring about the health not only of the body, but also of the spirit.[32]

Nordau believed that in order for Jews to fully recreate themselves, they needed to
become physically strong. This notion was influenced by both European national
movements that aimed to create a "new man" based on ancient Greek ideals[33] and
the German Physical Culture Movement that began in the early nineteenth century.[34]

The cultivation of the body held a central place in German culture. The Turnen,
or German gymnastic movement, played a significant role in connecting the
nurturing of the body to the nurturing of the nation, and the gymnastic clubs
served as important sites advocating nationalism.[35] Beyond gymnastics the German Korperkulture, or body culture movement, focused on a variety of areas of
physical development. The goal in all these arenas—gymnastics, physical education,
bodybuilding—was to generate a well-adjusted body that would epitomize the
characteristics of "physical beauty, harmony, symmetry, and perfection."[36]

Nordau adopted these concepts. A healthy body came to be intimately linked
to a healthy spirit and a healthy nation.[37] The discourse of muscle Judaism, as Todd
Presner shows, was integrally connected to a range of German ideologies at the time,
including discussions on regeneration, health, aesthetics, and nationalism.[38] Believing that the Jewish body had been ruined in the ghettoes of Europe, Nordau called
for its renewal.[39] Numerous Jewish gymnastic associations emerged, with almost
thirty in Central Europe alone by 1903.[40] Gymnastics was intended to cultivate both
the body and "a sense of nationality," and these features were viewed as "important
for the regeneration of the Jewish people as a whole."[41]

Zionists aimed to create a physique that represented the opposite of their view
of the Diaspora Jewish body. Instead of the bent-over, pale, feminized Jewish body,
stereotyped in European culture, this renewed Jew would be brawny and muscular
(Figure 2).[42] A critical objective of this construction was, in Judith Butler's terms,
to "perform" a male identity and promote a masculine image.[43] This emphasis on
masculinity remained part of not only the gymnastics groups in Europe but also
the Jewish and later Zionist youth movements in Europe and Palestine.[44]

In the Yishuv developing and presenting this new Jewish body was a central
component of the national aim to revitalize Jewish life and alter the Jewish image.
Physical activities were nurtured and encouraged and viewed as part and parcel of
the goal. There were no tensions surrounding this objective: All strands of Zionism
agreed on the need for strength and toughness.[45]

The significance of the cultivation of the body was even advocated by the
important theorist and leader of religious Zionism Rabbi Abraham Isaac Kook,

Figure 2. Jewish National Fund Poster, New York, 1930s. This image of a muscular and masculine worker encapsulates the aesthetic of toughness. Courtesy of the Library of the Jewish Theological Seminary.

Although Kook disagreed with secular Zionists on numerous issues, he shared this goal.

> The claim of our flesh is great. We require a healthy body. . . . We have neglected healthy and physical prowess, forgetting that our flesh is as sacred as our spirit. . . . Our return will succeed only if it will be marked, along with its spiritual glory, by a physical return which will create healthy flesh and blood, strong and well-formed bodies, and a fiery spirit encased in powerful muscles.[46]

The Yishuv also drew influence from trends in interwar Europe, where, following the devastation of World War I, a great emphasis on the building of the body beautiful developed, especially an increased stress on physical culture and the ideal of the strong male, not only in Germany but also in Britain and France in particular.[47] The muscular Christianity movement also emerged in the United States.[48]

The events discussed in this book show how the goal of fostering the body was applied in the Yishuv. The aesthetic of toughness, a term borrowed from Jan Nederveen Pieterse,[49] refers to the cultivation of a strong, tough, masculine body; it represents the negation of the Diaspora and the creation of the new Jew.[50] It emphasizes bodies that appear masculine, tough, free, young, and healthy—bodies that would be up to the task of building a modern nation and would be appropriate for the formation of the new Jew.

Inventing Traditions: Old Versus New and Religious Versus Secular

Despite their different features, times, and places, the four events addressed in this book grappled with essentially the same dilemma: how to fashion an "authentic" Hebrew culture. The Jewish community in Palestine, in Eric Hobsbawm's term, "invented tradition"; they were seeking to develop a culture that stood rooted in the Jewish past and would therefore be viewed as authentic, yet they simultaneously aimed to separate from the past and produce new customs. This quest for authenticity presents the paradox of invented traditions, because a new, constructed culture cannot simultaneously be old.[51]

As in other national movements, Zionists embraced both old and new aspects simultaneously. For instance, following the title of Theodor Herzl's well-known utopian novel, *Altneuland*, Yishuv leaders emphasized that they were building a new culture in an old land, as one Zionist poster proclaimed: "A Nation Reborn on Its Ancestral Soil" (see Figure 2).[52] In a similar vein, when modernizing the Hebrew language, Zionists stressed the "rebirth" of an "ancient" tongue. The burgeoning city of Tel Aviv took its name from this dichotomy, stemming from Nahum Sokolow's

Hebrew translation of Herzl's novel: "Tel," literally "hill" but with an additional meaning of an ancient site; and "Aviv," meaning "spring" or "renewal." The "new" Jew, who was to be fundamentally different from the "old" Diaspora Jew, was referred to as a new Hebrew in order to connect to the ancient Hebrews in the ancient land.[53]

Each of the events in this book wrestled with the tension between old and new. In all four cases the old-new dichotomy was acknowledged and embraced as the founders sought to create a novel society connected to its ancient roots. This tension—and the desire to be both ancient and modern simultaneously—has remained a feature of contemporary Israeli society.

The cases show how the founders tackled the process of inventing traditions, with four examples of new creations. These particular events offer a representative sample of different models of cultural construction: The beauty competitions for Queen Esther during Purim illustrate the refashioning of a Jewish holiday; the Maccabiah Games, stemming from the modern European Olympics, show the transformation of a Europe-based event; the National Dance Competition focuses on the formation of high culture; and the Dalia Festivals exemplify the production of folk culture.

Unfolding in an especially fervent and productive cultural milieu, these activities stood as integral components of a multitude of new celebrations and public activities in the Mandate era. Attention to public festivals emerged in the Ottoman period, when the most popular public celebration, according to historian Arieh B. Saposnik, was the Passover fair in Rehovot from 1908 until the outbreak of World War I; these fairs featured sports, gymnastics, and music.[54] Although the process began before World War I, it consolidated during the Mandate period.

During these years a wide variety of public festivals took place on the kibbutzim and in the cities. They shared the goal of celebrating the Yishuv, sanctifying the new society, and demarcating major achievements. Some were related to the Zionists' lives and activities in Palestine; they celebrated different milestones and landmarks, including Lord Balfour's visit for the inauguration of Hebrew University in 1925 and anniversaries of the city of Tel Aviv in 1929 (twenty years) and 1934 (twenty-five years).[55] Several large public funerals materialized for influential people from different walks of life, including Zionist leader Chaim Arlosoroff, Hebrew writer Yosef Haim Brenner, and Zionist thinker Ahad Ha'am.[56]

The Yishuv also created new national holidays, such as Yom Tel Hai (Tel Hai Day), commemorating those who fought to defend Tel Hai, a settlement in the Galilee, from an Arab attack in 1920. This event became a central national myth, which endures into the contemporary era, and produced a slogan: "It is good to die for our country," a tailored version of the last words of Yosef Trumpeldor, the central hero.[57]

The arena that provoked the greatest controversy was the refashioning of holidays based on or linked to traditional Judaism. Connected to the dichotomy between old and new stood the clash between religious and secular, terms used in contemporary Israeli society to differentiate between two broad groups: Orthodox Jews of all types (the religious sector) and non-Orthodox or nonobservant Jews, many of whom maintain a connection to symbols and practices from Judaism but do not adhere strictly to Jewish law (the secular sector).[58] In the Yishuv secular Zionists, and in particular the dominant socialist Zionists, sought both to break from Jewish tradition and to maintain a link with and assert the Jewish past. For secular Jews, Judaism was a source for the new culture, but it was to be altered even as it was appropriated. Thus they created new festivities that were an integral part of the effort to find ways of celebrating Judaism that they found more appropriate and meaningful. Secular Zionists viewed their innovations as in keeping with and in the spirit of Judaism. Religious Jews considered these innovations an abomination of Judaism. From the religious perspective the notion of creating a culture that did not require the observance of Jewish religious law was anathema.[59]

As socialist Zionists transformed classic Jewish holidays and created new celebrations, they shifted the hierarchy of the traditional Jewish holiday calendar. Dominant holidays in traditional Judaism, such as Rosh Hashanah, the Jewish New Year, and Yom Kippur, the Day of Atonement, were "widely ignored."[60] Simultaneously, relatively minor festivals were assigned greater importance and became central, such as Hanukkah and Purim. Both of these holidays fitted well with socialist Zionist goals: Hanukkah was associated with a struggle for national independence, and Purim was connected to a struggle for freedom.[61] Purim, as will be shown, became especially prominent in the Yishuv.

Beyond reassigning the relative value of the holidays, socialist Zionists invented new ways of celebrating them, changing traditional symbols and rituals to fit with secular Zionist goals and ideals.[62] According to this Zionist vision, the Jews, through their own work, would build a new society. They would not wait for the Messiah to come or for God to intervene in history. Secular Zionists thus shifted the supreme power away from God and focused instead on the strength of the Jewish people.[63] Adopting concepts from European nationalism, they began to construct a civil religion whose authority would rest in the polity. In George Mosse's terms, nationalism, both in Europe and in Zionism, served as a form of civic religion.[64] This civil religion emerged in the Yishuv to sanctify the ideology and practice of Zionism. Later it came to sanctify the state.[65]

One major shift in the nature of the celebrations was the emphasis on the outdoors. Although religious holiday celebrations took place in the synagogue and at home, secular Zionist festivities were usually held in public places. Because Zionists aimed to project rootedness to the land, the physical landscape held significance, and a wide range of outdoor festivals transpired.[66] As is evident through the events discussed in this book (three of the four cases took place outdoors), the festivals inscribed themselves into the landscape, in both the urban and the rural environment.

Another shift was a change in focus of the meaning of the holiday. As in European nationalism, new myths were established and placed in a historic framework to sacralize the political.[67] Thus secular Zionists shifted the emphasis of holidays, often focusing on their agricultural components, particularly on the kibbutzim.[68] Festivals connected to agriculture held an especially central place, such as Tu b'Shevat, or Arbor Day, a minor holiday in the traditional Jewish calendar that fitted well with the Zionist project and became an important festival.[69] In addition, rural components of traditional Jewish festivals were emphasized, especially for the three ancient pilgrimage festivals of Sukkot (Festival of Booths), Pesach (Passover), and Shavuot (Pentecost).[70] Shavuot, with the celebration of the first fruits—Hag Ha-Bikkurim—was especially popular.

In addition to refashioning traditional Jewish holidays, the kibbutzim also created their own festivals—connected to ancient Jewish life—to celebrate their agrarian existence, such as the sheep-shearing festival and the festival of the vineyards.

Another aspect of the changing nature of Jewish rituals consisted of the participation of everyone in song and dance.[71] Pageants, which incorporated theater, song, and dance, were popular forms that developed on the kibbutzim, particularly for the three ancient pilgrimage festivals of Sukkot, Pesach, and Shavuot. Because, in traditional Judaism, attending the synagogue was the appropriate form of celebration, the pageants represented a break. They were secular celebrations that presented an alternative to religion-based practices. Yet they aimed to connect to Judaism by focusing on the biblical stories that formed the bases for these holidays, connecting themselves to the ancient Hebrews living on the land.

Secular Zionists viewed their innovations as appropriate. Religious Jews vehemently disagreed. As I will show, the controversies between these two sectors were great. In an emerging nation the decision of who would have the ultimate authority to resolve questions about Judaism in the public sphere was especially significant. The different approaches to Judaism continuously clashed, with varying visions of how the new society should look as well as how it should be structured.[72] A pattern developed during this period: In times of heated controversy the wishes of rabbinic leaders were granted by the socialist Zionist leaders of the Yishuv. Rather than succeeding in finding a comprehensive solution to the religious-secular split, the Yishuv did not generally address the matter, except when under duress, and even then on a case-by-case basis. In these instances of conflict secular Zionist leaders almost always granted authority to rabbinic leaders, because they aimed to mollify their protests and to keep them within the nation-building process.[73]

The tension between religious and secular remained unresolved in the Mandate period and stands as a source of ongoing conflict in contemporary Israeli society. The patterns created in the Yishuv in this era—aiming to avoid the matter and granting ultimate authority over the role of Judaism in the public sphere to rabbinic leaders—endure.

Creating New Forms: East Versus West and the Aesthetic of Fusion

In addition to creating new traditions, the events discussed in this book also represent the development of new forms, which unfolded in an especially fervent and productive cultural milieu in all arenas, including language, literature, high and low arts, and sports.

Although significant cultural developments took place before the British Mandate era, such as progress in modernizing and disseminating the Hebrew language, the founding of the Bezalel School of Arts and Crafts (now the Bezalel Academy of Art) in Jerusalem by Boris Schatz in 1906, and the establishment of the Institute for Jewish Song (known as the Institute for Jewish Music) by Abraham Zvi (Ben-Yehuda) Idelsohn in 1910,[74] Hebrew national public culture expanded and crystallized under the British Mandate.

During the Mandate era the Hebrew language was solidified as the center of the Jewish national enterprise; it was proclaimed one of the three official languages in Palestine alongside Arabic and English in 1922. Hebrew literature flourished, with its center moving from Europe to Palestine in this era.[75] Universities launched: Technion University fully opened in Haifa in 1924, and Hebrew University was inaugurated in Jerusalem in 1925.[76] A Hebrew press and radio evolved: The daily Hebrew newspaper *Ha'aretz* was established in 1919, the worker's daily newspaper *Davar* was founded in 1925, and the Palestine Broadcasting Service began operations in 1936.[77]

In addition, numerous arts institutions developed during the Mandate period. For instance, in drama, the Ohel Theater, the socialist workers theater, opened in 1925, and the Habima (The Stage), the Hebrew-speaking theater company that had been founded in Moscow in 1917 and later became the national theater company, moved its base to Palestine in 1928. The Palestine Opera was founded in 1923. In the visual arts the center of activity moved from Jerusalem to Tel Aviv after 1929, and the art museum in Tel Aviv was established in 1931. In concert music the Palestine Orchestra was established in 1936, founded by violinist Bronislaw Huberman, with its first concert conducted by Arturo Toscanini.[78]

Achievements in film also abounded in this era, with sound films introduced in April 1930.[79] In addition, a vast array of developments in the folk arts arena took place.[80]

In all these fields and in the festivals discussed in this book, the Yishuv aimed to find its place between East and West and to interpret these categories, a central dilemma in a variety of components of Zionist life. Because they were geographically nestled in the Middle East but had a population whose dominant immigrants were also connected to their European roots, the Jews of Palestine remained ambivalent about where to situate the new culture between the East and the West. In the process of cultural definition, Jews in the Yishuv struggled to find their own voice and expression between perceptions of the cultural milieus of Europe and the Middle East. These perceptions were based on assumptions and assessments—themselves fraught with contradictions—of high and low culture.

On the one hand, the new society looked up to the West, a term that generally denoted Europe, particularly Western and Central Europe.[81] In aiming to establish a nation like other European nations, the Yishuv aspired to develop a culture that would be recognized by the West. At the same time, being situated in the Middle East, the Jewish community in Palestine wanted to validate its roots in the region. Adopting Orientalist notions of the East, they romanticized Arab society and believed that Eastern qualities provided authenticity. As the ancient home of their biblical roots, the Middle East was a source of their "true" culture.

Yet these constructions were not static and were permeated with contradictions. Eastern or Arab qualities were viewed as genuine, in the Orientalist vein, but at the same time they were belittled, viewed as primitive, and regarded as forms of low or folk culture. Similarly, Europe was esteemed as representing dominant high culture—the culture to aspire to—but at the same time it was denigrated for representing a passive, degenerating Jewish life in the Diaspora, or *galut*.

Moreover, an "internal Orientalism" was also applied to Arab and Eastern European Jews, as Derek Penslar and Ivan Kalmar have addressed, demarcating the "liminal" space between East and West.[82] Sephardim, as well as Middle Eastern or North African Jews (termed Mizrahi Jews),[83] were situated in between these constructions of East and West because they were both Jewish and a part of Arab culture, and for this reason the new society adopted an "internal Orientalism," an issue that continues to linger in contemporary Israel.[84] Oriental Jews were considered a "living testimony" of ancient Jewish life in the land.[85] In particular, as will be shown, Yemenite Jews were both belittled and seen as especially "authentic" representations of the Jewish biblical past.[86] Eastern European religious Jews were similarly viewed as Oriental. As Kalman and Penslar delineate, Diaspora Jewishness came to be Orientalized.[87]

These multilayered constructions and distinctions were continually inverted and interwoven with evaluations of high and low culture as the Yishuv used different and contradictory concepts in trying to fashion an authentic imagined past that would inscribe them to the land.

Although the Yishuv leaders remained ambivalent about both backgrounds—and the benefits and deficits of each were regularly evaluated—the founders sought to blend Eastern and Western cultures, to take what they viewed as the best from both worlds, even if these worlds were often contradictory. Authentic Hebrew culture came to be seen as resting on the appropriate mixture of these two cultural milieus. The aesthetic of fusion represents this cultural characteristic of aiming to combine Middle Eastern and Western influences.

Competing Sensibilities: Socialist Versus Bourgeois and the Aesthetic of Togetherness

During the British Mandate, socialist Zionism and in particular Labor Zionism gained political dominance in the Jewish community,[88] but a variety of different strands of Zionism competed for prominence.[89] One of the many forms that consolidated in this era was urban Zionism.[90]

The socialist Zionist political and social ideologies emphasized the collective; its best known institution was the kibbutz. Labor Zionism valorized the Hebrew worker, especially those who worked the land. Not only was tilling the soil endowed with spiritual meaning, according to A. D. Gordon's ideas, but the land itself was infused with significance. The early settlers believed that they came both to change the land and to be changed by it, as captured in the lyrics of a well-known folk song from the pre–World War I era: "We have come to the land to build it and to be rebuilt by it" (*Anu banu artza livnot u'lehibanot ba*).[91] This notion of the transformative potential of the soil and the importance of forging connections to it was further solidified in the educational system through a focus on *yedi'at ha'aretz*, or "knowledge of the land," which emphasized a close bond with the terrain through, among other aspects, hiking around the country.[92]

The prominence of agricultural labor in socialist Zionist thought placed dwelling in communal farming settlements on a higher plane than living in an urban environment. Yet throughout the Mandate period most Jews lived in cities and towns. However, this fact was deemphasized at the time as well as in the history, until recently.[93]

The city of Tel Aviv expanded dramatically during the Mandate period. At this time 40 percent of Jews settled in the "first Hebrew city," with its population growing from about 3,000 in 1920 to about 150,000 in 1940.[94] In the 1920s an immigration wave (referred to as the fourth aliyah) of Jews primarily from Poland (1924–1931) accounted for the significant enlargement of Tel Aviv. In 1925, the height of this immigration, the population of Tel Aviv increased by 50 percent and the number of buildings in the city almost doubled.[95] The city continued to grow in the 1930s when large numbers of Jews arrived mostly from Germany and Austria (1932–1939) (referred to as the fifth aliyah), fleeing the Nazis after Hitler's rise to power in 1933.

Especially as a result of the arrival of these middle-class Jews from urban environments in the 1930s, a distinctly urban culture and urban Zionism consolidated that consistently conflicted with agrarian values; socialist Zionists often viewed the new immigrants as bourgeois and incompatible with their ideology. Thus, for instance, the cultivation of decorated shop windows and cafes with jazz music and European salon dancing, such as the waltz and tango, went against the collective, ascetic, and agrarian ideals of the Hebrew worker on the kibbutz.[96]

In this book I use the terms *socialist* and *bourgeois* to denote competing sensibilities and cultural preferences rather than political party preferences. For instance, socialist Zionists lived in urban areas, of course. Yet, as I will show, these terms and concepts were used by members of the Yishuv to refer to opposing visions for a new Jewish society. Because socialist Zionism dominated and urban culture was deemphasized in favor of the romantic images of the rural, the label *bourgeois* was used in a derogatory way. Thus the conflict between "socialist" and "bourgeois" was connected to tensions between the communal and the individual and between the rural and the urban.

In addition, because the more urban population sought to generate high art, which would place the Yishuv within the purview of European nations, these forms were often seen as elitist and exclusivist by the socialist Zionist enterprise, as high art rests on the kinds of distinctions and valuations that socialist concepts eschewed. An ideology calling for a society without status and rank was fundamentally at odds with the establishment of cultural, artistic, and social hierarchies. The dichotomies established between high and low and East and West inherently conflicted with the socialist Zionist ideal of togetherness based on equality.

Yet, despite the ideological disputes in the Yishuv and the tensions within this goal of unity, the ideal of togetherness remained part of the national consensus and was viewed as necessary for the nation-building process. The aesthetic of togetherness rested most strongly on the dominant role of the socialist Zionist ideals of equality, sharing, and unity. It also stressed the goal of developing a national community and, to that end, encompassed the setting aside of differences among divergent sectors in the Yishuv with the aim of forging a modern nation-state. In the contemporary era the notion of Jewish Israelis being part of the same family remains strong, especially when the state perceives itself as threatened.

Coping with Turmoil: Celebration Versus Sorrow and the Aesthetic of Defiance

The period of the British Mandate was replete with political conflict as Jews and Arabs aimed to control Palestine.[97] When it assumed control over the Mandate, the British did not anticipate the severity of the internal conflicts between Arabs and Jews or the incompatible pressures that would fall upon them. To the British the development of Palestine as a prosperous and well-run country would provide the basis for easy governing. Their overall priority for this territory was the country's critical location as a backup to protecting the Suez Canal and its significance in defending the route to India, the most important element in the British colonial system, "the jewel in the crown," as it was often called.

But the British confronted a situation in which the Jews and the Arabs both sought to gain ultimate rule of Palestine. The British responded by offering each group a certain amount of autonomy and self-government. As the Mandate evolved, each of the three sectors—the British, the Arabs, and the Jews—were mostly disconnected and developed separate spheres. Throughout the 1920s and 1930s conditions in Palestine alternated between periods of quiet and times of violence; the Mandate period was a tumultuous era that faced economic and political struggles and was affected as well by worldwide developments.

In 1920–1921, 1929, and, most starkly, 1936–1939, the Arab community rioted, protesting the Jewish presence in Palestine. The future of the country was precarious and uncertain. This era also witnessed the progressive worsening of the plight of Jews in Eastern and Central Europe, following Hitler's rise to power in 1933 and finally resulting in the Holocaust.

On the one hand, members of the Yishuv were confronted with the overwhelming horror of what was transpiring in Europe, even though the full extent of the devastation was not completely known during the war.[98] On the other hand, the Yishuv intended to celebrate and honor its new society. The community therefore continually faced the question of whether or not it would be appropriate to hold festivals in light of trying and tragic events. The Jewish residents consistently debated the pros and cons of proceeding with planned celebrations and festivities.

On this issue a pattern developed that remains to the contemporary period. With few exceptions the Yishuv regularly chose to celebrate in the face of trauma: to continue with the process of rejoicing and honoring its efforts and its new life. The Jews in Palestine considered this decision defiant and a symbol and demonstration of their strength and resilience.

The Hebrew term *davka* came to represent this sensibility. The Hebrew word does not have an exact English translation; it loosely means "in spite of it all" and is generally used for emphasis. As described by sociologist Oz Almog, "The *davka* spirit is one of defiance, disobedience, standing one's ground, doing things out of spite and stubbornness."[99] The aesthetic of defiance refers to this characteristic that has sustained a lasting impact.

Between the Edges

In showing how the embodiment process unfolded and how the Yishuv addressed these different tensions in the period of the British Mandate, I also depict the ways in which life in the Jewish community in Mandate Palestine existed on the edge. As Ruth Jordan's memoir emphasizes, all aspects of life were in the process of being heightened during the Yishuv. In the chapters that follow I demonstrate the effects of living on the edge, not only between these divergent conflicts and the continuing attempts to resolve them but also with the daily uncertainties of the political climate. This quality too has become a legacy in contemporary Israeli life.

In the subsequent chapters I show how the tensions in Yishuv society were sometimes left unresolved and sometimes mitigated. A thorough discussion of the four events reveals the importance of debate in Jewish life in Palestine as well as the seriousness with which the members of the Yishuv treated their creations. Likewise my discussion demonstrates the manner in which the Jewish community in Palestine discovered how to celebrate and honor itself on its own terms.

A stylistic choice throughout the chapters that follow is the inclusion of an array of direct excerpts and passages from the time. To understand the era and the process of cultural production, it is necessary to hear the members of the Yishuv speak in their own voices. By listening to them, it is possible to gain a sense of their exaggerated language, their intense reactions, their frames of reference, and their lines of thought. These selections provide the texture of the process of cultural production and the tenor and flavor of the debates, giving the reader deeper insight into the passion, tension, and pitch involved in creating Hebrew culture.

The different aesthetics of toughness, togetherness, defiance, and fusion define Israeli culture today. Each of these aesthetics embodies Zionist ideology and illustrates how Zionist ideals were encoded onto the body. These cultural dynamics remain at the core of contemporary Israel, and understanding their roots is critical to comprehending Israeli society.

CHAPTER 1

Searching for Hebrew Beauty

The Queen Esther Competitions, 1926–1929

About one month before the Purim holiday, in the years 1926 through 1929, a beauty competition took place at an evening gala in Tel Aviv. This contest was a key element of the Zionist transformation of Purim, a minor and joyous festival in the traditional Jewish calendar. The winner of the competition was crowned Queen Esther, the heroine of the Purim story. Yet the creators of the beauty contest also changed the tradition by secularizing it and connecting it more closely to the national project.

Although short-lived, the beauty contest played a central role in the renewal of the celebration of Purim in Tel Aviv in these years. The selected queen took on an important symbolic position, for she came to represent the emerging nation. Female beauty was intricately linked with nationalism. The selected queens were not assessed in terms of their physical appearance alone. Instead, they were judged by how well they represented the Yishuv.

The Queen Esther competitions encompassed all the major tensions: old versus new, socialist versus bourgeois, East versus West, celebration versus sorrow, and religious versus secular. The beauty competition for Queen Esther represents the quest to define Jewish or Hebrew female beauty and raises questions about conceptions of gender in the developing society and debates about how women should be viewed in the Yishuv. The beauty contest also illuminates competing ideals of different sectors of Yishuv society, including those between socialist and urban Zionists and those between religious and secular Jews. Ultimately the beauty contest was curtailed because of religious objections, thereby setting a precedent that granted rabbinic leaders ultimate authority over the role of Judaism in the public sphere.

Purim in Tel Aviv: Old Versus New
The Zionist Transformation of the Holiday

The transformation of Purim in the Yishuv, in keeping with secular Zionist ideology, attempted to both maintain a link to Jewish tradition and create a new and modern celebration.

In traditional Judaism Purim celebrates a Jewish victory over those who wished to destroy the Jewish people. The tale, as told in the Scroll of Esther, takes place in the city of Shushan, the capital of Persia. Esther, a young Jewish orphan raised by her uncle Mordecai, is selected as the queen of Persia by winning a beauty contest held by the king, Ahasuerus. The book of Esther describes Esther as "beautiful and lovely" (Esther 2:7). After becoming queen, Esther plays an essential role in saving the Jewish people from their destruction by Haman, the king's viceroy.

Purim stands out as one of the most joyous and secular holidays in the traditional Jewish calendar. Because it is considered a minor holiday, Jews are permitted to work during this festival. In traditional Jewish observance the Scroll of Esther is chanted in the synagogue. Each time the name of Haman, the king's viceroy and the antagonist in this story, is recited, the congregants yell and make noises with noisemakers (groggers) to symbolically blot out his name.

The two primary elements of Purim, according to scholar Monford Harris, are "dis-order and merriment."[1] As a holiday of inversions, where Jews are encouraged and even mandated to act out of the ordinary, on Purim it is customary for Jews to dress up in costumes and masks, to become drunk, and to prepare Purim plays. A rich tradition of these comedies developed in Diaspora communities. Although wearing clothing of the opposite sex is forbidden by Jewish law, on Purim Jewish men may dress as women, and Jewish women as men.

As an inherently secular holiday that commemorates Jewish endurance, in the Yishuv Purim was viewed as particularly well suited to secular Zionist goals of transforming Jewish holidays. In fact, the Jewish National Fund (JNF), the organization responsible for buying land and constructing the Yishuv's infrastructure, considered the holiday "most closely related to the present upbuilding of Palestine, inasmuch as the special significance of Purim is . . . bound up with release from oppression and persecution."[2]

The new festivities were centered in the city of Tel Aviv. As the first Hebrew metropolis that prided itself on its secular character, Tel Aviv was an ideal fit and was considered the most suitable location to celebrate this holiday of joy and frivolity.[3] Moreover, Purim festivities offered an occasion to show off the young city and to revel in the accomplishments of the first national Jewish urban environment.[4] In addition, the celebrations presented opportunities for economic gains, including an increase in commerce and a boon to a range of businesses.[5]

The festivities incorporated a variety of sectors of Yishuv society, such as socialists, revisionists, urban and rural dwellers, religious and secular Jews, Yemenite Jews, Sephardim, and Ashkenazim. Other sectors of Mandate society also took part in the festivities, including Arabs and the British.[6] The scholar Hizky Shoham refers to Tel Aviv during Purim as an important "pilgrimage site" that drew in primarily local tourists and Tel Aviv residents, but also visitors from abroad.[7] Although workers participated, historian Anat Helman claims that Purim highlighted urban middle-class values, including "prosperity and individualism."[8]

From 1920 to 1936 the Purim carnival was a central event in Tel Aviv and the Yishuv at large. Prominent artists and writers of the day participated in the preparations,[9] and residents planned for the festival by decorating houses, cars, balconies, buses, and gates (Figure 3).[10] Many activities filled the city during the two- to three-day celebration, but the parade through the streets of Tel Aviv was the central moment of the carnival. Dignitaries, representatives, and businesses took part in the procession, which also featured bright and colorful floats (Figure 4).[11] The parade represented the vibrance and creativity both of the renewed holiday and of the Hebrew metropolis. In 1932 the parade served as the setting of a landmark film, a comedy short titled after the first two words of the book of Esther, *vayehi bimei*, "and it came to pass in the days of."[12]

Tel Aviv completely transformed in honor of Purim.[13] According to reports of the time, the entire population of the city seemed to be outside—on rooftops, on balconies, and in the street (Figure 5). At night the metropolis came alive with evening costume balls,[14] dancing galas in which competitions took place and prizes were awarded for costumes.[15] Outside, a significant element of the celebrations was dancing a stormy hora in the streets into the late hours of the night.[16]

European carnival practices strongly influenced the Purim celebrations. The procession itself, as well as such aspects as flower wars and the throwing of confetti at the carnival, was imported from Europe.[17] In 1928 the Tel Aviv Municipality's secretary, Yehuda Nadivi, attended the Oktoberfest in Munich to gain information on arranging a city fete.[18] The Yishuv openly compared itself to the European carnival and aspired to reach its level. Newspaper headlines illustrate this objective, especially the aim to emulate Nice: "Tel Aviv, the Carnivalesque's Future, Is to Be Our Eretz Israeli [Land of Israel] 'Nice'" and "As Nice and As Monte Carlo, Tel Aviv Is

Figure 3. Postcard with an image of the Adloyada Purim Parade, Tel Aviv, 1934, featuring the decorated streets and crowds standing on rooftops. Courtesy of the Department of Special Collections and University Archives, Stanford University Libraries. Eliasaf Robinson Tel Aviv Collection.

Figure 4. The Adloyada Purim Parade, Tel Aviv, 1934, featuring the floats and the procession. Photo: Zoltan Kluger. Israeli Government Press Office.

Figure 5. Crowds
Streaming through
Allenby Street during the
Adloyada Purim Parade,
Tel Aviv, 1934. Photo:
Zoltan Kluger. Israeli
Government Press Office.

Tomorrow."[19] Articles in the Hebrew press also expressed these goals: "It is necessary that our Hebrew city develop into the real Nice in the upcoming years."[20]

With their aims to combine modern European and Jewish customs, the planners adopted Jewish tradition and symbolism in a variety of ways. In seeking traditional concepts associated with the holiday, they chose to highlight joy.[21] The importance of cultivating merriment on Purim stems from a well-known rabbinic saying: The Talmudic rabbis proclaimed "Mishenichnas adar marbin be-simcha" (From the beginning of *Adar* [the month in which Purim takes place], we increase our happiness).[22] The planners strove to create a celebratory mood at the center of the festivities in Tel Aviv and used this saying to endow credibility and continuity to the new customs.

The committees organizing the Purim festivities made great efforts to ensure that the occasion would be happy and humorous for the public.[23] Poets created comic pamphlets and poems for the event, and newspaper descriptions focused on the festival and the lighthearted mood in Tel Aviv.[24] Despite the political and financial problems in the Yishuv during these years, the joyous atmosphere surrounding Purim endured and the holiday represented a time to set aside all the dilemmas of the day. As Lotta Levensohn, the American Jewish writer, described: "Are times hard in Tel Aviv, and does it bear the sad honor of standing in the front ranks of unemployment? Yesterday, yes; tomorrow perhaps. But not today. No, today all Tel Aviv is enjoying a family party in the streets."[25]

In addition to the emphasis on merriment, other features of the holiday also demonstrated an appropriation of Jewish tradition. The city adopted street names to reflect phrases from the Scroll of Esther, offering a connection to the Jewish source of the holiday. Allenby Street became Shushan Habira (Shushan, the capital); Herzl Street was Vegadol Layehudim (and it was great for the Jews); Nahalat Binyamin became Esther Hamalka (Queen Esther); and Ahad Ha'am Street was Ish Yehudi (referring to Mordecai, "A Jewish Man").[26] The children's components, which featured special events geared toward younger celebrants, such as a costume competition and singing and dancing, also took their names from traditional Judaism.[27] Titled the *Shacharit le-yeladim*, "morning service for the children," these festivities were named for the prescribed morning prayers.

The title of the Purim carnival likewise represented a link to Jewish tradition. Until 1932 the parade was called the carnavale. In December 1931, however, as part of the efforts to strengthen the festivities' "Hebrew" character, the Tel Aviv Municipality decided that the carnival must have a Hebrew name. To this end, it initiated a contest to select a new title for the carnival and offered a monetary prize for the winner. The committee, including writers and poets such as Y. Karni, Y. D. Berkovitz, Y. Fichman, and Y. Grazovsky, chose from more than 200 possibilities suggested by the public.[28] Some of the proposed titles included *Avivia* (spring), *Hag Esther* (holiday of Esther), *Purimia* (Purim), *Simchat Purim* (joy of Purim), and *Tor Esther* (age of Esther).[29] Prominent poets and writers of the day participated in this competition,[30] and the name suggested by the Hebrew writer Yitzhak Dov Berkowitz won. The parade then became known as Adloyada, after the Talmudic saying of the Babylonian teacher Rava: "It is the duty of a man to drink so much wine on Purim that he is incapable of knowing [ad-lo-yeda] the difference between 'cursed be Haman' and 'blessed be Mordecai.'"[31]

Queen Esther Competition

The beauty competition for Queen Esther was a central component of the renewal of Purim in Tel Aviv. It held such a significant role in the celebrations that one of the new names suggested for the carnival was in Esther's honor.[32]

The creator and organizer of the event, Baruch Agadati, a talented and eclectic artist, was involved with numerous projects in this period. Born in Bessarabia in 1895 as Baruch Kaushanski, he immigrated to Palestine in 1910. Considered the first modern dancer in the Yishuv, he presented his initial dance performance in Jaffa in 1920. Agadati was also a visual artist who studied at the Bezalel School of Arts and Crafts and a filmmaker who directed *Zot hi ha'aretz* (This Is the Land) in 1935.[33]

Beginning in 1926, about one month before the Purim holiday,[34] Agadati convened an evening ball at the Exhibition Hall[35] in Tel Aviv during which a Queen Esther was selected. The election gala remained restricted to a select section of Tel Aviv society. To attend, one needed to receive an invitation.[36] Each entrance ticket included a list of the candidates for queen and served as the ballot at the gala. At the end of the evening, at around 2 or 3 in the morning, the winner of the Esther competition was announced. At that time those present at the gala applauded the chosen queen and usually presented her with a bouquet of flowers and, in some years, a gift.

Candidates were nominated with fifty signatures that were submitted to the election or carnival committee. The committee members, who were prominent artists and writers, changed annually. Most years four to six candidates competed, and many years a runner-up was selected as well.

The election gala served as a preface to Agadati's masquerade and carnival balls, which took place during the Purim holiday.[37] According to the announcements, 50 percent of the proceeds of the gala went to the JNF. The selected queen assumed a series of responsibilities. At first, her primary task was appearing at Agadati's exclusive Purim carnival ball at midnight. Beginning in 1928, she also led the Purim parade and attended a ceremony at city hall held in her honor sponsored by the Tel Aviv Municipality.

As with the other elements of the renewed Purim festivities, the Queen Esther competition symbolized the incorporation of the old and the new. Agadati, as well as the other planners, wanted the Queen Esther contest to be both a specifically Jewish celebration and an event modeled after European culture. Agadati most likely adopted the idea of choosing a queen for the pageant from the European carnivals of Venice and Nice that were presided over by a king.[38] He may have also been influenced by the French folk festival of the Crowning of the People's Muse[39] and by the Miss America pageant, which began in Atlantic City in 1921. Staging a beauty contest was one more cultural feature that likened the Yishuv to European practices and confirmed its intention to become like other European nations.

The Tel Aviv municipal ceremony for the queen emulated European society. At this event in 1929 the queen entered formally. She arrived with Agadati in a decorated car, following a procession that included a line of motorcycles and a camel.[40] The orchestras played the "Hymn of Purim," and the crowd called out, "Long live the queen of Tel Aviv," reminiscent of the British call to their queen or king. Mayor Meir Dizengoff received the queen on the balcony of the Municipality with the following blessing:

> Today you are the queen of Tel Aviv, and your rule is from the Yarkon [River] to the borders of Jaffa–Tel Aviv. All of this crowd bows before your beauty and blesses you not as the queen of Tel Aviv alone but as the queen of all of Eretz Israel. In the style of Europe—herewith you are Miss Eretz Israel.[41]

In stating that the queen represented Miss Eretz Israel in the style of Europe, Dizengoff explicitly welcomed and embraced European society. After his speech, the orchestra played its tune again and the queen left the Municipality with her attendants. The formality and ceremonious quality of the event evoked the manner in which European queens and kings were received.

At the same time that many aspects of the Queen Esther phenomenon emulated European culture, they likewise included elements from Judaism. Agadati viewed the Queen Esther contest as consistent with Jewish tradition and practice. For him the competition was rooted in Jewish lore: In the Purim story Esther herself became queen through a beauty contest.

Many of the gifts presented to the queens, as well as their crowns, incorporated Jewish symbolism. Lilia Tcherkov, the first queen in 1926, was given a ceramic vase decorated with olive branches and a pair of golden lions bearing the crown of beauty. According to curator Batia Carmiel, Agadati borrowed the Jewish symbol of lions carrying the tablets with the Ten Commandments, a well-known image in Jewish ceremonial art. However, rather than placing the tablets between the lions, he instead inserted the crown of beauty on the decoration of the vase.[42] Tsipora Tsabari, the queen of 1928, also won a ceramic jug with these symbols. In addition, Tsabari's crown included a Star of David, the symbol of the Zionist movement,[43] protruding from the right side. Mayor Dizengoff presented her with a silver Hanukkah menorah from Poland that, like the vases, featured two lions holding tablets in a shape that signified they would contain the Ten Commandments. However, they instead had an inscription to Tsabari (see Figure 8).[44] Chana Meyuhas-Polani, the queen of 1929, wore a crown created by the Bezalel School of Arts and Crafts and specially commissioned by Agadati. This crown, with silver filigree, included traditional symbolism, such as the two tablets with the Ten Commandments and the Zionist sign of the Star of David (see Figure 10).[45]

Another Jewish construction included the character of the declaration of the queen's reign. By proclaiming her ruler over Tel Aviv "from this Purim to the next

Purim" (*mi-yom purim zeh ad yom purim ha-ba*), the pronouncement emulated a well-known phrase from the evening service (Kol Nidrei) on Yom Kippur (Day of Atonement), the holiest day of the Jewish year: *Mi-yom kippurim zeh ad yom kippurim ha-ba*, "From this Yom Kippur unto the Yom Kippur to come."[46] Yishuv members would recognize that this declaration was a play on words borrowed from Yom Kippur. Placing the queen's rule within the context of the Kol Nidrei service implanted a gravity and solemnity to her appointment. Even though the two holidays are completely different, this symbolic link served to assert and align her reign within Jewish tradition.

Beauty: East Versus West and Socialist Versus Bourgeois
The Selected Queens: Woman as Nation

Research on beauty contests across cultures shows that these competitions highlight issues of gender, power, and culture and reveal the societal dilemmas of the day.[47] As Colleen Ballerino Cohen, Richard Wilk, and Beverly Stoeltje suggest, "By choosing an individual whose deportment, appearance, and style embodies the values and goals of a nation, locality, or group, beauty contests expose these same values and goals to interpretation and challenge."[48] In the Yishuv as well, the beauty contests represented larger national issues and cultural ambivalences. The evaluation of Jewish beauty became connected to nationalism.

The Hebrew press described the stated purpose of the first beauty competition in 1926: "to select the most beautiful and typical Hebrew woman in Tel Aviv as Queen Esther for Purim 1926."[49] Embedded in this quest is a contradiction: The competition seeks the "most beautiful and typical" woman. The "most beautiful" woman implies someone who will stand out for her attractiveness and highlights her individuality. At the same time, the "most typical" woman refers to a candidate who will look like everyone else and thereby characterize Yishuv society. The national project was thus encoded into the goal of the competition. The chosen queen was supposed to embody the nation; her appointment aimed to signify the most "typical Hebrew woman."

Ironically, the contest also represents a discomfort with discussing physical attributes. For the most part the participants and commentators avoided addressing Jewish beauty, disregarding the physical characteristics of the contestants or winners. The women's bodies especially remained out of the bounds of the discussion. Rather, the only physical attributes mentioned, if at all, focused on the women's faces. Pictures of the candidates emerged in store windows and on flyers posted in the streets of Tel Aviv, but the press provided scarce and limited coverage on the contestants and the victors. In most years the newspapers neglected to describe the appearance of the candidates or the winner, recounting instead the number of votes each candidate received and the activities at the gala. Only in 1929, at the height of the phenomenon, did a head shot photo of the queen, Chana Meyuhas-Polani, appear on the front page of *Ha'aretz* and the second page of the Hebrew daily, *Do'ar ha-Yom.*[50] At this time as well, stamps materialized with a face portrait image of Meyuhas-Polani.[51]

The well-known journalist Uri Kesari emerged as perhaps the sole writer to address the presumed beauty of the candidates, yet even his descriptions failed to provide an account of the women's actual appearances.[52] In 1932, after the cancellation of the Queen Esther pageant, Kesari published an article in the illustrated biweekly magazine *Kol-noa*[53] titled "Mi-Esther ad Esther" (From Esther to Esther) in which he presented a portrait of each of the annually selected queens. In this piece he included head shots of two of the queens; he also incorporated a photo from head to waist of two of the queens and a runner-up. The only figure whose full body appeared belonged to Baruch Agadati. Given that the piece centered on the queens, the presentation of a full-length shot of just a man's physique suggested uneasiness with women's physiques.

Lilia Tcherkov, the first queen in 1926, was Eastern European. She had long, wavy dark hair and dark eyes and eyebrows (Figure 6).[54] Uri Kesari described Tcherkov as follows: "She was a woman, and with her supreme smile it was as though she could change the map of the world, she was beautiful. . . . She was chosen for Esther, for the beauty queen. The beauty queen of a proud, upright nation!"[55] In this account, Kesari links the queen's prettiness to a national notion. Rather than defining Tcherkov's appearance, Kesari claims that she represents a "proud, upright nation." Thus he offers a conception of the nation rather than one of female beauty.

Riquetta Chelouche, the second queen in 1927, was a Sephardic woman of medium height with long, dark straight hair and dark eyes and eyebrows (Figure 7). She was descended from the North African elite: Her grandfather, Aharon Chelouche, arrived in Palestine from Algeria in the nineteenth century and became active in founding the Neve Tzedek neighborhood in what was then Jaffa; her father and uncle, Avraham Haim and Yosef Eliyahu Chelouche, developed a store and factory in Jaffa that was involved in important building projects; Yosef Eliyahu Chelouche also served as one of the early founders of Tel Aviv; and her uncle Ya'akov Chelouche became the first manager of the Anglo-Palestine bank.[56] The Chelouche family played an important role in Tel Aviv, and Kesari highlighted this prominent lineage in his description.

The second Purim Queen, the second Esther of Tel Aviv, was one of our coveted girls.

Figure 6. Lilia Tcherkov, winner of the Queen Esther competition in 1926. This photo appeared in Uri Kesari's article in *Kol-noa*, March 21, 1932. Courtesy of the National Library of Israel, Jerusalem.

Figure 7. Riquetta Chelouche (later Gobernik), winner of the Queen Esther competition In 1927. Courtesy of her daughter Diana Berner.

A native, golden woman, daughter of the daughter of a golden woman, and her father and her father's father were of the proudest locals.

She came and stood before the judging people:[57] this is the vigorous and upright body, these are her burning and demanding eyes, and this is the family tree of one of the most respectable Sephardic families.[58]

As with Tcherkov, Kesari fails to provide a detailed description of Chelouche's appearance. Yet he does note her "upright" posture, a symbol of the "new Jew," and her gaze, also denoting power. He as well references her darker skin tones, differentiating her from Ashkenazic women. Overall, though, he focuses primarily on her ancestry as a member of one of the prominent Sephardic families.

Tsipora Tsabari, the queen in 1928, was a Yemenite woman known to be impoverished (Figure 8). She had dark skin and long dark hair. Her victory gained extensive coverage at the time, and she became an important symbol for the Yemenite Jewish community. As with the other queens, rather than discussing Tsabari's appearance, most contemporary descriptions focused on other attributes, emphasizing instead her position as a destitute Yemenite woman whom writers and residents were accustomed to seeing riding on her donkey and selling milk in Tel Aviv (Figure 9). Uri Kesari portrayed her in his piece as follows.

She was beautiful (in the name of Allah)! That dark and peppery Yemenite, whom Agadati the magician brought down from her donkey and put a royal crown on her head. Only yesterday she was selling milk and carrying it from house to house, and here less than twenty-four hours later Dizengoff received her at the Municipality. . . .

Queen! She was a little bit shy, when they announced that she will "rule over Tel Aviv." But the red in her cheeks added grace to her tanned skin, which was a mixture of the plums and the apples in her body and her eyes.

When you looked at her, you were compelled to bite your lips with your teeth. This was a "product of Israel," gentlemen, one hundred percent! And had all our produce in the country been like her—there wouldn't be a need to fight against foreign products.[59]

Kesari's use of the invocation "in the name of Allah" emphasizes Tsabari's connection as a Yemenite woman to the Arab rather than European world. Although he describes Tsabari's skin tones, he otherwise neglects to provide details of her appearance. Kesari's portrait also includes sexual overtones and overtly reveals that he wrote explicitly for a male audience, such as "when you looked at her, you were compelled to bite your lips with your teeth . . . gentlemen." These innuendos represent unfamiliarity with discussing beauty and sexuality directly and highlight the demeaning nature in which Kesari reviewed the queens.

Figure 8. Tsipora Tsabari, winner of the Queen Esther competition in 1928, with her gifts: a ceramic vase; a wreath of flowers with a banner marked "Municipality of Tel Aviv to Queen Esther"; and a Hanukkah menorah with the inscription, "To Esther the Queen, Tsipora Tsabari, from Dizengoff, T"A [Tel Aviv], 1928." Eretz Israel Museum, Tel Aviv Collection.

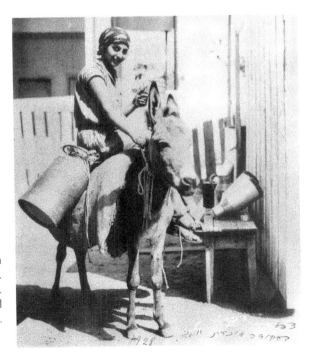

Figure 9. Tsipora Tsabari on a donkey selling milk, 1928. Photo: Shimon Korbman. Eretz Israel Museum, Tel Aviv Collection.

In addition to focusing his description on Tsabari's ethnicity as a Yemenite Jew, Kesari also depicts her as a "product of Israel." During this era, as the Jewish community aimed to strengthen its economy, frequent advertisements encouraged Yishuv residents to buy only local merchandise. On one level Kesari's portrayal illustrates that the queens were viewed as commodities: Tsabari was seen here not as a person but rather as an item that represented the nation. On another level Kesari's remark confirms that Yemenite Jews were perceived as "authentically" Hebrew, such that he deems Tsabari "one hundred percent" of the society. Alluding to the Yishuv's campaign against foreign products, Kesari situates Tsabari within that discussion, presenting her as a local commodity. As with many of the other queens, Kesari's depiction represents a conception of the emerging nation rather than one of female beauty.

Chana Meyuhas-Polani, the queen in 1929,[60] offered a stark contrast to Tsabari, her predecessor (Figures 10 and 11). Unlike Tsabari, who grew up in a poor, unknown Yemenite family, Meyuhas-Polani emerged from a well-established, wealthy Ashkenazic family. It was not coincidental that an Ashkenazic woman triumphed on the heels of a Yemenite victory. Likewise, the vice queen that year, Yaffa Lederman, was Ashkenazic. In contrast to Tsabari's donkey riding in Tel Aviv, Chana Meyuhas-Polani descended from an intellectual Ashkenazic lineage: Her father, Yosef Meyuhas, served as a writer and head of the municipal committee for the Jews of Jerusalem, and her maternal grandfather, Yehiel Michael Pines, was a Hebrew writer and a religious Zionist.[61] Rather than "rescuing" a poor girl, in 1929 the competition voters

Figure 10. Chana Meyuhas–Polani, winner of the Queen Esther competition in 1929, in the Adloyada Purim Parade. Central Zionist Archives.

Figure 11. Program for Agadati's masquerade ball during Purim, 1929. On the left-hand page is a photograph of Chana Meyuhas-Polani, winner of the Queen Esther competition in 1929, demonstrating the centrality of Queen Esther in the festivities. On the right-hand page is the program for the evening's activities, including a variety of live bands and dancing. In the upper left-hand corner of the page are the words *mishenichnas adar marbin be-meholot* (from the beginning of *Adar* [the month in which Purim takes place], we increase our dancing), which is a play on words that Agadati has taken from the Talmudic saying *mishenichnas adar marbin be-simcha* (from the beginning of Adar, we increase our happiness). Courtesy of the Department of Special Collections and University Archives, Stanford University Libraries. Eliasaf Robinson Tel Aviv Collection.

bestowed honor and royalty on a wealthy high-status woman. A sense of backlash prevailed from the earlier annual event in which Tsabari, a Yemenite woman, reigned, as though the voters were trying to assert a Nordic model and realign themselves with European culture. Kesari's description of Meyuhas-Polani demonstrates this effort.

It seemed clear, that in the selection of the new queen we wanted to take revenge on the West and to show it that we also have beautiful women in the style of Europe.

We chose an Esther for the queen of Purim who was a fair woman, with hair the color of gold. . . .

. . . And it was as if her beautiful and dreaming eyes requested an asylum from all the noise and tumult. This was a queen reluctantly, this was a woman of a higher level, as if she didn't want all the commotion and all the numerous ceremonies. . . .

. . . The people chose her. That year the people wanted to have a fair Esther, a modern Esther of German "illustration," a wonderful angora cat Esther, who immerses each morning in blue waves and abandons her body to the rays of sunshine and the granules of sand.[62]

Kesari's portrayal, which also overlooks Meyuhas-Polani's actual appearance, highlights class and status issues; he regards her as of a "higher level." Moreover, Kesari interprets Meyuhas-Polani's selection as the epitome of the Yishuv's ability to emulate Europe. In claiming that "we also have beautiful women in the style of Europe," Kesari demonstrates that this continent serves as the cultural model and the standard by which the Yishuv judges itself.

Within this European image, Meyuhas-Polani specifically represents a model of Aryan beauty: She is fair, with hair of gold. In addition to her blond hair, Meyuhas-Polani is also lighter skinned than several of the previous queens.[63] Kesari claims that the "people wanted that year . . . a modern Esther of German 'illustration,'" signifying that they pursued a representation of an Aryan Jewess. As with his portrayal of Tsabari, Kesari's account of Meyuhas-Polani also includes sexual euphemisms. His remark of the people choosing an Esther "who immerses each morning in blue waves and abandons her body to the rays of sunshine and the granules of sand" perhaps describes a sexual fantasy. The metaphoric and euphemistic nature of this portrait, just as the one of Tsabari, signifies the uneasiness and perceived inappropriateness of writing about a woman's body.

The Absence of a Consensus/The Absence of a Beauty Ideal

The analysis presented so far shows that the Yishuv failed to develop a standard for the "most beautiful and typical" Hebrew woman. The contestants looked different each year, annually symbolizing the society's concerns. Female beauty remained a construction of Yishuv society: There was no ideal woman. Rather, the chosen queen became the object of a cultural creation. Because Yishuv society was uncomfortable with discussing female beauty in general, the selected queen became a vehicle for addressing national concerns.

Even when the elected queen's actual attractiveness was questioned, the discussions still lacked a standard or a definition of beauty against which she was judged. In 1928 and 1929 questions arose over whether the chosen queen indeed represented the best looking candidate. Tzvi Lieberman, a writer and prominent member of the non-Marxist workers' party Hapoel Hatzair,[64] expressed this concern, claiming that many people believed that the runner-up in 1929, Yaffa Lederman of Rehovot, was much prettier than the winner, Chana Meyuhas-Polani. Lederman, like Meyuhas-Polani, was an Ashkenazic woman, but with dark hair. Lieberman asserted in *Ha'aretz*:

> But I was astonished to hear many people undermining the elections and claiming that the runner-up deserved to be queen. I went to see the picture of the queen on Herzl Street. Dozens of people are standing around me, looking seriously at the picture, and here I hear many people saying:
> —The runner-up is prettier than the queen.
> I went to Nahalat Binyamin to peep at the picture of the runner-up, and here too I hear the same rebellious opinion![65]

Lieberman's comments confirm the absence of a general consensus on which of the two finalists epitomized the most beautiful woman for the Yishuv. He too neglects to address the actual physical attributes of both the queen and the runner-up.

Similarly, Uri Kesari believed that the best contestant never became queen. He thought Miriam Levinska, the runner-up in 1928, was the most beautiful woman of all the queens through the years (see Figure 13).

> And there was one more. She was only chosen as a vice queen. Not important! She was the queen, from then and forever. . . .
> Nineteen springs were her life. Straight, tall, caressing eyes. A body?—like this Eretz Israel has not seen before. And after her—they won't see again.
> This was a girl for whom the ground is beneath her feet, the sky, the sun prayed to her, dreamed about her at night. The waves of the sea sang to her songs of love in the morning, afternoon, and evening.[66]

Although Kesari describes Levinska's physique when he states that she is "straight and tall," he does not fully delineate her appearance. Instead, he incorporates sexual euphemisms. Moreover, his belief that Levinska was the most beautiful woman suggests the absence of a consensus over the winner. Once more he neglects to provide a concept of a standard of beauty or an explanation of why he thinks she is prettier than the rest. Beauty remains undefined, not even discussed.

The quest to select the most beautiful and typical Hebrew woman did not ultimately result in the creation of a beauty ideal. The attributes of beauty remained vague and indeterminate; they were not delineated or depicted, even when questions emerged over the validity of the beauty of the elected queen.

Socialist Versus Bourgeois

The beauty contest also highlighted competing Zionist visions, especially between socialist and urban Zionists. Socialist Zionists expressed discontent over the way in which the Queen Esther contest was conducted; they believed it opposed their ideals of equality. Moreover, the election gala to select a Queen Esther raised class issues; it represented a middle- to upper-class bourgeois activity restricted to a select few.[67] As an event in which the elite of Tel Aviv arrived dressed in evening attire,[68] danced primarily European salon dances,[69] and held a competition in which one candidate prevailed, the election gala demonstrated urban Zionism and was an affront to socialist values.

Tzvi Lieberman described his concern over the event in *Ha'aretz.*

> All the people in all the ranks do not participate in her election, only a handful of ticket holders, that is: those who have the means to buy tickets and a portion that receives the right to choose from different councilors for the candidates for queen. Anyone who grants greater "voting rights" is victorious. The more tickets—the more beauty.[70]

By advocating for the opening of the elections to all classes, not only the upper echelons of Tel Aviv society, Lieberman calls for a democratization of the process. The beauty contest, in his view, is hindered by the restrictions on who can select the winner.

Not only did the contest clash with socialist Zionist values in structure, but it also contradicted these ideals in its attitude toward women, viewing women as objects rather than subjects. The complete absence of the image of the *halutza,* the female pioneer, in the beauty competition was a significant issue (Figure 12). In a society that, in theory, idealized the worker, the nonexistence of this model from the contest scene illuminated the competing visions of socialist and urban Zionists. Further, holding a competition of this type in which one woman would be chosen was antithetical to socialist notions of equality. Moreover, convening a beauty contest was also contrary to the notion of fostering a "modern" woman in the Yishuv, because the nature of the event itself placed women in a traditional, objectified role. The bourgeois and socialist sensibilities thoroughly diverged from one another.

The writer Yitzhak Schweiger, who also opposed the Queen Esther competitions from a socialist Zionist standpoint, argued adamantly against the very idea of a contest because he thought it conflicted with the ideals of the worker and of the new Hebrew woman. In an article whose title referenced Passover, "Dayenu be 'esther hamalka'" (Enough of "Queen Esther"),[71] Schweiger claimed that the custom was

Figure 12. Members of Kibbutz Ein-Harod working in the field, 1934. These women portray typical images of the *halutzot*, female pioneers, represented toiling the land. Photo: Zoltan Kluger. Israeli Government Press Office.

"stupid," "tasteless," and "flawed and contemptuous." Women in the Yishuv, in his view, came to Palestine to create a new society; the beauty queen contest clashed with the objectives of the budding culture and the working woman. His argument concluded with the effect of the pageant on young men.

> And the saddest part is, that also many of our young men, in the workplace, started already to follow after this wicked folly [the beauty contest], and of their souls they won't ask: what is it for the workers at all, and to the working person of Israel here especially, and specifically in its current situation of the working sister—what is it to them and to the cultivation of "this supreme value" of the "splendor of the daughters of Zion," this, "the splendor" that is known to us since the days of Isaiah. . . .
> Get rid of the stupidity from our midst![72]

For Schweiger the competition stands in opposition to the ideals of the worker and the working spirit. In its idealization of physical beauty, it conflicts with the goals of the new society that, in his view, should idealize and emphasize labor rather than beauty.

The contest, then, was a direct affront to socialist Zionist ideals in a variety of ways; ultimately it did not promote the aesthetic of togetherness. This perhaps was one of the reasons that a greater effort was not devoted to resuming the beauty contests even after they were canceled in 1930: They were not inclusive and infringed on the goal of bringing people together on an equal footing. In contrast, the Purim carnivals—which encompassed togetherness and community and, as will be shown later, were less offensive to the religious sector—resumed after their cancellation in 1930 and continued until 1936.

East Versus West: The Aesthetic of Fusion

The beauty contest represented the aesthetic of fusion. By alternating between queens of Sephardic/Arab Jewish or Ashkenazic descent, the Yishuv aimed to include those from both backgrounds. The comments of philosopher Mortimer J. Cohen highlight the manner in which the beauty contests represented this cultural ambivalence: "Not always is the most beautiful young girl crowned Queen Esther. Sometimes she is chosen for beauty, but sometimes from patriotic motives, and at other times even to strengthen local pride. One year an Ashkenazic girl is chosen, then perhaps a Sefardic [sic] beauty."[73]

The queens' costumes at the carnival and the galas also illustrate an amalgamation of Eastern and Western motifs. Riquetta Chelouche, a Sephardic woman, arrived at the ball wearing "a fashionable European gown, jewels characterized by an eclectic combination of Eastern and Western styles, and a crown resembling a North African Jewish bridal headdress embellished with artificial pearls and a forehead ornament from the Balkans."[74] She was also photographed against an "Eastern" background. Similarly, Chana Meyuhas-Polani, an Ashkenazic woman, wore "a Roman tunic, Oriental harem trousers, and Oriental and European jewelry."[75] The clothing and ornaments worn by the queens testify to the aesthetic of fusion.

In addition, Tsipora Tsabari, the Yemenite queen, came to be portrayed at times in a European manner. For instance, in a photograph in a humorous pamphlet titled *Hefker* (literally "anarchy," referring to the topsy-turvy nature of Purim), Tsabari appears in European clothing (Figure 13). Without the caption clarifying her Yemenite ethnicity, Tsabari's origins remain unclear from the image alone. The photograph attempts to construct the image of an Ashkenazic woman in contrast to her Yemenite background. The beauty queens—both Eastern and Western—symbolize the aim of combining these cultural milieus.

The reactions to the election of Tsipora Tsabari in 1928 highlight the politics of East and West in the Yishuv, confirming that Yemenite Jews remained peripheral,

ה פ ק ר

8

וימליכוה תחת ושתי ... בתל־אביב

Esther the Tel-Aviv Purim Queen (right) and her Vice-Queen (left).

■

استير الملكة (يمين) ووزيرتها (شمال)

■

אסתר המלכה (מימין) ומשנה למלכה (משמאל)
לפורים בתל־אביב.

מרים לוינסקה — אשכנזית

צפורה צברי — תימנית

ותימני זקן עומד בשוק ומתפאר בפני קהל שומעים: — גם מלך־ישראל מקרב התימנים יצא למלוך!..

Figure 13. In the humorous pamphlet *Hefker*, an image of Tsipora Tsabari, identified as Yemenite, is shown on the right and an image of Miriam Levinska, the runner-up, identified as Ashkenazic, is shown on the left. The title at the top of the page is a play on words from the Scroll of Esther (Esther 2:17): "And she was queen instead of Vashti [the queen preceding Esther] . . . in Tel Aviv." The bottom line states: "An old Yemenite man stands in the marketplace and boasts to an attentive audience: and also a king of Israel from the Yemenite community will rule!" The caption represents the pride of the Yemenite community with the selection of Tsipora Tsabari as Queen Esther. Printed page from the pamphlet *Hefker*, 1928, 8, A-30/403 of the Zalman Pevzner Collection, Goldstein-Goren Diaspora Research Center Archive, Tel Aviv University.

separate, and belittled in the dominantly Ashkenazic society and represented the Ashkenazic approach of "internal Orientalism." Within the Yemenite sector Tsabari developed into an important symbol and source of communal pride. Yet the mainstream Ashkenazic sector viewed Tsabari's victory as unexpected and as an effort to elevate the status of the Yemenite community in the Yishuv. *Ha'aretz* described her appearance in the parade.

A great wave of excitement ran through the crowd as the Yemenites appear in that Carnival with their "Queen." This was indeed a special surprise, the likes of which had not been seen in the carnivals of the previous years. The whole affair of the "Queen" assumed an almost "serious" air. This Yemenite community, consisting chiefly of the poorest of the people, who do all the hardest work and eke out the merest existence, suddenly saw themselves as "redeemed." The election of the "Queen" from one of their own placed them on a level with the other communities and they decided to celebrate the "day's reign" of the daughter of their own community with full pomp and circumstance.[76]

Several Ashkenazic writers, including the *Ha'aretz* one just quoted, openly addressed the lower socioeconomic status of Yemenite Jews and viewed Tsabari's victory as a moment of shifting the disparity. In a similar surprised and demeaning tenor to the *Ha'aretz* depiction, A. Avi-Shulamit claimed:

> I will never forget the day when they put the crown of royalty on the head of an orphaned Yemenite lady. . . . Each day beforehand we would see her at sunrise riding on her donkey with her milk jugs. And suddenly, overnight—queen of the city of Tel Aviv and its daughters. In the same day, it seems, the last divide fell between the big and privileged tribes of Israel and the poor and small tribe, which chose out of its own good will the modest task of supplying caretakers and cooks for the people of Israel. . . . It was so nice to meet these Yemenites and to feel that on this night the shame of "rich and poor" was lifted from Israel.[77]

Mortimer J. Cohen's description likewise emphasized the impression that the Yemenite Jewish community gained new status through Tsabari's election. Among various portrayals of Purim in Tel Aviv that mythologized Tsabari's success, Cohen interpreted her victory as a Cinderella story.[78]

> Once a Yemenite maiden of Neve Zedek, a quarter bordering on Tel Aviv, was crowned queen. It was, indeed, a Cinderella story of a poor orphan girl who was queen for a day. The joy of the Yemenites was unbounded. At last they had come into their own. They were now considered the full equals of other Jews. Thus, the selection of the queen is used to foster the sense of Jewish unity. Parodying a well-known statement of the rabbis [the rabbis had said that all of Israel would have a part in the world to come], a wit in *Kerobez*[79] [a pamphlet issued especially for Purim] declares: *Kol Yisrael yesh lahem helek be-Esther ha-Malkah*, which means that all Israel is united in the pride they share in glorious Queen Esther.[80]

As other writers had done, Cohen also addresses Tsabari's socioeconomic status; the crowning of Tsabari, in his view, represents the Yemenite community's realization of equal status to its Ashkenazic counterpart. He takes this notion one step further and interprets the selection of Tsabari as a symbol of Jewish unity.

Given this Ashkenazic attitude toward Yemenite Jews, it was not surprising that an Ashkenazic woman, Miriam Levinska, was chosen as runner-up in a year in which a Yemenite queen reigned. Levinska was fairer and had long hair and dark eyes. The humorous pamphlet *Hefker*, discussed earlier, printed adjacent photographs of Tsabari and Levinska (see Figure 13). Below each of their names appears a label identifying their background as Yemenite and Ashkenazic, respectively.[81] The overt differentiation between their respective origins illustrates the continuing consciousness of ethnicity.

Within the Yemenite Jewish community, the election of Tsipora Tsabari became a significant source of pride and a cause for celebrating—and promoting—their ethnic identity. Their reactions and participation illustrated their desire to become an accepted part of the dominant Ashkenazic Zionist enterprise at the same time that it confirmed they were separate from it. In the carnival that year, Yemenite Jews participated in the parade, emphasizing the strength and energy of their sector. Horsemen led the Yemenite procession,[82] carrying a blue and white flag with the inscription, "And the Lord God shall blow the trumpet and shall go with the whirlwinds of Yemen" (Zechariah 9:14).[83] Through this display the Yemenite sector incorporated the classic Zionist symbol of the flag while simultaneously focusing on Yemen, emphasizing their community's biblical history by means of the inscription. Their procession also included a float with their own orchestra playing "national folk songs," characters from the book of Esther adorned in an "Oriental-Hebrew" style, camel riders and horses and donkeys, floats with Yemenite men and women singing and dancing, and a car with "Queen Esther's maids." According to the *Ha'aretz* depiction, "On all sides the air rang with merry shouts from the cars:—'Long Live the Queen!' 'Long Live the Yemenites.' 'Long Live the People of Israel!'"[84] The mix of shouts themselves, the costumes, and the songs exhibited the combination of celebrating the Yemenite community specifically alongside all of the Jewish people.

The choice of Tsabari in 1928 garnered such a great influence on the Yemenite Jewish sector that in subsequent years Yemenite Jews selected their own Yemenite Purim queen. In March 1929 the Yemenite Jewish community held their own gala—separate from the Agadati event where Chana Meyuhas-Polani won—at which it elected Rachel Haberi with 227 votes.[85] In the carnival procession that year, *Do'ar ha-Yom* noted that the Yemenite Jews "stood out" with their own beauty queen and orchestra.[86] The Yemenite sector thereby established its own place in the Ashkenazic-dominated Purim festivities.

Indeed, the Yemenite Jewish community continued to elect its own queen even after the cancellation of Agadati's ball.[87] Evidently, the religious community expressed greater concern with the Ashkenazic population because even after the Agadati gala was canceled, the Yemenite event remained unencumbered; there did not appear to be any debates surrounding the Yemenite queen. The separate

Yemenite competition endured longer than the Ashkenazic one precisely because the Yemenites were viewed as peripheral in Yishuv society.[88] The contest for Queen Esther brought Yemenite Jews into mainstream Yishuv society only briefly; they still remained on the margins.

The Battle over the Queen: Celebration Versus Sorrow and Religious Versus Secular

The Queen Esther competition sparked a controversy regarding Jewish tradition, raising questions of whether valuing and focusing on beauty was acceptable and permissible in the emerging nation. Moreover, it generated debates over who had the authority to legitimize new customs. Deliberations on the issue, between different literary figures, journalists, and rabbis, aired in the Hebrew press, on public signs, and in special Purim pamphlets. The dramatic tenor of these debates epitomized the deep tensions in the Yishuv over the appropriate role of Judaism in their society.

The contention over the beauty contests was part of the larger debate over the transformation of Purim in Tel Aviv more broadly and the appropriate ways to celebrate the holiday in the Yishuv. By early 1929 religious dissent mounted against the renewed Purim celebrations in general and the Queen Esther competition in particular. This opposition followed from the expansion of activities around the queen and the impression of the lost modesty of Tsipora Tsabari during her European tour. However, the event having the strongest effect on the future of the custom was the August 1929 Arab riots.

Throughout the Yishuv period the emerging society regularly deliberated on the propriety of holding celebrations during difficult times. In this vein discussions took place over whether it was appropriate to rejoice—and, if so, how to celebrate—in the wake of the riots. As will be shown in subsequent chapters, the Yishuv generally chose to celebrate. However, this instance was an exception. A variety of deliberations ensued over whether to hold the carnival that year. In a confidential letter to a range of Zionist institutions, Mayor Dizengoff presented the arguments for and against the festivities at that juncture. On the one hand, staging the carnival would show that the Jewish community continued to persevere despite the riots; the Yishuv would not lose the economic benefits of the event, particularly in the city of Tel Aviv; and it would further demonstrate resilience by refraining from canceling customs that had already become a tradition and brought joy to the Yishuv. At the same time, many thought the Yishuv should remain in mourning after the riots and refrain from planning festivities; the carnival could present an opening for conflict because times were tense; and many settlements would be left without enough protection when their residents traveled to Tel Aviv.[89]

The JNF approved the festivities. The Zionist Executive, however, while attesting to the carnival's importance, believed it should not take place that year because of some of the reasons Dizengoff outlined in his letter: the troubled mood in the country in the aftermath of the riots and the concern that the festivities would generate conflict during such tense times.[90] Dizengoff thus canceled the carnival procession.

The mayor next turned to a deliberation on the Queen Esther contest that year. In his decision he formulated a clear distinction between public and private space. He stated in his correspondence with the JNF and the Zionist Executive that although the Municipality controlled public space—thereby canceling the carnivals and all activities in the streets—the Municipality did not maintain jurisdiction over the Queen Esther beauty contest precisely because it took place in private and closed arenas.[91] In his letters on the same day to Rabbi Kook, the Ashkenazic chief rabbi of the Yishuv (during the Mandate period the British established the Orthodox rabbinate of Palestine, consisting of a Sephardic and an Ashkenazic chief rabbi), as well as the chief rabbinate of Jaffa and Tel Aviv, Dizengoff emphasized the same distinction, adding that the mayor would not receive the queen that year as in the past. Aiming to appease religious leaders, Dizengoff stated he would convey their concerns to the organizers and advise them to "avoid this matter." However, because the queen was selected in a private gala, Dizengoff stood firm in his public and private demarcations: "We have to be clear that we do not have the right to forbid this event."[92]

These negotiations ensued during a period in which the young city of Tel Aviv was still in the process of defining itself and the Municipality was determining its appropriate role in a variety of deliberations. By the late 1920s the Municipality had already established the division between public and private space.[93] Despite Dizengoff's firm stand on paper, he nonetheless urged Agadati to cancel the event because of the rabbinic dissent. Agadati eventually yielded to the pressure, and the beauty competition was canceled in 1930 and thereafter.

The very nature of Tel Aviv's official Purim activities was on trial in these years. In 1930 the future of the city's Purim festivities remained unclear. Proponents of the celebrations hoped that the holiday would return to its former stature in the years to come.[94] In 1931 the carnival procession resumed, but, despite initial efforts to resuscitate the popular contest, the Queen Esther election gala was never reinstated.[95] The pressure from rabbinic leaders to abolish the custom—which began before the August 1929 riots and increased in their aftermath—ultimately led to the curtailment of the beauty contest and set a precedent for future battles over the role of Judaism in the public arena.

Opponents of the Competition

Opponents of the Queen Esther innovation, including journalists and rabbis, believed that the practice remained fundamentally at odds with Jewish tradition. They viewed the competition as inauthentic, and some even labeled it an abomination of Judaism. Moreover, they thought that the creators lacked the authority to alter the tradition in this way.

The Hebrew writer Alexander Ziskind Rabinovitz initiated the debate in the press. A well-known figure in the Yishuv, Rabinovitz was strongly attached to both socialism and the Jewish tradition and maintained close ties with Rabbi Kook.[96] In March 1929 (after the election gala but before the Purim celebration), Rabinovitz warned against the custom of the selection of a Queen Esther in his regular column in *Davar*. Prefacing his argument with a defense of the character of Queen Esther in the original story, he claimed that it was a miracle that Esther included herself in her people's suffering. The focus on Esther for a beauty queen competition in the Yishuv, however, was problematic for Rabinovitz: "And nevertheless, the heart suffers. And the words of Shimon and Levi emerge: as a prostitute will you make our sister? Lord of the universe! . . . Take mercy on the daughters of Israel and do not hand over our festivals or our fun to the evil ones."[97] In his argument, Rabinovitz used biblical references and exaggerated language. Believing that the selection of a Queen Esther was immodest and in conflict with Judaism and the biblical past, Rabinovitz concluded his piece with a call to Menahem Ussishkin, the head of the JNF, to cancel his support of this new practice.

Y. Avizohar also viewed the custom as inconsistent with Jewish life. He took issue with the focus on a woman's beauty rather than on her other traits and characteristics, claiming that the contest neglected the important qualities of the new Hebrew woman. Raising the question of how a practice should become a custom in Jewish life, Avizohar asserted in *Ha'aretz*:

> Is there any point to all of this and to the mass cheers for the Hebrew woman not for her good deeds, not for her strength, not for her healthy and successful children that she gave birth to and cultivated, but rather just for the fact that she was born with a pretty face? Is there not in this public and loud applause for beauty a disrespectful attitude to the person herself, to her essence and her soul?
>
> And I know, they'll say to me, "they even do this like that in Europe." But what

is fine for others is not always fine for us. To whom is it not clear that our attitude
toward women was always different from the Aryan attitude. Even our famous women
did not become prominent by virtue of their beauty. I know that one can come to
me with dozens of verses from the Tanach [Bible] and the Talmud, but we don't live
according to verses, we live according to customs, and this custom does not have a
single basis or root in Jewish life.[98]

Avizohar thus concluded that the Queen Esther competition was inappropriate
because it did not have a precedent in Jewish custom. Moreover, he opposed the
emulation of European society, asserting that the Jewish people put forward different
attitudes toward women.

Rabbinic leaders stood even more adamantly against the phenomenon. They
believed that it was an abomination of Judaism. In January 1929 the chief rabbis of the
Jaffa and Tel Aviv District (the Ashkenazic chief rabbi Shlomo Hacohen Aharonson
and the Sephardic chief rabbi Ben-Zion Meir Hai Uziel) sent a letter to Menahem
Ussishkin. Imploring him to refrain from involving his organization in the custom,
they argued:

> And we ask ourselves with surprise when this shameful tradition of choosing a pretty
> girl for Queen Esther and arranging new or old modern-day dances was set. Did
> something like this come out of Israel since it became a nation, or is this the Israeli
> renaissance to bring something foreign like this among us in the name of tradition
> and in the name of the redemption of the land?
>
> By no means! A tradition like this has not been and will not be in Israel, and the
> glory of the JNF will not come from this path, that on the one hand will redeem the
> land while the other brought a tradition like this into our lives that stains the shape
> of Judaism. . . .
> This deed is evil in our eyes.[99]

In their use of exaggerated language, stating that the practice was "shameful" and
"evil" and "stains the shape of Judaism," these rabbis raised the level of opposition.
By claiming that the custom was "foreign in the name of tradition," they asserted
that the contest was not only out of keeping with Judaism but also, more seriously,
a false representation of the Jewish tradition.

Interestingly, in 1928, only a year earlier, rabbinic authorities had resolved a
religious issue in favor of the queen. Ordinarily in Jewish law, a mourner is forbidden to partake in festivities. The queen that year, Tsipora Tsabari, was officially in
mourning for her father and sister, and questions emerged over whether it would
be appropriate for her to appear at the carnival. *Ha'aretz* reported:

Although she [Tsipora Tsabari] is a mourner (because her father and sister died, after she was chosen for "queen"), the Yemenites didn't give up—the young generation in particular—on her "kingdom." The rabbis, to whom they presented this question, gave permission in this case because of the clear reason in the *Shulchan Aruch* [Jewish law code] that "a king doesn't behave as a mourner."[100]

In this case, rabbis[101] consented to the appearance of Tsabari in the carnival through the use of the Jewish law code of the *Shulchan Aruch*, by which they treated Tsabari as a true ruler. Thus only a year before the heated religious debates ensued over the Queen Esther competition, rabbis sanctioned Tsabari's presence in the parade by finding a loophole in the law.[102]

In January 1930, following the announcement for the Queen Esther competition in the Hebrew press, rabbinic leaders urged Mayor Dizengoff to cancel the contest.[103] Rabbi Kook sent a letter to Dizengoff requesting the mayor's response in connection with the "removal of the monster of the selection of a beauty queen from among Eretz Israeli Judaism."[104] Kook assumed that he, as Ashkenazic chief rabbi, had full authority over Judaism in the Yishuv.

In January 1930 rabbis in Mea Shearim, an ultra-Orthodox neighborhood in Jerusalem, called for attendance at a sermon against the selection of a Queen Esther, also referring to the practice as evil.[105] The talk's announcement, titled "Evil in Israel," appeared in florid, rabbinic Hebrew rather than the modern Hebrew used by journalists.

> In the last few years they entered a terrible breach in the holiness of Israel, a terrible evil: the selection of a beauty queen in Eretz Israel.
> . . . In this year at a time when the blood of the dead is still wet and the tears have not yet been wiped off the faces of thousands of Israel, at a time when miserable widows and depressed orphans are still crying from the calamity of the hardship of their lives, the licentious ones of our nation are organizing gatherings of debauched laughter and lightheadedness. . . .
> . . . And we are a holy nation, should we allow this abuse, abuse of the holiness of Israel and abuse of the troubles of Israel . . .?
> . . . It is incumbent upon us . . . to look for ways to remove this terrible shame from us and from the holy land.[106]

As with the letter written to Ussishkin, these rabbis viewed the custom as "evil," a "terrible breach of holiness," and an "abuse." They believed that proponents of the Queen Esther competition acted against Judaism and the Jewish people. They even took the debates a step further by claiming that the custom and its promoters were calamitous and destructive.

Queen Esther's Advocates

By contrast, supporters of the innovative Purim practices in Tel Aviv believed strongly that the custom was "authentically" Jewish. In addition to Baruch Agadati, proponents included such prominent figures as the Hebrew writer Avigdor Hameiri[107] and the journalist Aharon Ze'ev Ben-Yishai, a writer for *Ha'aretz* as well as the editor of *Yedioth Tel Aviv* (Tel Aviv News).[108] These proponents, well versed in Jewish tradition, viewed themselves as working within the boundaries of Judaism. Their goal was not to reject but rather to interact with and modernize the festival. They saw themselves as having the authority to renew Jewish tradition, and they exhibited a high level of creativity in their responses to the dissent.

For proponents of the custom the idealization of beauty was acceptable and legitimate: It represented one more facet in becoming like other European nations. Avigdor Hameiri argued that a beauty queen should be permissible in the Yishuv, just as in other countries. He criticized opponents of the contest when he remarked in 1929:

> Only for us is enjoyment forbidden. All the nations of the universe that carry the burden of wars and peace on their shoulders . . . also find it possible and permissible to have a little fun with sports, with boxing competitions and with beauty pageants. . . .
>
> And among us—it is forbidden to choose a Queen Esther. Because—old age always finds objective arguments for its hatred of the youth. There is a "commandment," *vesamachta bechagecha* [and you shall rejoice in your festival]. They are "obliged" to fulfill the commandment as a rule, by Halacha [Jewish law], according to the strict laws of the *Shulchan Aruch*. But to rejoice from the heart—heaven forbid.[109]

Hameiri attacked the religious leadership for not sanctioning joy in the celebration of Purim; he claimed that they were not truly prepared to fulfill the commandment to "rejoice on your holiday." Because Purim is a minor holiday in the traditional Jewish calendar, this commandment is actually not fully applicable. Nonetheless, Hameiri used the language and the concepts of traditional Judaism to criticize the religious authorities and to imply that they themselves were not faithful to traditional Judaism.

Like Hameiri, A. Borrer, the pen name of Yitzhak Lufban, the editor of the weekly *Hapoel Hatzair*,[110] also claimed that enjoying beauty was permissible, just as in European nations. In 1930 he contended in the literary weekly *Ketuvim*:

> Due to the riots in the month of Av [a month in the Hebrew calendar], the joy of Purim was darkened this year and the carnival was canceled, and an anger even emerged about the custom of the election of the queen, which was declared as a foreign branch among us. (What hasn't been declared as a foreign branch?) Even in the case of the queen, there is no justice in the voice of criticism. We have to look at the selection of the queen through a mirror of all of the enlightened people in the European countries, who see it as a justified cause for celebration and a possibility for an expression of thanks from the people and the tribe toward the beautiful and characteristic human type, because beauty is also a decisive power in the war of existence.
>
> Let us hope that these clouds that have darkened our lives this year will go away.[111]

Because beauty contests constituted a respectable characteristic of enlightened European countries, Borrer believed that holding this event was one more element in becoming a nation. He also took issue with the opponents' claim that the custom was inauthentic, stating sarcastically that all new forms were declared foreign. Presenting the opposition as "clouds" that "have darkened" the Yishuv, Borrer did not find legitimacy in their arguments.

Proponents viewed the Queen Esther contest as a harmless and innocent celebration that fitted with their sense of Judaism. Like the opponents, they used exaggerated language and form. In 1930 Ben-Yishai published a subversive poem in *Ha'aretz* titled "Eulogy for Queen Esther" (he signed it Rabbi Tarfon, a famous rabbi in the generation after the destruction of the Second Temple).[112] This creative parody focused on the innocence of both the custom and Esther. In the original Hebrew the second and fourth lines of each stanza rhyme with one another.

Bad news we have been told:
By virtue of public workers and righteous ones
"Queen Esther" will not be chosen
This year, as a custom of the old timers . . .

Queen Esther won't be chosen
. . .

She won't be brought anymore to the Purim galas
. . .

She won't be brought to city hall

. . .

Oy ve-ach! At the right of the righteous ones
Came the termination of "Queen Esther,"
We didn't know from where she came
Also we won't know to where she has left . . .

But nevertheless I wonder:
"Queen Esther" what is her crime?
An orphan she is and the daughter of Israel,
A relative of Mordecai and in the end a woman . . .

Of Haman, Zeresh, and all the rest
The enemies of Israel please depose
(They are still ruling with a heavy hand!),
And to Esther it is best to give a rest . . . [113]

This poem reveals Ben-Yishai's clever usage of modern Hebrew. By signing the verse as Rabbi Tarfon, he asserts that the celebration was within the bounds of Jewish tradition and history. Ben-Yishai emphasizes Esther's innocence and puts forth his view that the termination of the custom was unjust. He also asserts that the focus of rabbinic leaders should not be on Esther but rather on the real evil ones of the story—Haman, Zeresh (Haman's wife), and the rest. His concluding line contends that the debate over Esther should be left alone—the Tel Aviv festival does not cause harm to anyone.

Agadati's Response

In response to rabbinic dissent, Dizengoff entreated Agadati not only to cancel the Esther elections of 1930 but also to announce publicly that he would not hold them in the future. Agadati complied, even though he had not changed his mind about the value of the competition. In a letter published in both *Davar* and *Do'ar ha-Yom*, Agadati announced the cancellation of the contest.

Without entering into the arguments on the question of the selection of a Purim queen and without changing my mind on the suitability of this selection to the character of the Purim holiday and on the form of the elections, I decided to cancel the election of a Purim queen at the gala . . . and to leave the issue of the elections alone also in the future.[114]

Although he consented to discontinuing the competition, Agadati, the performer, developed a dramatic response to its termination. During Purim in 1930 a Queen Esther appeared at the carnival ball, even though the competition had been canceled that year. *Ha'aretz* reported: "At midnight there was a surprise: the lights were suddenly turned off and the hall was half-darkened, and a 'Queen Esther' was brought onto the stage on a royal throne, and immediately disappeared."[115] A manifesto, appearing in the form of a Megillah, a scroll emulating the one for the book of Esther, was then distributed to the crowd. Agadati wrote this manifesto in the name of Esther in which "she" defended herself and proclaimed her innocence to the people of Tel Aviv. The first section of the 1930 manifesto echoed Ben-Yishai's poem. Writing in a florid biblical style, "Esther" says:

> I would not presume to know why or wherefore, but an anger was unleashed against me this year from the rabbis of Israel and their public workers, that on this Purim they will not choose one of the daughters of Israel for Queen Esther and she will not come before the public on this Purim holiday. I would not presume to know why this anger was unleashed at me, a daughter of Israel who loves her people and is connected to them and ensures their well-being all of the days. And they, the sons of Haman, are still living and existing, and also Zeresh still walks and walks mincingly on her legs and winks her eyes at every persecutor and enemy on the right and on the left. And I, what is my sin and what is my crime? . . .
>
> . . . My rest did not last, and then opponents to me arose from inside the camp as well. They saw in the election of "Queen Esther" a custom that hurt the religion, heaven forbid. And they have different arguments in their mouths! And a decree was issued from above: Do not let a man of Israel give his daughter for "Queen Esther" this year.
>
> I was shamed and ashamed, my people, that this is what happened to me. . . . Will this indeed be my reward for all the good that I have done for my people? . . .
>
> Happy holidays to you, then, my dear brothers and sisters. Be happy, be cheerful, and be merry. Do not let your spirits drop. The God of Israel will not abandon us, and all of the power of the evil will soon be cut off . . . . Pay attention to that, my people, and do not let your hands weaken; build and raise the homeland of Israel, renew the holidays, and also remember well Queen Esther.
>
> Goodbye until next Purim!

Your sister
Who loves you with all of her heart and soul
And misses you a full year
Queen Esther[116]

By focusing on the innocence of Esther, this creative manifesto advocates the legitimacy and harmlessness of the custom. Emphasizing that Purim is supposed to be a joyous holiday, the proclamation argues that the Esther phenomenon goes hand in hand with that directive. Not only does the declaration express surprise and hurt that the religious community contested this festival, but it also reverses their argument: Whereas opponents claimed the celebration was shameful to Judaism, the manifesto instead declares that Esther herself was disgraced in the process of canceling the activities in Tel Aviv. Rather, the "evil," conventionally associated with the figure of Haman in the Scroll of Esther and those seeking to destroy the Jewish people, was conferred on adversaries of the practice. By emphasizing the righteousness and rightful place of Esther both in Jewish tradition and in the city's Purim festivities, the declaration asserts that the celebration is "authentically" Jewish.

Purim 1931 constituted the final effort to resuscitate the Esther tradition. Although Agadati's pre-Purim gala refrained from holding a competition for a Queen Esther that year,[117] instead Agadati selected a queen himself. During Purim he arranged a dramatic ceremony, calling for the return of the pageant. At 6:30 on the eve of Purim, Agadati's private choice for Queen Esther, Rachel Blumenfeld,[118] joined one of the processions of the parade toward the Tel Aviv Municipality. She entered accompanied by funeral escorts, representing a death march and bestowing a sense of urgency and gravity to the moment. Upon their arrival at the Municipality, Mayor Dizengoff received Queen Esther and her entourage.

Just as in the previous year, Agadati crafted a manifesto, likewise written in the form of a scroll and in the name of Esther. Building on the theatrical tenor, Dizengoff then publicly read the proclamation in his office (Figure 14). Later that evening, at the stroke of midnight, the queen appeared with her funeral escorts at the masquerade ball and the declaration was distributed there as well.[119] "Esther" states in the manifesto:[120]

In the time of our suffering and misery in the Diaspora, they would choose a "Rabbi for Purim," a king for an hour who would give instruction and rule on this day. And in recent years in our awakening country they switched, according to the custom of the generation, the "Rabbi of Purim" for a "Queen of Purim" who would rule on this day and would rule without boundaries. There is no doubt that all of you, all of the

Figure 14. Meir Dizengoff reading "Queen Esther's" manifesto before the queen and her escorts at his office at the Tel Aviv Municipality, 1931. Photo: Avraham Soskin. A. Soskin Collection, Eretz Israel Museum, Tel Aviv.

citizens of this city and all of her pilgrims and guests, will admit that the tradition nevertheless continues.

... And one thing I ask and request from you: Return the crown of the kingdom to its old place, continue the tradition from year to year, and choose a Purim queen for Israel.[121]

This declaration, and the drama surrounding it, was the final plea to revive the custom. The ceremony was a creative and theatrical response to dissent against the practice. As with the 1930 declaration, Agadati used florid language to emphasize his point. He also, as before, focused on the justified place of choosing a queen, and of Esther herself, in Jewish history and tradition. His knowledge and awareness of Jewish custom and tradition permeated the different symbols and references in the manifesto reading. Agadati again illustrated his belief that the pageant was Jewish, acceptable, and worthy of continuation.

Conclusion

The Queen Esther competitions embodied all the cultural tensions: old versus new, socialist versus bourgeois, East versus West, celebration versus sorrow, religious versus secular. Proponents of the renewed Purim festivities aspired to create new ways to observe a traditional Jewish holiday. Members of the Orthodox community were opposed to these new forms of observance. The locus of the celebrations endured in Tel Aviv, the symbol and center of urban, bourgeois Zionism. Moreover, the approach to women as objects rather than as subjects went against socialist Zionist values; yet the concept of a beauty contest remained part and parcel of urban Zionism and the desire to emulate European practices. Here, rabbinic authorities agreed with socialists: They too found a beauty contest offensive, but for different reasons.

The contest for Queen Esther embraced the aesthetic of fusion. Queens from both Ashkenazic and Sephardic or Arab Jewish backgrounds were selected and embraced. Moreover, the queens' costumes embodied the amalgamation of East and West.

As with many of the events in this book, a debate ensued over the propriety of celebrating during difficult times. In this instance in 1930, an exception was made to the Yishuv's general pattern: Following so soon after the August 1929 Arab riots, the Purim parade was canceled. However, the following year, returning to its more normative decision to celebrate, the Yishuv resumed the parade, which continued until 1936.

In contrast, the Queen Esther contest, also canceled in 1930, did not return. Ultimately, the religious-secular dispute was the strongest area of contention and led to the curtailment of the practice. Beyond Queen Esther, the renewal of Purim in the Yishuv unleashed the question of who had the authority to determine how the holiday would be observed. A. Avi-Shulamit's comments about the Purim festivities highlighted this issue in 1932.

> But it is good for the holiday that it isn't yet frozen, and there is still space for arguments about its forms. It is good for the holiday that it still has more room for improvements. The upcoming years will certainly explain to us the problems and the questions: is it nice and fair to choose a Queen Esther . . . in honor of Purim, if there is a need to have a carnival procession, and so forth. Life itself—and not just a higher authority—will show us the forms of this holiday.[122]

Avi-Shulamit's words express the unclear future of the new celebrations. For him, life in the Yishuv will decide the final outcome rather than God or the rabbis. The civil society, in his view, maintains the authority to determine what will ultimately be appropriate for the holiday.

Even though the two sides debated back and forth, the rabbinic leaders proved victorious: The Queen Esther competition was eliminated.[123] The triumph of the religious community set a tone for the emerging state: In issues relating to the celebration of Jewish holidays, rabbinic leaders maintained authority.

CHAPTER 2

Promoting Sport

The First Maccabiah Games, 1932

The first Maccabiah Games, a nine-day sports festival in Tel Aviv held from March 29 to April 6, 1932, was a Jewish Olympics. Directly influenced by European culture, the games were modeled after the modern Olympics first staged in Athens in 1896. They included the usual diversity of Olympic sports competitions for men and women, such as track and field, gymnastics, hockey, soccer, basketball, tennis, rugby, handball, wrestling, fencing, swimming (in Haifa),[1] and boxing (in Haifa).

Jewish athletes from twenty-seven nations participated in the first Jewish international athletic games.[2] Unlike the other events in this book, the Maccabiah Games were organized in conjunction with Jews living in the Diaspora; they were arranged by the Maccabi movement, a sports association for Jewish youth with branches around the world as well as in Palestine. Thus the Maccabiah Games developed through an already established institution and international movement.

However, the Maccabiah Games maintained political Zionist implications. As in European national projects, sports were not viewed merely as a leisure activity; rather, they were a central component of nationalization and of the Zionist refashioning of the Jews.[3] The emphasis on the public display of Jewish strength was used to demonstrate the capabilities of the Jewish people. Staging the games in Palestine furthermore served as a means of bolstering the international Zionist movement and increasing the number of Jewish residents in the country.

The event also aimed to exhibit the achievements of the Jewish community in Palestine and to promote and solidify the Yishuv as the center of Hebrew culture. Indeed, the Maccabiah Games belonged to part of a trio of festivals in Tel Aviv in the spring of 1932: The games were preceded by the Purim carnival (Adloyada) and were immediately followed by the Levant Fair, a trade fair that exhibited Yishuv products (Figure 15).[4] These festivals occurred alongside one another to show off the Yishuv, to boost tourism and the economy, and to bring a large number of visitors to the country with the hope that they would choose to remain as permanent residents.

The Maccabiah Games highlighted numerous tensions: old versus new, socialist versus bourgeois, celebration versus sorrow. However, unlike the other events in this book, they did not attempt to incorporate Middle Eastern culture; the games conformed to European sports practices. Moreover, the Maccabiah Games were the only event with official British support and participation: Arthur Wauchope, the British high commissioner appointed in 1931, served as patron of the games and appeared at the opening and closing ceremonies. The 1932 competition is also the single event in this book that Palestinian Arabs boycotted, viewing the games as a Zionist militaristic display.

Figure 15. Postcard by the Tel Aviv Municipality endorsing tourism. With the byline "Come to the Land of Israel in the Spring," in Hebrew and German, it promotes the city of Tel Aviv as the center of Hebrew culture and advertises the Purim festivities, the first Maccabiah Games, and the Levant Fair in 1932. Courtesy of the Department of Special Collections and University Archives, Stanford University Libraries. Eliasaf Robinson Tel Aviv Collection.

Within the Yishuv, political ramifications emerged over who participated in—or chose to refrain from—the games. One of the central tensions of the Maccabiah Games was the conflict between socialist and urban Zionists. In contrast to the renewal of Purim, a religious protest did not materialize over the event, demonstrating that the cultivation of the body remained an uncontested goal in the Yishuv. The aesthetic of toughness was central: It was promoted and lauded.

As with the Queen Esther competitions in the 1920s, the potential benefits and disadvantages of the Maccabiah Games were debated, and those discussions addressed the political ramifications, the timing of the event, and how the Yishuv would present itself both internally and externally. After the first games the competition was considered a successful event for the Yishuv and for the city of Tel Aviv.

Creating a Jewish Olympics
Old Versus New: Modern Europe, Ancient Greece, Ancient Jewish Life

The Maccabiah competition directly modeled itself on European culture, emulating the modern Olympic Games founded by the French baron Pierre de Coubertin (1863–1937). Initially, Yosef Yekutieli, the founder of the Maccabiah Games, wanted the Jews to appear as members of a Jewish team at the Olympic Games rather than as participants on teams of the nations in which they lived. Yekutieli asked Coubertin if the Jews could indeed participate as Jews, but Coubertin replied that it was not possible because a territory or a nation was necessary.[5] Yekutieli then developed his idea for a Jewish Olympic Games. As he explained:

> The world organization, which includes thousands of members, and among them wonderful sportsmen, has not as yet taken part in an international world Olympiad and the reason for that is that in these games only territories and not national bodies take part. It is true that many of our members have taken part and distinguished themselves in various Olympic Games, but they did not appear as Maccabians—Jewish sportsmen who have the blue-white flag—but as Englishmen, Americans, Canadians, Germans, etc. The only means of joining in the international Olympic Games is by joining as Eretz-Israelians. But this would necessitate great preparations and vigorous action.[6]

At the same time that the Maccabiah competition modeled itself according to the Olympic Games and modern European conceptions about sports, the Yishuv also aimed to connect the event to earlier times. Viewing antiquity as endowed with authenticity, the organizers turned to the ancient Jewish world and to ancient Greece, home of the original Olympic Games.

The Yishuv perceived itself as following in the ancient Olympic tradition. Beginning in March 1932, the *Palestine Bulletin* featured eight special articles about the history of the Olympic Games in ancient Greece.[7] *Ha'aretz* likewise published articles discussing the connection between the Olympics and the Maccabiah competition.

In imitation of the Olympics, the Yishuv intended to stage a Maccabiah Games every four years. The leaders also wished for the event to remain in Palestine, just as the ancient Olympic Games always took place in Olympia, in contrast to the modern Olympics, which change location. This objective was also linked to Ahad Ha'am's notions that the Land of Israel should become a spiritual and cultural center for Jews in the Diaspora. Of course, although Ahad Ha'am intended spiritual or high cultural developments, the Maccabiah Games instead used athletics to situate the Land of Israel in the center of the Jewish world.

In addition to incorporating aspects from ancient Greece into the competition, the Maccabiah organizers aimed to instill a Hebrew character. In seeking to construct an "authentic" "Jewish" Olympics, they drew from Jewish history and tradition. The event served as a national sports festival, which, like Purim in Tel Aviv, was viewed as a national holiday. Reminiscent of the three pilgrimage festivals in traditional Judaism, wherein work is not permitted on the holiday's first and last days, work was canceled in Tel Aviv on the opening and closing days of the festival (March 29 and March 31 [even though sports competitions continued through April 6, the official closing ceremony was held on March 31]) to make it possible for the city's residents to participate in the celebrations.[8] Similarly, newspapers referred to the event as a *chag*, the Hebrew term used for a traditional Jewish holiday.

Jewish history and symbolism was an integral part of the event. In seeking images for the Maccabiah Games, Yekutieli and other Maccabiah organizers especially turned to the Bible. The opening ceremony included the dispatch of 120 doves, 10 for each of the 12 tribes of biblical Israel, thus linking the event with the biblical past. These doves were viewed as the central symbol of the initiation of the games.[9]

Maccabiah organizers also turned to ancient fighting figures, such as the Maccabees themselves, who are celebrated on Hanukkah for their revolt against the ancient Greeks with the aim of reinstating religious freedom. They thoroughly overlooked the irony that in ancient times the Maccabees were fighting against Hellenization, which heavily valued sports. They also turned to Bar Kokba, the leader of a rebellion against the Roman occupation of Palestine in 132–135 C.E. In this way they aimed to connect to—and to align themselves with—a particular ancient image: one of strength, might, courage, and resilience. As Yael Zerubavel shows, Zionists turned to particular moments in the ancient Jewish past, and the Bar Kokba revolt in particular was seen as representing active Jewish resistance.[10] Yekutieli arranged for the first games to take place on the 1,800th anniversary of the Bar Kokba revolt. The newspaper *Do'ar ha-Yom* heralded the event's inauguration, situating it in the direct line of ancient figures: "Today our youth from all parts of the world will demonstrate the health of their bodies, the flexibility of their movements, their gymnastic prowess, the ancient Israeli spirit of Joshua and Gideon, the spirit of the Hasmoneans and Bar Kokba."[11]

Selecting a Name

Unlike the Queen Esther contest, these athletic games did not represent a modernized way of celebrating a traditional Jewish holiday. Yet the title of the games connected to the Jewish holiday of Hanukkah, and the athletes at the Maccabiah Games were viewed as direct descendants of the ancient Maccabees, the heroes of the Hanukkah story, again disregarding the irony. Before the competition, however, this title was contested. In February 1932, a month before the opening of the games, the name Maccabiah was debated in the press. At the same time that the selection of the name Adloyada for the Purim festivities was being deliberated, voices of discontent emerged over the chosen name for the Jewish Olympics.[12] The process of how the title Maccabiah was chosen or who exactly suggested the name remains unclear. The initial designation was Maccabiada. Some accounts claim that Yekutieli picked the name, and others indicate that the writer K. (Kadish Yehuda) Silman chose Maccabiah Games over Maccabiada.[13] Itamar Ben-Avi, a prominent journalist and the son of Eliezer Ben-Yehuda, the formative figure in the revitalization of modern Hebrew, also claimed that he suggested the name.

The conversations about the appropriate title for the games centered on an intention to create a name with a Hebrew meaning and resonance as well as a connection to both the ancient Greek and Jewish pasts. As with the renewal of Purim, these discussions illustrate how Hebrew culture and the creation of a modern Hebrew language were intertwined. Ben-Avi proposed that the event be called Zionade, believing that this title incorporated Jewish content into the ancient Greek Olympic character. Just as the ancient Greeks labeled their event Olympiade after Mount Olympus, the home of their pantheon, the Yishuv should call its event Zionade after Mount Zion in Jerusalem, the important site in ancient Jewish life.

> When the Maccabees first expressed the thought of a Hebrew "Olympiada" in the country, some of their leaders turned to this writer with the question of how to translate this name to Hebrew.

—Of course—they proclaimed with the strength of the excitement—we want to emphasize that this is a great honor for the "Maccabees."

—"Maccabon" or "Maccabiah"—returned the asked.

The last name was that which was chosen by the majority who decide in the Maccabi movement.

Everyone admits today—and the one who offered it also—that "Maccabon" and "Maccabiah" are not the correct terms for this holiday. Had they listened to my advice, they would have given it the more ringing name "Maccabi-ad," from the meaning "eternity" and "holiday" according to the second word. And one more thing—"Maccabi-ad" is close to "Maccabiada," and in French they say "Olympiade" and not "Olympiada." Let the French decide this time, as they decided our words many times.

It is more correct, though, than all to call the event "Zionade" (Sionade).[14]

Ben-Avi's clever use of language bears a resemblance to the debates over the Purim queens. He demonstrates the kind of cultural concerns and underpinnings that were behind the selection of a name: the desire to emulate the Europeans and to find a "correct" or "authentic" solution.

Like Ben-Avi, K. Silman found the name Maccabiah inappropriate.[15] He too aimed to find a fusion of a Hebrew with a Greek connotation.

Recently there has been much bandying around of the name Maccabiah Games. . . . I do not know who coined this name, but it is obvious that it does not fit the event. Maccabiah means: a woman or girl who is a Maccabi [organization] member, and no more. I think that there is still time to correct this mistake. I suggest the Maccabion (along the lines of Sanhedrion), or Maccabi-on (as in Pantheon, etc.), and its meaning is Maccabi, the power ("on"). Maccabiah also indicates the diminutive, whereas Maccabion or Maccabi-on suggest the vastness of the enterprise. During the upcoming months it will still be possible to enter this change of name, if the Maccabi [organization] agrees to do so.[16]

Silman's initial suggestion of Maccabion is linked to the concept of the Sanhedrin, the rabbinic legislative and judicial body in the aftermath of the destruction of the Second Temple, and his other option of Maccabi-on is connected to the pantheon, the collective of Greek gods and goddesses. Thus he too plays with the words' resonances, double entendres, and significance, seeking to create this intermingling.

The debates over the name Maccabiah symbolize the aim to demarcate and generate authentic Hebrew culture. The discussion also shows the close tie between the development of modern Hebrew and cultural creations. Representing the old-new tension, the Yishuv wanted to place the new and modern event within the context and lineage of ancient history, enabling the imagined ancient past—both Hebrew and Greek—to infuse the new Maccabiah Games with authenticity.

Political Zionist Objectives: Promoting Jewish Immigration

The Maccabiah Games were closely connected to one of the central goals of the Yishuv during the British Mandate: to encourage Jewish immigration to Palestine to increase the Jewish population.

As part of the aim to strengthen the international Zionist movement, the Maccabiah Games sought to foster a strong tie to the Yishuv among Diaspora youth. Yosef Yekutieli expressed these objectives: "The Jewish youth from abroad who will visit the Maccabiah will breathe the atmosphere of the beloved fatherland, will hear Hebrew spoken, and will go back full of courage and energy to continue in the country of his birth the work of the nation and the redemption of the country."[17] In the same vein, the journalist who signed his articles "H.L.H." stated: "The Maccabiah comes to awaken the spirit of the Diaspora youth. They will see the land with their own eyes, will feel themselves under the wings of the motherland—and will keep its spirit and its love even when they return to their stepmother."[18] Although interchanging genders in their references to Palestine as fatherland or motherland, both writers express the Zionist notion of the transformative capacity of experiencing the land and its culture through the senses—seeing, hearing, breathing, feeling.

Because seeing the land was perceived as an important means of promoting Jewish immigration, a special Maccabiah Games committee arose to arrange trips throughout the country.[19] Henrietta Szold, a prominent American Zionist best known as the founder of Hadassah, traveled to the games and delivered an address before the Maccabees, as the athletes were called. She encouraged members to tour Palestine during their visit.

> The hallowed land is spread out before you in its bridal charm. It invites you to go forth and view it after your peaceful contests have been fought. Drink in its inspiration. Learn from its beauty as well as from its ruggedness and its resistance, that the Jew worthy of living upon it must make himself a complete man, forgetting no part of his people's heritage, and also rejecting nothing that is human. Note the health and buoyancy of its children. Listen to their Hebrew prattle, the new value they have inherited. See their young, sturdy parents reveling in a renewed value, in the labor from which prejudice kept them throughout many centuries in almost every country of the civilized world.[20]

Szold's urging of the visitors to take in all aspects of the Yishuv is steeped in Zionist rhetoric and concepts: the presentation of the new Jew, the transformative capacities of working the land, the emphasis on youth. It was hoped that the land itself—and the Jewish society developing on it—would entice the visitors to remain.

To this end, hospitality was heavily encouraged. The city of Tel Aviv wanted to present a positive picture of life in Palestine, and a warm welcome was viewed as one avenue for creating a first-rate impression. In the weeks preceding the Maccabiah Games, residents of Tel Aviv were urged to be hospitable to their guests. In an article in *Do'ar ha-Yom* in February 1932, Yehezkel Friedman entreated:

> Here those who stand behind the scenes have a lot of work before them, work full of effort and responsibility. Upon you is thrown the task of hospitality. According to the measure of hospitality we judge a man, his family, his people, his country. We, the workers behind the scenes, need to come close to our friends and guests who come from the Diaspora, to accompany them everywhere and to show them the beauty of our country, our work, and our energies that we have invested here. . . . We need to show them that we are building a new Hebrew here, a Hebrew that is not like those in the walls of Warsaw or Berlin—a Hebrew who knows what he is striving for and what is the purpose of his existence here in the country. . . . Explain to our guests morning and night all of these things and plant in them the seed of love for the country, root the idea of homeland in them, root it to such an extent that at the time that these youth will have to return to the Diaspora and will arrive at the seashore in order to get on the boat, their hearts will beat and a question will peck in their brain:
>
> Are we going home or leaving it?[21]

As is evident, Tel Aviv's residents were expected to take an active role in the proceedings. Their hospitality was viewed as a medium through which to instill Zionist ideology and to promote the achievements of the Yishuv.

To immediately welcome the visitors, Tel Aviv residents flocked to the Jaffa port to greet the multitudes of incoming tourists. Although municipal functionaries requested residents to stay away from the harbor and instead greet the visitors inside the city, a large number still descended on the port. In addition, the city made extensive special arrangements to accommodate its guests. According to Chaim Wein,[22] an active leader and teacher in the sports arena who took part in the activities, these plans included the preparation of tents, private rooms, and classrooms for the athletes.[23] All these efforts, it was hoped, would promote Jewish immigration.

Although the first Maccabiah Games ultimately succeeded in this goal[24] and although many visitors illegally immigrated to the country through the event,[25] in the months preceding the games, beginning in November 1931, disputes over whether the Maccabiah Games would actually increase settlement appeared in the Hebrew press. Some writers, such as the journalist from *Davar* who signed his articles "N.," warned that visitors would form an incorrect impression of the country.

> Is this connection and this awakening that the Maccabiah might bring us . . . [the one] that we need? Will not everything be swallowed up by empty festivities, by blasts of victory, by meetings, by parties, by galas, by journalistic descriptions that are a little bit exaggerated—also fake? Won't these youth go away from here with the wrong impression of life in the country, from its suffering, from its difficulties, from the strict test that each new Hebrew immigrant has to take? And we—aren't we going to be left afterwards, when the holiday has passed, with a bitter feeling of double neglect? . . . Surely both we here, and the Jew in the Diaspora, are not seeking a drunkenness of senses, but rather a national purpose. If the Jews are seeking one more thing, indeed it is first of all a shelter, a real shelter, a place where they can live a life of honor and work. . . . One hundred Jews settling, fifty Jews settling—this is the only real comfort.[26]

N. argues that the games will present a superficial portrait and worries that Diaspora youth will not see the "real" Yishuv, which was marked by suffering and hardship. This position also highlights different attitudes between socialist and urban Zionists: Workers believed that the toiling of the land was central, whereas urban Zionists applauded achievements in the city. For N., success was measured by immigration; if the games did not achieve this aim, he thought they would be meaningless.

Those who favored staging the games warned against the opposition to the Maccabiah competition among some journalists, stating that their views were based on a Diaspora mentality. Referring to the voices of resistance in exaggerated language as the "voice of slavery," the journalist H.L.H. claimed that the opponents aimed to "create a new Diaspora" in Palestine.[27] H.L.H. further argued that by seeing the Yishuv "*davka* in its desolation," Diaspora Jews would be more encouraged to lend a hand and immigrate to Palestine. This debate brought the different attitudes to the surface, not only toward the Maccabiah Games themselves but also toward the work in the Yishuv more broadly and to divergent Zionist priorities.

Displaying the City of Tel Aviv and Promoting Hebrew Culture

The Maccabiah Games presented an opportunity to exhibit the young Hebrew metropolis and to promote achievements in Hebrew culture. Just as it had for the Purim celebrations, the city of Tel Aviv, with approximately 50,000 residents,[28] ardently prepared to host the event and to create a festive atmosphere for the city and its visitors. As with the Purim festivities, the Tel Aviv Municipality played an active role in creating and defining a public community and in controlling the public sphere. Following the instructions of the Tel Aviv Municipality, the city's residents decorated their homes, balconies, and cars with blue and white flags, greenery, and flowers[29] so that by opening day, the *Palestine Bulletin* noted, "in Tel Aviv all the cars are decorated with some emblem connected with the Maccabiah."[30]

A holiday feeling and a festive air permeated the whole city.[31] The writer Aharon Ze'ev Ben-Yishai described the atmosphere.

> The colours of the town most visible to all is: blue-white. From the blues of the heaven, the balconies of the houses, from each auto or motorcycle, and from the hat and chest of each Maccabee there flow the four Hebrew letters (Maccabee)[in Hebrew, the word Maccabee consists of four letters]. They are waved in all kinds of forms and styles and they are also engraved in the hearts of all these wonderful youths who pace gaily in the streets of the Jewish city.
>
> And the guests stroll about in the streets of the town as if somewhat intoxicated, as if daydreaming, like descendants of Columbus who opened a new country.[32]

Ben-Yishai's reference to Christopher Columbus distinctly sets the scene in terms of exploration, discovery, and, ultimately, the creation of a new state. The visitors had the opportunity to revel in the "new Hebrew city."

The Maccabiah Games were connected to the urban growth of Tel Aviv and presented an example of the integration of the city's culture and physical space. Because the culture and the city grew and developed simultaneously, many structures were created specifically to support the burgeoning culture, including the new national stadium for the games.

The decision to build the stadium in a sandy area near the estuary of the Yarkon River in northern Tel Aviv (the point where the Yarkon River enters the sea to the north of Tel Aviv) was made only about two months before the games began by Mayor Dizengoff's assistant, Israel Rokach (Figure 16). Given that the stadium was far from the city at the time, private companies paid for roads to link the area to the city. Because the land was owned by the Mandate, the city of Tel Aviv asked the previous British high commissioner, Sir John Chancellor, to lease the space for the stadium. Since the English supported sports activities, they gave the land to the Tel Aviv Municipality for free.[33] The British endorsement of athletics directly resulted in an actual land increase for the Yishuv.

The building of the stadium also served an economic function, because it increased employment. Work continued on the stadium around the clock in the

Figure 16. Construction of the stadium for the Maccabiah Games. Joseph Yekutieli Maccabi Sports Archive, www.maccabi.org/museum.

weeks preceding the event; the structure was finally finished only a few hours before the opening ceremony.[34] The engineer in charge, Shlomo Arazi, later described the process of building the stadium: "On the night of March 29th and on the following morning, hundreds of workers were still finishing the field and barracks. On that same afternoon, the big audience present at the opening ceremony was amazed to see the smooth fine surface, which less than two months before had still been a desolate desert. Even we, the constructors were amazed—accomplishing this work on time was a real miracle!"[35] The stadium was made of wood and could seat 5,000 people; its level track was prepared for field events.[36]

The Maccabiah Games also provided an opportunity to promote Hebrew language and culture. The Yishuv wanted to present itself in the best light, exhibiting its achievements in the construction of a new society in a variety of arenas. Just as with the Purim carnivals, Hebrew writers played a part in the festivities. Authors and luminaries such as Yehuda Karni, Nahum Sokolov, and Avigdor Hameiri created songs and poems in honor of the games. In the evenings, after the sports competitions, a series of cultural events and galas were held; they were intended to foster and instill a Hebrew character to the proceedings. At Mugrabi Hall, Habima performed a variety of plays: *Uriel Acosta*, *Twelfth Night*, *The Sacred Flame*, and *The Golem*. At Ohel-Shem Hall the singer Hanna Kipnis presented favorite Eretz Israeli songs. The schedule also included an evening performance by the well-known Yemenite singer Bracha Zefira and the pianist and composer Nahum Nardi.

In addition to formal performances, evening hora dancing in the streets added to the festive atmosphere. Hora dancing also celebrated and demarcated the successful completion of the games: The closing procession ended with singing and hora dancing at the Herzliya Gymnasium.[37]

Integrally connected to the promotion of business and the economy, the event inspired a range of memorabilia: special Maccabiah Games emblems, posters, badges, uniforms, and flags.[38] Stamps featuring the image of the Maccabiah Games poster likewise materialized.[39] A competition also developed to determine the design of postcards for the games. Judged by the Maccabi administration and Yishuv artists, it reflected a further intermingling of the sports and arts arenas.[40]

The Opening and Closing of the Maccabiah Games

A parade through the burgeoning metropolis at both the opening and closing of the games also showcased the city of Tel Aviv (Figure 17). On Tuesday, March 29, 1932, at approximately 1:00 p.m., the opening procession began at the Herzliya Gymnasium, the first Hebrew high school and the central landmark of the city at the time. Mayor Meir Dizengoff, astride a white horse, led the procession through the heart of Tel Aviv on the way to the stadium.[41] Dizengoff was followed by the captain of the parade, Yehoshua Alouf, organizer of the Games and physical education teacher at the Herzliya Gymnasium, with two fencing champions from Poland and Egypt walking beside him.

The representatives of the Maccabi organization[42] followed, and then the different Maccabi delegations, each with a Hebrew flag, a flag of its nation of origin, a brass band, and its own costume.[43] Participating delegations included Austria, Great Britain, Bulgaria, Germany, Danzig, Denmark, Greece, Yugoslavia, Lebanon, Syria, Latvia, Egypt, Lithuania, Poland, Czechoslovakia, Rumania, Switzerland, and Palestine.[44] After the Maccabi groups came the scouts, Betar (the Revisionist sports organization), and the schools.[45] About 3,500–4,000 participants, ages 5 to 60, marched in the parade; they were cheered and applauded by onlookers following every part of the procession.[46]

Unlike the haphazard procession during Purim, the Maccabiah parade consisted of formal marching. The groups were lined up and organized in distinct rows, and they marched in sync. As the athletes passed through central avenues, such as Ahad Ha'am, Allenby, and Eliezer Ben-Yehuda Streets, they experienced the Jewish urban environment.[47] The procession then continued along the Mediterranean Sea, taking in Tel Aviv's natural setting on its path to the newly built stadium.

The Maccabiah Games highlighted an interesting interplay of Zionism and other nationalisms. Each group proudly represented its country of origin, but the

Figure 17. The parade through the streets of Tel Aviv at the opening of the first Maccabiah Games. Joseph Yekutieli Maccabi Sports Archive, www.maccabi.org/museum.

athletes also reveled in their joint identities as Jews and in the Zionist aspirations for their own nation-state. The games strove to assert that the Jewish people indeed constituted a modern nation.

Because the road was not large enough to accommodate all of the crowds, the parade caused a huge traffic jam.[48] Representing the event's international stature, the *New York Times* reported on the proceedings and commented on the significance of the congestion: "The huge stadium, built within the past seven weeks, was crowded beyond capacity, 25,000 persons cramming all available accommodations and creating what was probably the biggest traffic jam in Palestine since Pontius Pilate inaugurated the Roman games at Caesarea in Northern Palestine 2,000 years ago."[49]

Once inside the stadium, which was decorated in blue and white and filled with Hebrew flags,[50] a grand march of all the national teams with their flags proceeded (Figure 18). The British high commissioner, Sir Arthur Wauchope, attended the opening ceremony, with a formal arrival and departure. Additional noted officials and honored guests who sat on the main stage with a British flag overhead included representatives of the Yishuv and of the national institutions, such as Mayor Dizengoff, Lord Melchett and his sister Lady Erleigh, consuls of different nations, and the Sephardic chief rabbi of Tel Aviv–Jaffa, Ben-Zion Meir Hai Uziel.[51] Representing

British rule and Zionist aspirations, the English anthem "God Save the King" as well as "Hatikvah," which was to become the national anthem of the state, were played at both the opening and closing ceremonies.[52]

At 3:30 the national flags were lowered (Figure 19). At 3:40 three trumpet blasts heralded the opening. On the third blast the Maccabiah flag was raised, followed by a brief greeting from Dr. Herman Lelewer, head of the Maccabi World Union. The 120 doves were then released to mark the official beginning of the Maccabiah Games. This opening ceremony was viewed as one of the high points of the games. It included a mass marching, drill, and gymnastics display as well as track and field presentations and appearances by Jewish Boy Scouts and Maccabi motorcyclists (Figure 20).[53] At the end, the delegations marched formally out of the stadium (Figure 21).

Although sports competitions continued through April 6, the official closing ceremony took place on March 31. The concluding event, especially the mass gymnastics display, was also one of the highlights of the games. Noted officials present at the ceremony included the British high commissioner Sir Arthur Wauchope; Colonel Frederick H. Kisch, who served as chairman of the Palestine Zionist Executive from 1929 to 1931; Mayor Dizengoff; and Maccabi representatives.

Zionist goals were evident throughout the city and the proceedings, from the

Figure 18. Maccabi members marching in the stadium at the opening ceremony for the first Maccabiah Games. Joseph Yekutieli Maccabi Sports Archive, www.maccabi.org/museum.

Figure 19. The opening ceremony for the first Maccabiah Games at the stadium included the singing of "Hatikvah" and the lowering of the flags. Joseph Yekutieli Maccabi Sports Archive, www.maccabi.org/museum.

Figure 20. The gymnastics display at the opening ceremony for the first Maccabiah Games. Joseph Yekutieli Maccabi Sports Archive, www.maccabi.org/museum.

Figure 21. The delegations marching through and exiting the stadium at the end of the opening ceremony for the first Maccabiah Games. The Maccabi Tel Aviv delegation is featured here. Joseph Yekutieli Maccabi Sports Archive, www.maccabi.org/museum.

blue and white flags to the singing of "Hatikvah" and the honoring of important Zionist figures. After the closing event at the stadium, a grand procession of approximately 5,000 Maccabees walked back to the Herzliya Gymnasium, where the parade had begun on the opening day. On the way they passed by the cemetery where representatives placed wreaths on the graves of Ahad Ha'am, Max Nordau, and victims of the Arab riots.[54] Zionist ideology and symbolism were directly encoded into these activities.

Although the organizers' Zionist goals were more important to them than the results of the competition itself, the winners of the games were as follows: Poland came in first followed by the United States in second, Austria in third, Czechoslovakia in fourth, and the Palestinian Jewish contingent in fifth place.[55]

Creating a Nation of Muscular Jews
Embodying Muscle Judaism: Jews and Sports in Palestine and Europe

The goal of rebuilding the Jewish body was an integral part of the Maccabi organization that began in Europe in the late nineteenth century. Its slogan, "A healthy soul in a healthy body," reflected Max Nordau's call for a muscle Judaism.

The Yishuv adopted several conceptions about sports from European society and its increased sports activities in the interwar period. Athletics had been integrally connected to nationalism in Europe since the early nineteenth century, particularly with the development of the German gymnastics movement. For Jewish communities participation in sports offered conflicting messages.[56] Athletics served as a medium through which Jews could assimilate into their societies, but they also were an arena in which Jews faced anti-Semitism when they were barred from several sports associations.[57] According to historian Michael Brenner, "In both instances—inclusion and exclusion—athletic activity was more than a marginal addition to their lives. The interwar period was not only a time of rising anti-Semitism, but also a high tide for sports enthusiasm."[58]

Jews in Diaspora communities rose to prominence in many athletic arenas in the interwar era and were recognized as Jews. In the field of boxing they especially excelled in Europe and the United States.[59] They also achieved fame in a variety of sports, including weight lifting, swimming, and soccer.[60] In addition, Jews proudly formed self-identified Jewish sports associations in Europe, such as the well-known Hakoah in Vienna.[61]

The cultivation of athletics was viewed—both in Europe and in Palestine—as a way of transforming the Jewish people; the traditional focus on the mind that was evident in the time-honored study of religious texts gravitated toward a greater emphasis on the body. These ideas were presented in a Maccabi movement pamphlet published in London after the first Jewish Olympics; the writer applied the language of regeneration prevalent in the period.

> The first task of the [Maccabi] Movement is to bring about the physical regeneration of our people, to draw Jewish youth away from their constant preoccupation with things of the mind, to make them aware of the potentialities of health, strength and beauty that is inherent in their bodies, and thereby to assist in laying the foundations of a healthier, stronger, [more virile] Jewish race.[62]

Although similar conceptions about athletics and its role for the Jews in Palestine emerged, the cultivation of sports in the Yishuv was directly and overtly linked to the national project. It was seen as an important component of becoming a "normal" nation, a healthy nation, and a nation like other European countries.[63] The *Palestine Bulletin* called on the Yishuv to understand the importance of fostering sports and shifting Jewish attitudes toward physical activity.

> In many countries young Jews have formed themselves into Maccabee Sports Organisations with zeal and enthusiasm, a reaction against the old Jewish view that study was all important, sport a heathen pastime and a waste of valuable hours that might be better spent over the pages of the Talmud.
>
> As a Palestine Maccabee said to me, "If Jews want to be recognized in the world to-day not as a strange survival of Bible times but as a living people, they must have a strong sport organisation like any other people. They must be prepared to play other peoples and they must acquire a sense of sport for sport's sake."[64]

Yosef Yekutieli similarly viewed the promotion of athletics as a necessity for Jewish national revival.

> The value of sports in the life of nations now-a-days is very big, one can even say that it is indispensable to any people wanting to lead a national life among the other nations. It is doubly important for us, the Jews who are now awakening to national consciousness and are trying to build the ruins of their country.[65]

Drawing on the importance of sports in European national projects, Yekutieli considered the nurturing of athletic activity to be directly correlated to the Jews' capability to successfully create a nation.

Sports associations in the Yishuv were also connected to—and at times originated in—Europe. The Maccabi association emerged in Europe in the late nineteenth century with the first Maccabi sport club founded in Constantinople in 1895,[66] followed by Maccabi clubs established in Berlin and St. Petersburg in 1898.[67] The movement reached Palestine in 1906, with a group called Rishon Le-Tzion in Jaffa. After World War I the Maccabi movement developed rapidly, and in 1921 it was centralized through the establishment of the Maccabi World Union in Berlin.[68]

Athletic organizations in the Yishuv also adopted European conceptions, especially the politicization of sports associations. In Europe nonpolitical Jewish sports clubs emerged, but there were also Zionist, Bundist, and other groups that saw their roles as both ideological and physical.[69] The Maccabi organization in Palestine viewed itself and its mission as connected to the Jews in the Diaspora and to the mission of spreading Zionism.

> The aim of the Maccabi [movement] is the development of and looking after the physical aspect of the Jewish youth in the Diaspora and Palestine. This development goes hand in hand with the spiritual development according to the well-known proverb "Mens Sana in Corpore Sano" [a strong mind in a strong body], which is the Maccabian motto.
>
> The Maccabi movement, as a Zionist nonpolitical sports organization, absorbs the youth from all ranks.... The Maccabi, therefore, serves as a bridge from assimilation to nationalism.[70]

Sports offered a means by which to promote Zionist ideology among Diaspora youth and provide a Jewish national identity.

As in Europe, sports associations in the Yishuv were divided according to different political affiliations. Hapoel, the workers' sports organization, was established in 1925 as part of the Histadrut (General Federation of Labourers in the Land of Israel) and as a challenge to the Maccabi organization. Although the Maccabi association viewed itself as representing all of Yishuv society, Hapoel considered it bourgeois. Betar, founded in 1924, was the sports club of the Revisionist Party. Later, in the 1930s, a sports organization for the Orthodox community was established, called Elitzur; it was founded in 1939 with the goal of creating a religious community that was also physically fit. Even though these sports organizations catered to different sectors of Yishuv society, they were all unified in their fundamental goal: the creation of a strong and healthy Jewish body. Yet they also politicized and divided the sports arena.[71]

Encoding the Masculine Ideal: The Aesthetic of Toughness

The Maccabiah Games signified the culmination of the work of the Maccabi organization in Europe and Palestine and the realization of Nordau's call for a muscle Jewry. References and allusions to Nordau were prevalent in Maccabi organization literature and speeches, as well as in newspaper accounts of the event.[72]

Viewed as a testimony to the health and virility of the Jews in Palestine, the first Maccabiah Games embodied the aesthetic of toughness and promoted a masculine image. Although women participated in the sports contests, the event valorized a body standard for the ideal man, based on the ancient Greek model—strong, tough, and muscular. The athletes represented and fostered the masculine model. They ran, boxed, fenced, and so on and in the process personified this ideal of the ancient male Greek athlete. There were no disputes or questions over how the athlete should appear; this image remained uncontested.

The Maccabiah athletes presented a contrast to negative stereotypes of the feminized Jewish body and were thought to give evidence of the transformation of the Jews. A journalist for the *Palestine Bulletin* lauded that "boys and girls who came from many countries bore a glorious testimony to the virility and vigor of the present Jewish regeneration."[73] Another reporter described the reaction of English tourists to the Jewish body seen in the closing display.

> Behind me sat a group of English tourists. They were as surprised at everything they saw. What struck them most was the splendid health and physique of the Palestinian Maccabees. "Look!" said Tourist A to Tourist B, as thousands of young Maccabees filed by, "How healthy they look! Every one of them." It was also added that many did not look like Jews—a common fallacy that Jews must be brunettes. Palestine seems to breed blondes.[74]

The emphasis on blonde hair enhanced the image of the ancient Greek ideal as well as the Aryan model. These notions resembled discussions over the selection of Chana Meyuhas-Polani as Queen Esther.

The masculine image fostered in the Maccabiah Games was viewed in stark contrast to the image of the Diaspora Jewish body. Many in the Yishuv feared that the Diaspora physique—seen as weak, sickly, and, indeed, feminine—would be recreated in Palestine. Paradoxically, although Jews in the Diaspora also participated in sports and attended the Maccabiah Games, cultivating the body in the Yishuv was presented as a characteristic of the new Jew and a marked distinction from Diaspora Jewish life. In December 1931, H.L.H. lauded the efforts of the impending Maccabiah Games, stating, "The Jewish youth, who dreams the dream of the redemption and devotedly fulfills the vision of generations, wants to see the land of its longings, as it takes her sons under its wings as they free their bodies from the webs of the Diaspora."[75]

To further promote the new Jewish body, visual images illustrating the strength and physicality of the Jew in Palestine appeared in a variety of posters, pamphlets, and advertisements. Although women participated actively in the games, as noted earlier, only male figures were featured in these images. The front cover of *Haitztadion* (The Stadium), a pamphlet published in the fall of 1931 to prepare the Yishuv for the Maccabiah Games, features a sketch of a man running forward with his head raised high (Figure 22). This athlete wears only shorts and sneakers, showing off his muscular body. His right arm is crossed in front of his body, highlighting his upward gaze, evoking pride.[76]

These ideas were similarly publicized in an advertisement in 1934—in the aftermath of the first Maccabiah Games and in preparation for the second Maccabiah Games of 1935 (Figure 23). Promoting a lottery to earn a free Studebaker car, the ad presents a picture of a Maccabi athlete holding up an automobile. The Maccabi athlete is portrayed in a superman veneer: male, strong, brawny, and capable of lifting a vehicle. Dressed in shorts and a tank top with a Star of David in the middle, the typical outfit of a Maccabee, his head is raised high, exhibiting his pride. This ad also conveys the male, macho, virile image of muscle Judaism.

The muscular Jew was overtly tied to the nation. Highlighting the blue and white colors of Zionism, the official poster of the Maccabiah Games shows a male brawny figure, standing upright and tall, holding a flag with a Star of David (Figure 24). With national goals at the forefront, the flag is the most heavily emphasized aspect of the poster. Representing the close connection between Hebrew writers and the national project of the Maccabiah Games, Avigdor Hameiri crafted a song for the event: "Hymn for the Maccabees." This hymn bears the message that the strong Maccabee will be the herald of the new nation. Echoing Judah Leib Gordon's

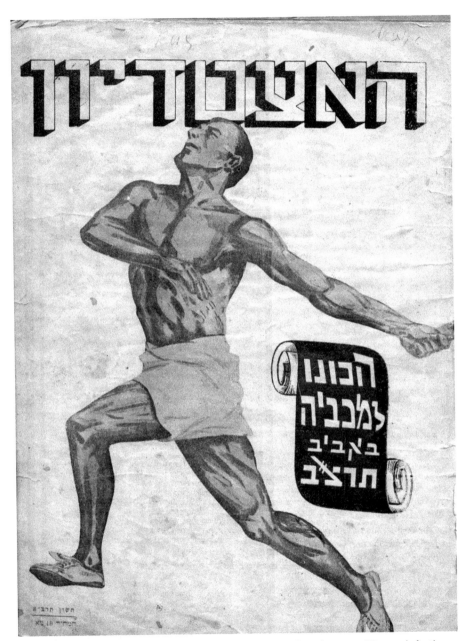

Figure 22. Cover of *Haitztadion* (The Stadium). The scroll on the right states: "Get ready for the Maccabiah in the Spring of 1932." Joseph Yekutieli Maccabi Sports Archive, www.maccabi.org/museum.

Figure 23. Advertisement that appeared after the first Maccabiah Games and in preparation for the second Maccabiah Games of 1935. The ad promotes a lottery to win a free Studebaker car. The top of the ad states, "Donate!" At the bottom is written, "A Studebaker car for the donors to the fund of the second Maccabiah Games!" Broadsides and Posters Collection, V. 1985/3, Archives Department, National Library of Israel, Jerusalem.

famous poem, "Awake, My People," Hameiri calls for the youth to arise and nurture their bodies, as shown by the following excerpt.

Awaken youth and straighten your head
Open your eyes sleepy one
Know, our future is hidden in your blood
The soul of the nation is in your fresh body!

Maccabee, Maccabee
Strengthen your muscles and make the blood courageous!
Maccabee, Maccabee
Be the leader for the glory of the nation![77]

Hameiri's hymn epitomizes the notion that the health of the nation is dependent

Figure 24. Poster for the first Maccabiah Games. Joseph Yekutieli Maccabi Sports Archive, www.maccabi.org/museum.

on the cultivation of the body. The refrain emphasizes the bond between building the nation and the aesthetic of toughness.

Henrietta Szold also referred to the importance of maintaining robust bodies as the building blocks for a strong nation. When she addressed the Maccabees at the welcoming reception the night before the opening of the games, she proclaimed:

> Your slogans, your aims, and your achievements proclaim that you have discovered in Israel's storehouse a neglected truth: that the soul that would be strong and sane and noble must be housed in a body that is vigorous and healthy and well-proportioned and upstanding. You express with peculiar emphasis the truth we all accept, that the return to the land is the opportunity for return to normal humanity, and that normal humanity is not a disembodied spirit, but an aspiring spirit encased in solid flesh and vivified by fast-coursing blood. We salute you as the apostles of the normal.[78]

Szold directly links the development of the body to the national revival, emphasizing the Zionist concept that strong physiques create a "normal" people.[79]

The potential national restorative effects of cultivating the body were also delineated by the journalist Shalom Ben Baruch in February 1932. In discussing the possible benefits of the Maccabiah Games, he argued for its healing capacities.

> First of all, comfort and encouragement. What the people of Israel need—both the masses and the upper class—is a little bit of healing and mental recovery! The wonderful view of thousands of young men and women straight and proud in their national togetherness, in their beauty and strength . . . will bring satisfaction to the whole nation itself.[80]

Thus the aesthetic of toughness was universally promoted.

Sports and Militarization

Another aspect of physical fitness that the Yishuv adopted from Europe was the relationship between sports and militarization. As Gideon Reuveni has shown, this connection began in Central Europe after World War I when the role of sports shifted from a leisure activity alone to a means of building national strength. These notions were adopted by the European Jewish community.

> It was claimed that by being strengthened physically, Jews could gain in self-confidence and assertiveness, and this not only made the ability to put up a fight a central element

of the concept of masculinity, but at the same time it legitimated the organization and application of physical strength as a political instrument. In this deeper sense, sports was a medium that militarized Jewish society.[81]

These concepts reached the Yishuv and informed ideas about sports. Yosef Yekutieli referred to the defense implications of the Maccabi movement: "Furthermore, vital importance is ascribed to the existence of the Maccabi in Eretz Israel for the security of the Jewish inhabitants."[82]

The connections between the Maccabiah Games and militarization were noted by members of the Yishuv. Particularly given the political climate in Palestine, the cultivation of a strong, masculine body bore consequences for security activities. Ben Baruch emphasized these links in his discussion of the potential effects of the Maccabiah Games: "The massive demonstration of the Maccabiah Games will serve as a pole of defense for us. Our hope has not yet been destroyed to defend ourselves and push back those who attack us. . . . Blessed will be those who participate in the Maccabiah Games, who will emphasize our real force in front of the whole world."[83] The defense implications of the Maccabiah Games also represented the aesthetic of toughness. These connotations were noted as well by Palestinian Arabs, as I discuss later in this chapter.

Questions About Timing: The Aesthetic of Defiance

At their conclusion the Maccabiah Games were heralded as a great achievement, but in the months before the competition a series of debates ensued as to whether the event should take place at all, especially given the political circumstances in Palestine and the Diaspora following the 1929 Arab riots, the world economic crisis, and the rise of anti-Semitism in Europe.

In the fall of 1931 questions emerged over whether the Yishuv stood ready to host the Maccabiah Games or even whether it was an appropriate time to schedule a sports pageant. Avigdor Hameiri believed that Palestine was not yet ready financially or organizationally and that the Maccabiah committee should not speed up the process: "As to the 'Maccabiada' itself—indeed again it is logical, that *davka* they shouldn't hurry to do it; that they should wait a few more years. Not because our athletic youth are not good enough in their skills and in their diligence, but because a project like this demands more than just skill and diligence."[84] Focused on the importance of representing the Yishuv in its best light, Hameiri believed it should wait to host the games.

Rabbi Benjamin, the pen name of journalist and writer Yehoshua Hatalmi,[85] also thought that the Maccabiah Games should not take place at that time, but for different reasons. He believed that a celebration was inappropriate because it was a bad period for Jews in the Diaspora and Palestine. An article in the Revisionist weekly newspaper, *Hazit ha-Am*, summarized Rabbi Benjamin's views.

> And his arguments: we find ourselves in a confusing situation in the country, without order and a lack of security.... We are in a constant state of fear. This is the situation in Eretz Israel. And in the Diaspora: campaigns for Israel collapse, in the whole world a wild hatred of Israel rages, many enemies of Israel rose up to swallow the people of Israel, and the conclusion of these things: in an emergency, in a time of mourning, you do not arrange festivities. Only Nero the crazy plays at the time when Rome burns.[86]

The writer of this unsigned *Hazit ha-Am* article, who criticized these attitudes, believed that times were always difficult and that the Yishuv nonetheless needed to push forward both with the Maccabiah Games and with the cultivation of the body.

> Indeed, it is impossible to deny that much of the reasoning and anxiety over the situation is evident in the words of this important writer. But this should not distract us from the fact that we are always found in a state of war with the whole world.... No! In spite of it all we will come up to Israel. Faces forward ... and the inspiration of the holiday will come, when they will pass in front of us in the procession in the streets of our beautiful city, ... battalions of our strong sons like oak trees that were not uprooted from their places, and upright like cypresses filled with plenty of spiritual and physical strength. And the joy of life flows in them like an inexhaustible fountain....
> And therefore forward to the work of the nation![87]

The Maccabiah committee addressed these issues in its communications with the Yishuv. In its announcement informing the public of the upcoming event, printed in *Do'ar ha-Yom* and posted in the streets,[88] they acknowledged that times were bad. Nonetheless, the committee advocated moving forward with the planning, arguing that the Maccabiah Games would provide beneficial outcomes. The proclamation noted that the Maccabi World Union meeting similarly raised these concerns but overcame them precisely because those present believed that the positive effects would outweigh the negative. As the announcement declared:

> In front of our eyes stands the Jewish reality in the Diaspora in all of its tragedy....
> ... At the meeting in Prague this question was asked:
> Are we entitled in this period to materialize the Maccabiah Games? There are those who answer in the negative, that the time is not appropriate for holding such

a tremendous enterprise, and others responded in the positive saying we must not surrender to the destructive influence of despair. Precisely this time—the time of weak hands and failed blessings—is the right time to carry out the project, make it even greater and make it into the moving force of the overly conservative Zionist movement.

The positive direction won out and the Maccabiah will take place. We may expect a few thousand Maccabees from abroad to whom will be added a greater number of tourists, coming to visit the country and to see the demonstration of Muscle Jewry.[89]

Public support, understanding, and interest were viewed as critical. The committee reasoned with the public, seeking to influence its attitude toward the forthcoming event as well as prepare it.

Whether the Maccabiah Games should or could take place at that time continued to be contested and remained a question until a month before the games. The Maccabiah committee in Palestine did not even begin its official preparations for the competition until November 1931, only four months before the opening, even though work for the event had already commenced in the Diaspora. According to Yekutieli, although the Maccabiah Games had been discussed for some time, many did not really believe they would materialize.[90]

The decision to hold the Maccabiah Games embodies the aesthetic of defiance. Moving onward with the event was viewed as synonymous with moving forward with the work of creating a modern nation. The defiant notion that precisely in this time of difficulty the games should take place represents this aesthetic: Even though times were bad, it was necessary to persevere and to embrace the national project.

Mass Calisthenics: The Aesthetic of Togetherness

Creating a display of unity, the mass gymnastics pageant during the closing ceremony at the stadium represented the aesthetic of togetherness and was heralded as one of the highlights and inspirational moments of the Maccabiah Games. About 2,500 gymnasts, men and women, participated in the exercises performed to Hebrew songs.[91] A song and exercise booklet was printed specifically for this occasion.

The gymnastic display featured almost fifty rows of fifty athletes each, all wearing the blue and white colors of the Zionist movement. The *Palestine Bulletin* emphasized these colors and the symbolic effect of the drill.

However much I may have been interested in the contests, high jump, throwing the discus, running for men, running for women, what impressed me most was the Drill Display. There was nothing very advanced about it. Just a few simple movements.

But the total effect was inspiring. The different groups of Maccabees were dressed in different colors and as they marched in their thousands from the track on to the field they presented a picture the most colorful I have ever seen.

This color effect was used to the very best advantage by those responsible for the display. At one moment the whole of the Stadium was an ocean of azure blue and blue and white, fringed with golden sand, the Scouts' khaki provided the sand.[92]

This presentation illustrated part of the enactment of the Zionist message, creating a portrait in bodies of the emerging nation.

Each person stood separately in his or her own place in line, but they performed the movements in unison. These exercises, which stemmed mostly from Swedish gymnastics, were linear and straight. Although music accompanied the rhythmic display, no directions were given. Each participant learned the order and the timing of the movements in advance, just as in a performed dance.

All the journalists reporting on the event expressed their high regard for the ceremony. It symbolized Jewish regeneration par excellence. An article in the *Palestine Bulletin*, titled "Maccabiah's Inspiring Climax: Symbol of Jewish Regeneration," reinforced this theme.

Before a crowd of spectators, thousands upon thousands of fine upstanding young Jewish men and women marched into the Stadium to-day and gave a display of massed drill which no one privileged to witness it will ever forget. Nothing like it has ever been seen in Palestine before. It was a perfect symbol of the national regeneration of the Jewish people and there were many in the crowd who were visibly touched to the core.

The English and Jewish flags were flown over the Stadium entrance and in the Stadium itself the flag of the Maccabees fluttered above the performers. The brown earth was matched by the tanned Maccabees, rank upon rank of uniformed gymnasts, thousands of swinging arms, bodies inclined, knees bent all without a word of command. The whole scene presented a perfect example of organizing ability, discipline, and rhythm.[93]

The portrait of people in absolute harmony with one another, without anyone giving directions, provided a visual display of the ideals of socialist Zionism.

The symbolic effect of these exercises was togetherness and unity. The synchronized mass performance of these simple movements produced a cohesive image. Several journalists were struck by the ability of all the participants to move in unison without any signals, even though they all came from different countries and spoke a variety of languages. Avraham Rivlin addressed this theme.

The closing of the Maccabiah—how great it was, how beautiful.

The stadium was filled and varied with a sea of heads, noisy waves of humans, graceful girls and boys. A "babel" of languages. . . . People from all over the world. But they were all united not only in their variegated costumes but also in their thought. The faces are different. But the hearts of all of those standing and exercising here are given to one aim: the benefit of the Hebrew youth and the benefit of the Land of Israel. For this they pounded their feet, some hundreds of people of Israel left the Diaspora and its bitterness for a short time and came to the land that also contains a Jewry of muscles—a "Muscle Judentum" as Max Nordau the great dreamed of.

How wonderful were the different exercises on the field of the huge stadium. The public in tens of thousands stood fascinated and surprised. The whole thing was done in rhythm and in order, even though thousands of the exercisers were from different cities, and most of them did not know one another.[94]

Max Nordau's claim that a strong nation could only be built on the foundation of strong bodies seemed to be proven by this athletic display. Even though the participants arrived from different countries, their synchronized movements asserted that Jews constituted one people, capable of creating a modern nation. The unity of movement signified a singularity of purpose. The goal of nation building was embodied in the athletes, and the socialist Zionist aim of togetherness was enhanced. The display offered inspiration and was viewed as a great national achievement.

The Politics of Participation

Not only were different sports associations tied to divergent political affiliations in the Yishuv, but the sections of Yishuv and Mandate society that took part in the Maccabiah Games were also politicized. The participation—or lack thereof—of different sectors in the Mandate demonstrated a variety of attitudes toward Zionism, sports, internal Jewish politics, Arab-Jewish relations, and the politics of the Mandate.

Socialist Versus Bourgeois: Hapoel's Abstention and the Breach of Togetherness

The politicization of sports associations in the Yishuv resulted in controversy over the Maccabiah Games. Although Jewish unity remained one of the significant goals of the games, it was not completely achieved because of the political and class issues between the Maccabi and Hapoel sports associations.

In the months preceding the Maccabiah Games, the Maccabi organization and Hapoel negotiated over Hapoel's potential participation in the games. These discussions reflected the politics between the two sports associations.

The differences between the memberships were directly linked to the divergent attitudes of socialist and urban Zionists. The Maccabi group saw itself as a Zionist and nonpolitical organization representing all of Yishuv society, whereas Hapoel viewed the Maccabi association as bourgeois. To them, the Maccabi organization was identified with the urban bourgeoisie and Hapoel with socialist Zionism. As Haim Kaufman states, "Hapoel identified Maccabi with the 'citizens' camp and argued that it could not associate a sports federation with an organization representing farmers and employers whose interests conflicted with those of the Histadrut."[95] According to Kaufman, the Maccabi organization viewed Hapoel as separatist, because it promoted sport along sectarian lines for workers only. In his view, for many socialist Zionists sports in general was considered inferior to actual physical labor, but workers nonetheless took part in sports activities. Historian Anat Helman likewise argues that sports were considered middle class and hedonistic.[96]

In July 1931 the Maccabi organization invited Hapoel to participate in the Maccabiah Games. According to Hapoel, its two requirements for agreeing to engage in the project were (1) the participation of Hapoel in the planning and administration of the Maccabiah Games and (2) invitations to working youth and scouts in Palestine as well as to Diaspora sports associations operating in the spirit of Hapoel. Hapoel also wanted to change the name of the games and to participate in the competition with its own flag and costumes.[97]

The discussions between the Maccabi organization and Hapoel broke down on February 4, 1932, and ultimately Hapoel did not participate in the games. Believing that the competition did not represent all the Zionist sports youth, Hapoel decided it could not take part.[98] By contrast, Betar, the sports organization of the Revisionist Party, joined the games.

In the weeks preceding the Maccabiah Games, the matter was addressed extensively in the Hebrew press. Hapoel in particular sought to uphold its position. A. Yair of Hapoel defended the organization's view.

> Suddenly Maccabi changed its rationale. Instead of making the Maccabiah Games a gathering of Hebrew sport without a difference between organizations and inviting all of the Hebrew sports associations, the representative of MWU [Maccabi World Union], Mr. Friedenthal, announced that it was a gathering for Maccabi alone. With this announcement he made a deceit of the agreement of MWU in Berlin, which says, "The Maccabiah is a world gathering of Hebrew sport in Eretz Israel."
>
> We need to say openly: It is not correct that Hapoel decided not to participate

in the Maccabiah Games. The truth is that Maccabi does not give Hapoel a chance to participate.[99]

The disagreement was centered on organizational politics. Each side viewed the other as responsible for the breakdown of negotiations.

Throughout discussions over the dispute, the aesthetic of togetherness was invoked and used to try to convince both parties to work with one another. Even before Hapoel made its final decision, the question of its participation in the Maccabiah Games and the debate between Hapoel and the Maccabi organization raised the issue of Jewish unity. In November 1931 Avigdor Hameiri warned against the absence of an agreement between the associations, positing that this rift could cause great shame in the upcoming event.

> And if the management of the Maccabi has not brought all this into consideration and has decided nonetheless to speed things and to have the world athletic holiday— indeed one should assume that at least the foundation of foundations was clear to it: the unity of the Hebrew youth in the country to this project. It needed to clearly know that this desire was the general wish, that in the fundamentals of the celebration there was camaraderie and excitement among the Hebrew youth in the country. It needed to know first of all, if there was the possibility here in our blessed land, to arrange something with the participation of all the youth who are torn and tattered in party rags.
>
> It needed to be sure first . . . if "Hapoel" is capable at this one historic moment of making a sacrifice for the nation: to give up a few percentages of its stubbornness in this matter or another—but also if "Maccabi" itself is capable of such a sacrifice?[100]

Believing that both groups should be able to compromise for the sake of the nation-building process, Hameiri viewed their inability to reconcile as a symbol of the problem of Jewish internal politics.

> I don't know the details of the argument between the two sports associations but that they are both Hebrew and they are both Eretz Israeli. I spoke by chance with the members of the "Maccabi" and I also heard the words of the members of "Hapoel." And I had to see the disaster that the highest sports principals . . . [are not at] the foundation of their arguments. And I also had to see another disaster, that . . . every one of them is sure that he is *davka* one hundred percent right. . . . It would not even occur to one of the sides to see the shame for generations that this matter might bring upon us.[101]

Hameiri deeply focused his criticisms on the image of the Yishuv and the potential of the games to promote political Zionism and Jewish immigration. Alluding to the importance of representing the Yishuv in its best light, he declared:

> And the Maccabiada nevertheless proceeds and is arranged without the two sides seeing the national disaster that this "festival" can bring upon us in its revealing to the eyes of the whole world our private parts and our Jewish shame in all of its party nakedness. . . .
>
> And if the celebration proceeds and is arranged, indeed maybe it will be necessary for the two sides to hand over the matter to neutral arbitration that is sincere and straight, that understands the extent of the disaster that the Maccabiah can cause if it is arranged without straightening the conflicts between Maccabi and Hapoel.[102]

Arguing against party politics and stubbornness, Hameiri believed that these conflicts could cause disaster. If Hapoel did not participate in the Maccabiah Games, he feared that the lack of Jewish unity would be exposed and would harm both the games and the Yishuv itself.

Like Hameiri, Itamar Ben-Avi also warned about the potential problems these divisions could cause. He too used exaggerated language, claiming that the split could precipitate "ruin" and "failure" and would be "poison."

> The question is only, if the internal disagreements will cause the failure even before it starts? The question is, especially, if Hapoel will blow what Maccabi has founded and if the triple Hebrew demonstration [referring to the Adloyada, the Maccabiah Games, and the Levant Fair that spring] will not turn into a terrible and frightening internal destruction?
>
> We are not here to decide with whom the justice lies in this civil war . . . [but we] can properly appreciate all of the scandal that could erupt from a class hatred that goes and eats at the flesh of all of our projects in the country. If we still have the flare and if we still believe in the cooperative directions for all levels of our people, then we need to put an end, while there's still time, to the poison that goes through the veins of the new generation during its national revival.[103]

Ben-Avi then called on the Maccabi organization to make compromises for the sake of national unity, but he did not place blame on either side. Like Hameiri, Ben-Avi sought compromise and consensus and feared the ruin that could result if an agreement was not reached. The critical importance placed on fostering Jewish unity—and the centrality of the aesthetic of togetherness—was invoked.

Hapoel's decision not to participate in the games was viewed by some members of the Yishuv as an affront to Jewish unity and a serious impediment to national revival.

H.L.H. was especially incensed by the lack of solidarity. He wrote in hyperbolic language:

> But a sword was struck in its heart. And *davka* not from outside. The hands of a friend, supposedly, forged it. Hapoel does not want to celebrate with the celebration of the nation. . . .
>
> For us the question is much deeper and penetrating to the depths of our sad soul than the participation or nonparticipation of Hapoel in the national world gathering. . . . The tear goes through all of our lives and our national revival. We have turned into two peoples. . . . All the efforts for our revival as a national unit are about to go to nothing. . . .
>
> Our nation has not yet coalesced enough and already the moles that undermine the future of our nation have been seen. What is the purpose of the sports association of Hapoel? The athlete writes on his flag: "A healthy soul in a healthy body." . . . From a sports perspective there is no difference between a bourgeois and a worker. The sports associations of the nation's various classes have one purpose: to fight against Hitlerism, Heimwehr, and so on. Who does Hapoel want to fight?[104]

Hapoel's abstention from the games was viewed in a dramatic fashion by many in the Yishuv. For H.L.H., Hapoel's abstention signified a much larger issue than the participation in the sports activities: The unity of the nation and the quality of the Hebrew revival were at stake. Hapoel's lack of participation in the games epitomized a breakdown of the nation-building process. For him the class differences between the sports associations were insignificant compared to the objective of creating a new Jewish state. He believed that in the sports arena, there was no difference between a bourgeois and a worker—both labored toward the same goal of the cultivation of the body. Hapoel's abstention from the games illustrated the prevalence of class differences, the politicization of sports, and its impact on the aim of generating a unified Hebrew culture. The centrality of the aesthetic of togetherness and the anger at its not being upheld added to the resentment of H.L.H. and others who agreed with him.

Religious Versus Secular: Rabbinic Approval and Support for the Maccabiah Games

In contrast to its opposition to the Queen Esther competition, the rabbinate approved of the Maccabiah Games. The Sephardic chief rabbi of Tel Aviv–Jaffa, Ben-Zion Meir Hai Uziel, attended the games and was one of the select members to sit on the stage at the opening and closing ceremonies. After the final procession he blessed the athletes at the Herzliya Gymnasium.[105]

The rabbinate's support of the Maccabiah Games was based on the condition that Sabbath laws would be upheld. Before the 1930s numerous religious-secular disputes ensued over the convening of sports events on the Sabbath.[106] In addition, in the months preceding the Maccabiah Games, the Tel Aviv chief rabbinate advocated for the availability and prevalence of kosher food for participants and visitors. In January 1932 *Ha'aretz* reported:

> The Tel Aviv Chief Rabbinate has asked the Maccabiah Games administration, which is about to contact Tel Aviv restaurants about providing food for Maccabi members and tourists during the Maccabiah Games, to deal only with kosher restaurants. The Rabbinate intends to recheck the restaurants, and during the spring festivities lists of kosher and nonkosher restaurants will be published.[107]

The Orthodox Hebrew Community Council of Jaffa and Tel Aviv also supported the Maccabiah Games on the condition that the Sabbath would not be violated during the proceedings. Its public letter to the Maccabiah Games secretariat—printed in both *Do'ar ha-Yom* and *Ha'aretz*—openly expressed their stipulations.

> We hereby are honored to inform you that the Community [Council] has decided to allocate the sum of 3 pounds for the Maccabiah Games. Unfortunately, our financial position does not allow us to participate in the Maccabiah Games with a sum that is appropriate to the value and size of this undertaking, and our small contribution serves rather as a symbol of our admiration for the project's importance. We feel it incumbent upon us to call to your attention that our participation and admiration is based on the assumption and complete assurance that the Maccabiah Games will create no act of desecration of our Sabbath nor profane any of the nation's holy tenets, and that the attempt at physical resurrection of our nation will not simultaneously cause its spiritual demise.[108]

This admiration and encouragement of athletic, secular games from the religious sector reveals the uncontested commitment to the cultivation of the body in the Yishuv.

This support, however, was also contingent on their stipulations being met. During the Maccabiah Games, the Orthodox community was satisfied that their requirements were upheld. Before the proceedings, in a formal response in the Hebrew press, Yekutieli confirmed that their needs would be addressed and verified that there would not be a violation of Sabbath laws at any of the events. No official sports activities took place on the Sabbath. On Friday evening, April 1, Sabbath services took place at the Great Synagogue and Ohel-Shem Hall in Tel Aviv. After the games the Hebrew Community Council of Jaffa and Tel Aviv further expressed its support of the competition by writing to the Maccabi administration, congratulating them on their achievement.

> The Community Council finds it a very pleasant duty to express to you our feelings of respect and admiration for the outstanding success of the Maccabiah Games.
>
> We, of course, foresaw that the Maccabiah Games might serve as an important, vitalizing factor in our country's rebuilding and independence, and that it would strengthen and tighten the link between our youth in the Diaspora and the past and future land of our nation. However, reality far exceeded anything we could have imagined; the Maccabiah Games were far more than exhibitions of strength and national devotion by youth: it became a tremendous spontaneous national celebration. It is still difficult to describe and predict the scope of its positive revitalizing effects on the rebuilding of our country and our home.
>
> Many and difficult are the hurdles and inhibitions in our path to the full rebirth and future of our nation, and what is needed is iron will, a Maccabi-like soul and muscles, in order to overcome the internal inhibitions and external obstacles.
>
> We are delighted to note that religious tradition was not trampled upon in this demonstration of national strength and pride organized by you.
>
> You have our blessing for what you have done and what you will do for the rebirth of our nation.[109]

The religious sector supported Jewish physical activity and the cultivation of the new Jewish body so long as it did not impinge upon traditional Jewish observance. Compared to the same community's vehement opposition to the Queen Esther competition, its considerable respect and approval of the Maccabiah Games is significant. The Orthodox community most likely endorsed the Maccabiah Games because its stipulations were both acknowledged and met and, unlike the Purim carnivals, the Maccabiah Games were based on an entirely secular event without a connection to or potential conflict with the celebration of traditional Jewish festivals. Moreover, the Maccabiah Games valorized strong, masculine bodies, even if they were housed in women, whereas the Queen Esther contests focused on female beauty with all its accompanying modesty concerns from the perspective of Orthodox Judaism. After the Maccabiah Games the Maccabi organization's use of the stadium for sports events taking place on the Sabbath was disputed.[110] Nonetheless, the Orthodox leadership's acceptance of the argument that a "Maccabi-like soul and muscles" was necessary for the building of the nation further illustrates the way in which the aesthetic of toughness was an uncontested virtue in Yishuv society.

British Support and Participation

The British supported and participated in the Maccabiah Games on the condition that Palestinian Arabs and local U.K. citizens were invited to engage in the competition. Openness to their participation was a stipulation set by the British high commissioner, Sir Arthur Wauchope, upon agreeing to serve as patron of the games. As he wrote to Dr. Chaim Arlosoroff, the head of the Jewish Agency:

> In reply to your letter of the 24th instant regarding the Maccabiad, I understand that entries from British-military and others, Police, British and Palestinian, and Arab Teams will be asked for and welcomed.
>
> On that understanding I shall be very glad to be Patron and to attend the Sports.[111]

As noted, Sir Arthur Wauchope and other U.K. dignitaries appeared at the games.

British support was significant, with both political and cultural ramifications. The English sponsorship represented to some an approval of the Yishuv's political Zionist aspirations. In contrast, the second Maccabiah Games three years later in 1935 were opposed by the British in part for these very reasons.

Culturally, U.K. support was an arena in which the Yishuv and the British shared similar interests. Although Yishuv culture in general developed separately without much influence from the British, sport was an arena that was important to them and one that they had an impact on. According to Tony Collins, "Britain is the birthplace of modern sports." Collins delineates how in the early nineteenth century games such as soccer emerged in the British public schools: "But, just as important as the codification and organization of individual sports, these schools also helped to define the moral attributes of sport. The concepts of sportsmanship, fair play, and athleticism were defined and propagated by them."[112]

In the 1920s in Palestine the British influenced the development of football (soccer) (which became the most popular sport in Palestine) and promoted the sport in both the Arab and Jewish communities.[113] Jewish teams played against their English counterparts.[114] Although historians debate the role of the British in the ultimate prevalence of football in the Yishuv, noting that many Jewish immigrants brought their appreciation for the game with them to Palestine and that, unlike in other areas of British rule, cricket, the British national sport, was not played in the

Yishuv,[115] football nonetheless offered an arena of common interest and exchange between the Yishuv and the British even before the Maccabiah Games.

At a time when Jews and Arabs in Palestine were trying to attain English support, the Maccabiah Games presented a portrait of Zionist and British agreement.

Arab Boycott

Palestinian Arabs protested the Maccabiah Games and entirely boycotted the opening ceremony. They viewed the games as a militaristic event and were concerned that the competition would bring large numbers of Jews into the country who would remain permanently as residents, just as the organizers hoped. The Arab community also thought that the Maccabiah Games symbolized and enforced the idea that the Jews had a right to a state within the territory of Palestine.

The Hebrew newspapers closely monitored the Arab press, noting and reporting on these reactions.[116] According to *Davar* and *Do'ar ha-Yom*, writers for the newspaper *Falastin*, the Arabic daily of Jaffa run by Christian Arabs, thought that all the Jewish athletes would stay in the country.[117] *Ha'aretz* similarly reported on *al-Jama'a*, an anti-Zionist paper, noting its urging of Arab institutions to refrain from participating in the "Zionist Maccabiah" and its disappointment that some Arabs chose to partake: "To our dismay—writes *al-Jama'a*—we have been informed that the young Christian association in Jerusalem decided to participate in the Zionist Maccabiah."[118]

Not only did the Maccabiah Games raise concerns in the Arab community, but it also posed questions in the Yishuv about Jewish-Arab relations. In the months preceding the games, in December 1931, the writer N. from *Davar* instigated a debate in the Hebrew press when he expressed his concern that the Arab sector would seek to imitate the Maccabiah Games. His comments also illustrate an awareness in the Yishuv that the Maccabiah Games could incite the Arab community.

> I am not that worried about the cry that the Arab newspapers will arouse certainly around this meeting. . . . This is not what I am worried about, as I know that there is no escape from this, and whatever we do, the Arab incitement will always find something to hold onto, but I am worried about another thing: of imitation by the Arabs. This we also knew: the Arabs follow in our footsteps, and in "external" matters rather than from real culture. . . . There are things in which they succeed less and things in which they succeed more; however, they always learn and react. I do not begrudge their studies if there is a real improvement in the working Arab settlement and a real benefit for the whole country. I wish the Arabs would learn to care a little for the health of the nation and its education, for the condition of the worker and

the status of the woman. But as was said, they learn more easily the external things rather than the real cultural things. . . . The meaning of the thing: in some time soon . . . there will be here in the country an Arab "Maccabiah" in Shechem and maybe even in Jerusalem. And even this will be done with great and loud preparations and with blasts of victory. Even this [Arab Maccabiah Games] will be composed of young Arabs and Muslims from all over the world. This spectacle displayed before the country is not pleasing.[119]

Others disagreed with this negative attitude toward the Arab community. Menachem Samburski wrote a response to N. in *Davar*, contending that competition should not be dreaded. He countered N.'s claims, stating that the Yishuv would not have accomplished anything if it had been only concerned with potential Arab imitation.

In *Davar* of December 1 . . . the author was opposed to the Maccabiah because of a fear that what we will do they will also do. With everything we have done in the country up until now, if we had to fear that the neighbors would also do it, was it then not worthwhile to have done it? We would have had to occupy ourselves only in the writing of the Torah, only then would we be sure that the neighbors would not do like us.[120]

Samburski believed that if the Arab sector wanted to create its own Maccabiah Games, it might even foster better Arab-Jewish understanding.

There is nothing to fear from competition. Let them also build colleges here, let them also have "Maccabiah Games." Indeed, let Torah grow, maybe this will hasten understanding between us and we will become closer to one another. We will not assimilate, but we will grow closer, for our benefit and for theirs.[121]

Like Samburski, H.L.H. thought that a potential Arab Maccabiah Games did not pose a problem. As he stated with confidence, "We don't begrudge our neighbors—let them also have a gathering of young athletes—this matter cannot change our position even a bit."[122] He believed that peace derived from mutual acknowledgment rather than trepidation. In his estimation the Maccabiah Games held the potential to promote harmony and understanding.

We think that the Maccabiah Games can bring peace. . . . At the Maccabiah, athletes from all the neighboring countries will participate. Even our neighbors in the land here were invited to our sports holiday. Peace will not come from fear but rather from recognition of the value of equality. Suppression never brought desirable results.[123]

Yishuv members weighed and debated the impact the games could have on the Arab community in Palestine. *Davar* writer N. stressed the importance of taking these political factors into account.

> I don't think (and I didn't say) that the Maccabiah gathering in Tel Aviv is an unjust thing that we are not entitled to do. And I do not think that it is without benefits. But I doubted if this gathering is worthwhile for us, in its development, with all the results, the positive and the negative, that it might bring us. And this accounting . . . is necessary, in my opinion, for Zionist politics and for the politics of every nation.[124]

N. concluded that the consideration of the effect of the Maccabiah Games on the Arab community was vital for Zionist politics. In the end, the Arab sector did not hold a Maccabiah Games of their own, and the Yishuv's Maccabiah Games became a huge success.

Conclusion

As Ruth Jordan, cited in the Introduction, noted, every aspect of daily life in the Yishuv had national significance. To members of the Yishuv sports were not just a pastime; they had deeper national, political, and social meaning.

The first Maccabiah Games in 1932 highlight the political climate in the Mandate era. The British supported the event; most Arabs boycotted it. Although the Maccabi association had begun in the Diaspora, the Jews in the Yishuv hoped that the games in Palestine would offer an opportunity to impress their Diaspora brethren and encourage them to immigrate.

The games embraced Nordau's philosophy of muscle Judaism, with its emphasis on strong, masculine bodies. Notions of German-based nationalism and the belief that robust bodies formed the basis of a solid nation were also emphasized. The aesthetic of toughness dominated the event.

The aesthetic of defiance also prevailed. There were discussions over the propriety of celebrating during difficult political times, but ultimately the Maccabiah Games took place.

Although the aesthetic of togetherness was showcased in the nature of the games, especially in the mass calisthenics, the presence of the socialist-bourgeois split played out in Hapoel's boycott. Even sports became a party to internal conflicts between different Zionist groups.

Because the Maccabiah Games developed from a European model, no opportunity for discussion or fusion of East and West emerged. Yet the continuing quest to create something new with elements of tradition is evident. The sponsors connected the games to the ancient Maccabees and thus to the holiday of Hanukkah. Because the Maccabiah Games were not used as an alternative means for celebrating the holiday and because no programs transpired on the Sabbath, there was no protest from the religious sector.

The Maccabiah Games were viewed as a great achievement and became a model for subsequent sports competitions. Three years later, another Maccabiah Games took place. In contrast to the 1932 games, the 1935 Maccabiah Games were officially opposed by the British. The second Maccabiah Games have been referred to as the aliyah Maccabiah because numerous athletes did not return to their countries of origin and remained in Palestine. A third Maccabiah Games was scheduled to take place in 1938 but did not materialize until 1950, after statehood. The games were delayed because of British fears that they would lead to increased illegal immigration and because of the Arab Revolt and the worsening situation in Europe. Although the aesthetic of defiance was temporarily defeated by British and international conditions in the late 1930s, the games resumed shortly after the establishment of the state and have remained an ongoing facet of contemporary Israel.

CHAPTER 3

Producing Theatrical Dance

The National Dance Competition, 1937

On Wednesday evening, October 20, 1937, a large audience gathered to attend the National Dance Competition at Mugrabi Hall, a well-known theater and cinema in the heart of Tel Aviv (Figure 25).[1] Gathered backstage stood many of the leading professional dancers of the day; some were prominent, and others were unknown to the Tel Aviv audience on the evening of the event. The program aspired "to discover *davka* the Hebrew, Eretz Israeli dance."[2] Each of the participants was asked to show choreography that represented "authentic" Hebrew dance, and the audience was invited to vote for the dancer whose work best fitted this goal.

The competition aimed to foster theatrical dance: dance by professional, skilled, or trained dancers that takes place on a proscenium stage. The terms *concert*, *theatrical*, or *professional dance* are all used to describe this form; in Hebrew, it was deemed *mahol omanuti* (artistic dance).

As a category, theatrical dance is intended to be a high art form.[3] The National Dance Competition, and the process of developing dance as high art, embodies several of the central tensions: old versus new, East versus West, and socialist versus bourgeois.

The old-new tension is embedded in the goal of the competition. With its stated purpose of finding the most inventive and "true" Hebrew dance (*ha-rikud ha-eretz yisraeli ha-mekori*), the competition endeavored to uncover a form that was both new and innovative but that was simultaneously rooted in the past. In deliberations over the event the meaning of the term *mekori* (original or genuine) was infused with the issue of cultural authenticity. The goal of finding a dance form considered both

Figure 25. Mugrabi Square, featuring Mugrabi Hall, Tel Aviv, 1934. Photo: Zoltan Kluger. Israeli Government Press Office.

authentic and original was fraught with tension because the concept of authenticity is ingrained in the past, whereas that of originality is entrenched in the present.

In attempting to create a high art form, the Yishuv endeavored to set distinctions between theatrical and folk dance and disputed what should belong under the rubric of high art. Folk dance, as I discuss in Chapter 4, also developed in this period. This form of low art usually refers to dance in which professionals and nonprofessionals alike can participate and that can take place in various spaces, not exclusively or primarily on an elevated stage. Because both forms emerged simultaneously, the demarcations of folk and theatrical dance in the Yishuv developed at the same time as the dances themselves. The National Dance Competition, as well as the Dalia Festivals discussed in Chapter 4, ignited debates about the appropriate content for each category.

Similarly, the process of setting distinctions between high and low art is linked to the tensions between East and West and to cultural assessments and assumptions about the two locales. Low culture was defined as folk, Arab, and Middle Eastern; in contrast, high culture was viewed as artistic, Jewish, and European. Whereas high art was deemed the goal, worthy of representation both abroad and in Palestine, low art was regarded as base and inferior.

In their efforts to create an authentic Hebrew dance form that would be considered high art, Yishuv members faced a paradox: They wanted a concert dance genre that would be considered artistic in European terms: choreographed, skillfully executed, evocative of European modern dance conventions during this period. At the same time they wanted dance that would be deemed authentically Hebrew: Middle Eastern, Jewish, evocative of biblical times or of their new life in Palestine. Dances considered authentic were deemed low art. Therefore they were seen as closer to folk dance and viewed as more appropriate for that category by both the artists and the critics of the time.

The aim to create a theatrical dance form also uncovered the tension between urban and socialist Zionism. The emphasis of socialist Zionism on equality was embedded in the structure of having the audience, rather than a professional panel of judges, choose the prizewinners. Yet the notion of selecting winners, ranking different dancers, and thereby establishing cultural and artistic hierarchies contradicts the socialist Zionist ideal of equality and its call for a society without distinctions, status, and ranks.

Creating a Theatrical Dance Form
Setting the Stage: Building Concert Dance

Within the cultural scene of the Yishuv in the 1920s, the creation of theatrical dance lagged behind developments in other arts. Theater, music, visual art, and literature gained prominence earlier: Bezalel, the academy for the study of fine arts, had been open since 1906; in July 1923 the Palestine Opera, which performed operatic classics exclusively in Hebrew, was established; in March of that year the daily newspaper *Ha'aretz* began its literature section; and in 1925 the Ohel Theater, the socialist workers theater, opened.[4]

These other arts were gaining popularity; however, theatrical dance was neither strongly featured nor organized but was by and large restricted to a few individuals. They included Baruch Agadati, discussed in Chapter 1; Margalit Ornstein, who opened the first major studio for dance in the Yishuv; and Rina Nikova, discussed in this chapter.[5]

In the 1920s the relegated state of concert dance in the Yishuv was addressed in the Hebrew press. In *Do'ar ha-Yom*, Ben Tzion Yedidya pleaded for the incorporation of dance in the artistic realm.

> Theatrical dance, which occupies such an important place in the world of European culture, is at a very low state among us, neglected and left to herself. The Hebrew public, which more or less understands the value of the rest of the art forms, the theater and the opera, drawing and sculpture, relates to theatrical dance with complete indifference and looks upon her as a stepdaughter.[6]

As discussed previously, the emerging Tel Aviv urban culture regularly compared itself to European society and followed that continent's models in a variety of arenas. With the creation of concert dance as well, the Yishuv aimed to produce a style that would be respected in Europe, and it viewed theatrical dance through the cultural hierarchies of that region. In this call Yedidya used Europe—and its high art forms—as an example to be emulated.

Even as the Yishuv aimed to create a theatrical dance type modeled along European lines, it also sought to produce a style that would signify its connection to the Middle East. Although Yedidya esteemed Europe as representing high art, he simultaneously derided it, viewing Jewish life in the Diaspora as having tainted the Jews and having caused them to disengage from their own culture. "Our people, like all the peoples of the East, is a people of movement which has a dancing soul, but the *galut* made us forget our splendid trait of expressing the stirrings of our heart through artistic movement."[7]

Yedidya also recognized the need to build an audience for concert dance and insisted that the educated elite assist in the process. In so doing, he reiterated the societal hierarchies: He associated theatrical dance with the cultural and educated community and distinguished this group from the masses. Yet he made a plea to the elite to bring the public closer to concert dance.

> There is not yet a basis and a tilled soil for dance, and that is why the loyal and devoted work of the pioneers of theatrical dance in our streets is so difficult. . . . The initial help to these artists needs to come from literature and the newspapers. It is imperative to explain and to illustrate to the broad public that dance is the father of all the artistic expressive movements of the human soul.[8]

Because the arts are usually described in the feminine, Yedidya's use of a male-gendered term seems to reinstate his drive to elevate dance within the arts hierarchy. By associating dance with maleness, Yedidya aims to add to its value. His assumption of the interplay between the newspapers and the public also illustrates the importance of these media in shaping Yishuv culture.

Different opinions emerged over the best way to attain a national concert dance form. Some journalists and cultural commentators, like Yedidya, called for the cultural elites to build the arts rapidly, whereas others believed that the arts should emerge gradually from the experience of living on the land. In a tone reminiscent of Ahad Ha'am, the dancer Margalit Ornstein called for patience in developing dance organically from the experience of the new society. She made this argument in 1929 in the literary periodical *Ketuvim*.

> Do not raise your voices to demand Hebrew art before we are Hebrews. Do not demand national expression in art before we will arrive at a specific expression in our daily lives. Do not make the end come sooner! One arrives at the art only with the strength of slow development and not with surprise and with haste. It is in the strength of a revolution to create comfortable conditions for new art that is different from before, but only conditions. Because the art itself needs gradation. Seven–eight years are not enough to remove the burden of the *galut* from the necks of the nation, especially if they have to derive its new strength and its spiritual food from the new land. A little patience! Because here this land of ours will nourish our youth, will give their arteries new juice, will open their eyes to see the Eretz-Israeli sun, the bright colors, the big lines in their scope, the mighty forces in the phenomena of nature—all of these will educate the nation to an art that is our own. And a "Jewish dancer" will arise from this.[9]

Ornstein shares Yedidya's assessment of the negative effect of the Diaspora on Jewish culture. Yet, instead of establishing a social hierarchy, her proposed route for the new art is more aligned with labor Zionism: It would emerge from the landscape and the youth's experiences in the land.

Concert dance was fledgling in the 1920s, but it began to progress in the 1930s as a result of both the continued efforts in Palestine and the large immigrations, including several dancers and artists from Europe, especially Germany.[10] Many concert dancers in Palestine were heavily influenced by the European theatrical dance legacy. Until the 1920s ballet prevailed as the dominant form of theatrical dance in most of Western Europe.[11] After World War I, though, a new dance form began to emerge whose center lay in Germany.

Many of the dancers in 1930s Palestine either arrived from or received training in Germany, the center of *Ausdruckstanz*, or German dance expressionism. *Ausdruckstanz* was a revolutionary movement in dance whose goal was to demonstrate the emotional world of the individual. Having developed in the one Western European nation without a strong ballet tradition, *Ausdruckstanz* stood in direct contrast to ballet: It was characterized by dancing in bare feet (unlike ballet with its satin toe shoes), strong facial expressions, and "free" movement, unencumbered by the rigid ballet technique. *Ausdruckstanz* was a new method of creating dance that focused on the individual expressing him- or herself from the inside out, as opposed to taking on a particular character, as in the ballets of the period.[12] Among the primary exponents of this new dance were Rudolf von Laban, Mary Wigman, Kurt Jooss, and Gret Palucca.

The National Dance Competition

The National Dance Competition generated a unique niche for theatrical dance in the Yishuv. Staged during a fervent period in the cultural arena, the competition occurred directly after the extremely successful first season of the Palestine Orchestra. Ten months after the inaugural concert of the symphony on December 26, 1936, the National Dance Competition was held, the same month that a song contest took place for Palestinian composers "of Jewish character musically."[13] In addition, in the following month of November, the Eretz Israeli Song Competition convened at the Ohel-Shem Hall in Tel Aviv; this competition sought to "find" the national Eretz Israeli song.[14] Beyond Palestine, in Europe, the 1930s featured dance festivals and congresses for both folk and theatrical dance.[15]

The seven participants in the National Dance Competition were (in order of appearance) Rina Nikova and her Yemenite Ballet Company, Eliza Vizer Levi, the Ornstein Sisters and Studio, Yardena Cohen, Dania Levin and Studio, Tehilla Rössler and Studio, and Elsa Dublon. With the exception of Yardena Cohen, all the participants had been born in Europe. The famous modern dancer Gertrud Kraus, who immigrated to Palestine from Vienna in 1935, was not a contestant. Because her arrival was a pivotal event in the concert dance arena in the Yishuv, her absence from the program remains unclear. Nonetheless, she attended the event.[16]

The evening presented dances with a variety of themes. Biblical influences could be seen in such dances as *Cain and Abel* (Ornstein Sisters) and *Dance of Esau* (Tehilla Rössler); dances with titles depicting life in Eastern Europe included *Ha-Shadchan* [The Matchmaker](Elsa Dublon) and *Mitzvah Dance* (Dania Levin and Studio). Some dances took inspiration from emerging Israeli folk dances, such as *Hora* (Tehilla Rössler) and *Debka* (one by Yardena Cohen and one by Nikova's Yemenite Ballet Company), and other works depicted Yishuv life and the local landscape, such as *Waves* (Ornstein Sisters) and *Valor* (Shoshana Ornstein and Studio) (Figure 26). Musical accompaniment was also varied, ranging from classical European music to Middle Eastern and emerging Israeli tunes.

Figure 26. The Ornstein Sisters in *Waves*, 1927. The Ornstein Sisters performed this dance at the National Dance Competition. Alongside the title of the dance in the competition's program, they included the note "an Eretz Israeli scene," informing viewers that they were presenting a dance based on the local landscape. Photo: Alfonso Himmelreich. Courtesy of Gaby Aldor and Resling Publishing Ltd.

On the evening of the competition, Mugrabi Hall's theater, which could seat 600 people, was full. Although scheduled to begin at 8:30 p.m., the spectators waited in anticipation until 9:00 for the opening curtain. The show represented the first time in which concert dancers from all over the country performed on one stage in front of a broad audience. Unlike most competitions, which featured a panel of professional judges, at this event the members of the entire audience chose the prizewinners. Just as with the Queen Esther beauty competition, each entrance ticket included a coupon with the names of the contenders. The audience was specifically instructed to vote immediately following the performance. At 12:30 a.m., when the show ended, each audience member marked a ballot to select the "most genuine" Hebrew dance; ushers came through the hall with boxes to collect the votes, and everyone waited for the results.

The Armon Theatrical Agency in Tel Aviv sponsored the contest and arranged for a ten-member supervisory committee, chaired by the playwright and lawyer Sammy

Gronemann.[17] Other members of the committee included journalists and two poets (Leah Goldberg and Saul Tchernichovsky). The committee's responsibilities included overseeing the evening and handing out the prizes, but their precise role remains elusive.[18]

The results of the contest were quite close. There were 576 votes in total, although 19 votes were disqualified.[19] Yardena Cohen, a native of Haifa, won first prize (a shield from the Tel Aviv Municipality)[20] with 176 votes; Rina Nikova, a Russian ballerina, and her Yemenite Company earned second prize (a silver cup sponsored by the cigar company Dovek) with 171 votes; and the Ornstein Sisters, twins from Vienna who immigrated to Palestine at age 10 with their mother, Margalit Ornstein, in 1921, received third prize (a silver medal sponsored by the Armon Theatrical Agency) with 156 votes.[21]

The three prizewinners that evening all received some level of dance training in Europe. A native of Haifa, Yardena Cohen was unknown to the Tel Aviv audience on the evening of the National Dance Competition. Cohen, a sixth-generation Palestinian on her father's side,[22] was the only contestant both born and raised in Palestine, but she too spent time training in Europe. Even though she was not a European immigrant, Cohen went to the continent from 1929 to 1933 to study modern dance in Vienna and Dresden. In Dresden she studied with Gret Palucca, one of the well-known German expressionist dancers of the period.

Rina Nikova stood among the earliest dance pioneers in Palestine, beginning her career there in the 1920s. She was thus already prominent both in Palestine and abroad when her Yemenite Company opened the performance. Born in St. Petersburg in 1900, Nikova received training in classical ballet. Initially a student at the Bolshoi Theater in Moscow, Nikova fled to Berlin after the Russian Revolution and while there gave performances and toured the smaller towns. She came to Palestine in 1925 and in that year founded the first ballet school there and became ballet mistress and prima ballerina of the Palestine Opera.[23] Until Nikova's arrival, the Palestine Opera, which was established in 1923, did not include any dancing (Figure 27).[24]

The Ornstein Sisters, Shoshana and Yehudit, twins born in Innsbruck, Austria, spent the first part of their childhood in Vienna and the latter portion in the Yishuv. In 1924, only a few years after their arrival in Palestine, their mother, Margalit Ornstein, opened the first studio in Tel Aviv that featured modern dance; it was the only school for modern dance in the Yishuv until the early 1930s.[25] Margalit Ornstein traveled with her daughters to Europe to study with well-known German expressionist dancers such as Rudolf von Laban, Elinor Tordis, and Gertrud Bodenweiser. Like Cohen and Nikova, the Ornstein Sisters received a European dance education.

At the time of the competition, the Ornstein Sisters, who were then directing the studio themselves, were well-known. Many members of the Tel Aviv audience had

Figure 27. Rina Nikova with her dancing partner, David Brainin, at the Palestine Opera. Photo: Zvi Oron. Central Zionist Archives.

seen them perform when they were teenagers or when they had studied dance at the studio, either with the twins or with their mother. In addition, the Ornstein Sisters organized several holiday pageants, particularly Tel Aviv's Purim celebrations in 1932. The Ornstein family had an established reputation in the Tel Aviv community. At the competition they performed three pieces together: *Waves, Cain and Abel*, and the closing dance in the show, *The Mirror* (Figures 26 and 28). They also presented pieces separately with their studio: *Jepthah's Daughter* (Yehudit Ornstein and Studio), *Shevet Achim Gam Yachad* (Brothers Dwell Together) (Shoshana Ornstein and Studio), and *Valor* (Shoshana Ornstein and Studio).[26]

The other participants also received dance training in Europe. Born in Poland, Tehilla Rössler, who came in fourth place, studied with Gret Palucca and Mary

Figure 28. Yehudit and Shoshana Ornstein in *The Mirror,* 1938. Later silver print. The Ornstein Sisters performed this dance at the National Dance Competition. Photo: A. Himmelreich. Courtesy of Igal Presler Collection, Tel Aviv.

Wigman in Dresden; she arrived in Palestine in 1933. Elsa Dublon studied with Hanya Holm at the Mary Wigman School; she arrived from Germany in 1936. Born in Turkistan, Dania Levin arrived in Palestine in 1922. She studied with Margalit Ornstein and later went to Berlin and studied Laban technique with Jutta Klampt.[27]

Artistic Process and Dancing: Old–New and East–West and the Aesthetic of Fusion

In creating concert dance in the Yishuv, as in other arts arenas, choreographers aimed to develop an authentic Hebrew style, a process that embodied the old-new tension. As in many invented art forms at the time in the Yishuv, in seeking to evoke an imagined ancient Jewish life, several choreographers turned to the Bible for inspiration. These depictions of the biblical past were encoded with complex evaluations of "Orient" and "Occident" that were similar to developments in other genres, such as the visual arts, music, and Hebrew literature.[28]

All three of the competition's prizewinners presented dances based on biblical themes. Yardena Cohen offered character types from biblical times in pieces such as *The Mourner: A Woman Whose Art Is to Lament* (Figure 29) and *The Sorceress: A Magician and Fortune Teller in Biblical Times and Today.* Cohen viewed the Bible as an important source of inspiration in her work, and her pieces evoked an imagined ancient Hebrew past.[29] She also dressed her musicians in white to further suggest a biblical scene.

Rina Nikova and her company performed *The Prophet's Sons,* a dance based on the biblical story of the meeting between the prophet Samuel and King Saul (see Figure 35).[30] The Ornstein Sisters performed two pieces based on biblical stories: *Jepthah's Daughter* (Yehudit Ornstein and Studio) and *Cain and Abel* (Ornstein Sisters). The dance *Shevet Achim Gam Yachad* (Brothers Dwell Together)(Shoshana Ornstein and Studio) also drew inspiration from the Book of Psalms (Psalm 133:1). The newspaper *Haboker* reported favorably on their selection, reiterating the notion that the Bible served as an appropriate source for new Hebrew dance: "Even for them the source of the Hebrew dance is the source of the Hebrew tradition itself: the *Tanach* [Bible]."[31]

In addition, in aiming to create authentic Hebrew concert dance, several choreographers turned to inspiration from the Middle East. Yardena Cohen and Rina Nikova embody the East-West tension. Internalizing Orientalist attitudes of the time, they both looked to the East as representing authenticity, but at the same time they remained conflicted about these sources and often viewed them as low art.[32] Their work represents the complicated and liminal space between East and West that Ivan Kalmar and Derek Penslar delineate.[33] Their artistic processes and creations embody the aesthetic of fusion because they combined influences from the two perceived cultural milieus in their work.

Although most of the dance contestants in the National Dance Competition are now recognized figures in Israeli theatrical dance history, the discussion here focuses on the work of Yardena Cohen and Rina Nikova as representative of the paradoxes

Figure 29. Yardena Cohen in *The Mourner.* Cohen performed this dance at the National Dance Competition. Courtesy of Irit Magal-Meltzer and The Dance Library, Tel Aviv.

of creating a new, yet original, Hebrew dance. This style sought to be viewed as high art, therefore Western, but it also strived to be rooted in the traditions of the Middle East.

Yardena Cohen

Yardena Cohen's artistic development embodies her complex relationship with and blending of the cultural milieus of Europe and the Middle East. In her personal accounts she emphasizes the deep level at which she felt like a foreigner and a stranger in Europe. She felt this estrangement most acutely when she saw Uday Shankar, the famous Indian dancer, perform in Vienna. As she recounted in a personal interview:

I was a stranger there. I remember I saw Uday Shankar, from India, and this was close to me. Drums, all of these things, and I was there and it was wonderful. And behind me sat Mary Wigman and Palucca, and they didn't see that I sat there, and they talked in German—I already understood. And so Wigman said: "This Palestinian of yours, she doesn't fit in at all here. She is very talented," as she said, "but she does not fit in with us." And I heard this, and I went to Uday Shankar behind her and I cried and I said to him in English, "I am a stranger. I am feeling so bad. And I don't know what to do." And he caressed me and said: "My daughter, I also passed through these crises in Europe. You'll return to your home, to your homeland, all of your roots will come." And this is how it was. And I still managed to thank him in a letter before he died in India.[34]

This meeting is a pivotal moment in Cohen's growth as a dancer: She was clearly identified with and embraced by the East, but Wigman and Palucca, the representatives of European culture, did not accept her. Shankar, the symbol of the East, on the other hand, took her in, encouraged her, and understood her plight. Cohen's feeling of otherness in Europe was intensified, and her sense of belonging in the East was reinforced.

After her experiences in Europe, Cohen viewed her dancing as a process of rebirth and awakening in which she sought to separate herself from her European training. When she returned to Palestine, Cohen first began to work with a pianist, a process that she found frustrating because she felt that she was "missing something essential, rooted."[35] She then slowly began to seek out Eastern instruments and located Sephardic musicians, among them Eliyahu Yedid and Ovadia Mizrahi, whose music sparked an awakening in her body.

> Back in my country, in my home, I was immediately attracted by the *genuine* Oriental drum that belongs here, by those ancient instruments. Now I made a new start, searching after old new ways. I began to talk in a new language, and I experienced a feeling of being re-created. My childhood—worlds that had remained latent through generations—I consider it as an atavism in me.[36]

Cohen cloaks her statement in Zionist terms: Her use of the phrase "old-new" echoes the title of Theodor Herzl's famous novel, *Alt-Neuland*. She interprets her move to Eastern instruments as a return to her origins, to her true self, believing, according to Orientalist notions, that the "genuine" Oriental drum and the "ancient instruments" deliver authenticity. She uses the term *atavism* to denote genuineness, and the word *latent* implies that she had uncovered something that was already there. In essence, the past, which Cohen saw as housed in the East, established legitimacy and provided the material with which she could be "reborn." The Eastern music, in her view, set the stage for her to create authentic dance.

Cohen also regarded her music choice as a rejection of the West in favor of the East. In her estimation her musical accompaniment distinguished her from her European counterparts. In describing her arrival at the theater before the competition, she depicted the reaction of the Sephardic custodian's family to her dancing: "They immediately entered into the secret of my work and didn't see in me another 'Ashkenazic' dancer with 'piano,' but one of them."[37] The piano signified the West and the Ashkenazim.[38] Cohen's musicians, on the other hand, represented the East and associated her with it.

Another element behind Cohen's choice of Sephardic musicians was her impression of their tunes as invoking biblical life. As with many Zionists aiming to project rootedness in the land, and especially for Cohen, whose paternal lineage had been there for generations, the East for her meant the connection of the Jewish people to the ancient Hebrew life in the current rebuilding of Palestine. In her search for Jewish biblical roots, Cohen viewed the surrounding Arab cultures, among which she had grown up, as sharing this biblical ancestry and Levantine culture.[39] She described her relationship to the Eastern style as follows.

> The Eastern style of mine on the stage, that is truly East. This I didn't learn in any place; this came to me from the blood. The intellect came from my parents. This is something else . . . when something came to me, they [my musicians] would say, "That's it, exactly"—meaning, they felt something from the nature, but with a spirit of culture [*tarbut*]. It is not a belly dance; it is a biblical dance.[40]

In this description Cohen conveys her belief that the Eastern style of her dancing emerged from inside her, rather than from her studies, and especially as an element separate from her European training. Furthermore, she establishes distinctions between her biblical dancing and belly dancing, implicitly placing her work into the rubric of high art because it has a "spirit of culture." She simultaneously views her choreography as embedded in the ancient East, though, because it has "something from the nature." Cohen aspires to be aligned with the "authentic East" and at the same time seeks to produce high art—two opposing objectives according to Orientalist concepts.

Yet, in her preparations for the National Dance Competition, Cohen discovered that she and her musicians had different expectations of how to prepare for a performance. The musicians upheld a Middle Eastern rehearsal style, a mode characterized by improvisations that would shift from rehearsal to rehearsal. Cohen was newly schooled in the European rehearsal model, demarcated by a set score repeated precisely each session. The musicians did not understand Cohen's need for a fixed program, because they believed that they should improvise and she should follow their tunes in her dancing.[41] Cohen and her musicians also maintained separate visions of how the musical group should dress for the performance at the National Dance Competition.

> When I informed my musicians that there was going to be a competition—they were very excited, but they were astonished to hear my suggestion that they should perform in original Eastern style, that is to sit on the stage on low stools, dressed in white tunics, as in ancient times. . . . For them, that all of their pride was in the "European" dress, it was not appropriate in their eyes to sit barefoot and "poor and miserable" on the stage in front of everybody, and they were about to rebel. As usual, also this time the explanation that this was a biblical style saved the situation. I claimed to them that our forefathers used to sit comfortably like this and please others with their tunes. And so I succeeded in convincing them.[42]

The difference in priorities between Cohen and her musicians, over both rehearsal style and costumes, is entwined with both parties' various interpretations and attitudes toward East and West. The musicians themselves, wanting to appear in Western garb that they viewed as more dignified, had adopted an internal Orientalism.

In her artistic process, Yardena Cohen personifies the tension between European and Eastern cultures. Cohen's attitude toward her musicians and toward the Eastern culture for which she searched was ambivalent. Adopting Orientalist concepts, on the one hand, she viewed her musical group as simple and unsophisticated; on the other hand, she was indebted to them and believed that they held the key to her art. As she stated about the competition, "My musicians boasted, not in vain, that 'if it weren't for us, there wouldn't be anything,' and I am grateful to them for giving life to my dances and for waking up my body from its sleep."[43]

Cohen also embodies this opposition in her artistic creations. German dance expressionism strongly influenced her movements. In a photograph of her dance *The Sorceress*, Cohen stands covered in a long, plain dark dress and a dark head covering (Figure 31). The only revealed parts of her body are those that are the most expressive: her eyes, mouth, and hands. Cohen's right hand is held above her head, her left arm is positioned at her side, and her face has a pensive and intent expression on it. In another photograph from this piece, Cohen crouches likewise with a determined look on her face, placing her hands in a similar configuration (Figure 30). Cohen's stance in Figure 31, her costume, her intensity, and, particularly, her hands held in a clawlike position are especially reminiscent of Mary Wigman's work (Figure

32). One of the preeminent German expressionist dancers of the period, Wigman believed that the hands alone could express any kind of emotion, and this clawlike position was one of Wigman's trademarks.[44] The similarity between photographs of Wigman's dances in the 1930s and Cohen's work is striking.[45] Although Cohen did not see Wigman perform and was unfamiliar with Wigman's *Song of Fate*, the resemblance between these images indicates a connection between the cultural milieus of Europe and the Middle East as well as Cohen's absorption of some of the styles of German dance expressionism.

These European movement qualities and body positions seem to dominate the form of *The Sorceress*. At the same time, however, at the dance competition Cohen presented her work with an Eastern veneer, as evidenced by the subject of the pieces, the accompaniment of Sephardic musicians, and the costumes. Although her attire in *The Sorceress* was European, it also included Middle Eastern qualities: Cohen's head covering was an Arab-looking headdress, and she wore a large, heavy bracelet associated with the East.[46] In addition, in other dances, such as *The Wedding Dance*,

Figure 30. Yardena Cohen in *The Sorceress*, 1933. Cohen performed this dance at the National Dance Competition. Photo: Hella Fernbach. Courtesy of Judith Brin Ingber from her photo collection.

Figure 31. Yardena Cohen in *The Sorceress.* Courtesy of Irit Magal–Meltzer, Ruth Eshel, and The Dance Library, Tel Aviv.

Figure 32. Mary Wigman in *Song of Fate* from her 1935 group work *Hymnic Dances.* Jerome Robbins Dance Division, New York Public Library for the Performing Arts.

Figure 33. Yardena Cohen in *The Wedding Dance*, 1937. Cohen performed this dance at the National Dance Competition. Photo: Hella Fernbach. Courtesy of Judith Brin Ingber from her photo collection.

Cohen wore a veil and exposed her midriff, also elements that evoked the East (Figure 33).

Dance historian Joan L. Erdman believes that "'Oriental dance' was an occidental invention."[47] The term *Oriental dance* was first used by Europeans and Americans to denote ballet dances considered Eastern in character. In Erdman's words, as of the 1920s, Oriental dance "conjured up expectations of exotic movements, glittering costumes, flowing lines, sublime dedication, and minor mode or strangely tuned music."[48] Erdman describes several features that Western audiences perceived as Eastern. Included among them were "opaque veils," "vibrant jewelry," and, often, uncovered midriffs for women. All of these attributes were evident in Cohen's outfits.[49] Yardena Cohen's costumes, then, featured the elements that the audience would associate with the East. In this way Cohen superimposed Eastern qualities onto a European dance structure. Cohen's dancing, like her artistic process, represented the aesthetic of fusion.

On the evening of the competition, Cohen captivated the audience. She was an unknown solo dancer, without a studio to back her up, performing alongside several of the prominent dancers of the day. At this time Cohen was a young and flexible dancer who exhibited fluid and lucid movements with graceful lines. She had a small waist, long arms and torso, and flowing auburn hair. In each of her dances she had an idea or a feeling, which she demonstrated with distinctness and with clear intent. The element that seemed to stand out most for Cohen on this evening was her powerful presence, which dominated the stage. Cohen believed strongly in her work and was able to transfer that conviction to her audience through her movement and her charisma as a performer. With her four Sephardic musicians dressed in white and playing live music on stage, Cohen transported the audience to a different world—one that evoked an imagined ancient Hebrew past—a mix of biblical and Eastern images. She performed four dances: *The Wedding Dance: How Does One Dance Before the Bride*; *The Mourner: A Woman Whose Art Is to Lament*; *A Village Dance: Debka*; and *The Sorceress: A Magician and Fortune Teller in Biblical Times and Today*.[50] In each of these pieces, Cohen depicted diverse characters and brought to the stage her interpretation of ancient biblical life.

In a personal interview Cohen related that her sister, Ruth Jordan, described her as the "Isadora Duncan of the East."[51] Cohen's work and artistic persona certainly maintained a Duncan-esque sensibility. Like Cohen, who grew up along the Mediterranean shores of Haifa in the Bat Galim neighborhood, Isadora Duncan, the famous American modern dancer of the early 1900s, matured on the Pacific coast in Northern California.[52] These two dancers carried with them both freedom of movement and flowing lines, influenced by a childhood by the sea with its open space and sinuous waves.

Duncan, a solo performer who captivated audiences in the United States and Europe, sought to portray elements of the ancient Greek past in her dancing. Greatly influenced by ancient Greek art and myth, she performed dressed in a Greek tunic with bare legs and bare feet. A dance revolutionary, Duncan opened up new ways of moving and of viewing movement in America at the time.[53]

Cohen, like Duncan, used ancient history—in her case the imagined ancient Jewish past—as a form of influence in her work and created her own technique. Also similar to Duncan, she sought to capture this past through her movement and used it as a source of inspiration.

Rina Nikova

Rina Nikova, like Yardena Cohen, similarly aimed to blend East and West in her work. She too wished to evoke an imagined ancient Jewish past and incorporate biblical stories, themes, and movements into her dances. Initially trained in classical ballet, Nikova began to change direction in the late 1920s, when she started to look for sources to create original Jewish dance. Because she believed that the Bible was the heart of the Jewish people, Nikova became dedicated to its revival in dance and sought to establish a "true Hebrew ballet, based on the Russian technique."[54] In 1928 Nikova staged a biblical ballet and traveled to America with the "special purpose of developing Palestinian ballet art there."[55] Leon Blumenfeld enthusiastically described her in *Dance Magazine*.

> Again the apple of the public's eye, Nikova conceived the Biblical ballet. She studied and restudied the Bible. She visited the original scenes of many of the episodes, studied them, and returned with what she had been developing into a native dance. Russia has its sombre, heavy-hearted ballet. America has its acrobatic, skyscraper-like dances. Palestine, thanks to Nikova, will have its Biblical ballet—a sort of Renaissance, if you will.[56]

When Nikova returned from America, she embarked on the development of the Palestine Singing Ballet with her Yemenite ensemble. In her Yemenite Company, established in 1932, Nikova aimed to combine her ballet background with the movements of Yemenite dancers.[57]

Nikova became fascinated by Arab life and viewed herself as part ethnographer. Just a few years after the well-known Russian Jewish writer and folklorist S. Ansky undertook ethnographic expedition to depict the shtetl in Eastern Europe (1912–1914), Nikova, in her role as researcher, traveled throughout Palestine observing dances and movements of Yemenite Jews and of the local Arab community.[58] Adopting an internal Orientalism, Nikova viewed the Yemenite Jews as maintaining a genuine form of Judaism,[59] and she was especially interested in their movements. The newspaper *Haboker* described her work: "She went around the whole country and looked for dresses of the neighborhoods and villages that are farthest away, studying the gait of the women, checking the load that they carry on their heads, and the influence of the heat and the rain on their movements."[60] Further remarking on Nikova's process, the writer claimed, "And in her studio she dresses this folklore in dance clothing. This is true research of Eastern dance in its entirety, from Jaffa to Tehran."[61]

Facing the incongruity of Orientalist attitudes, Nikova looked to her Yemenite

Jewish dancers for a reflection of true Jewish life, even as she also viewed their movement as low art. This outlook was illustrated in a program bill introduction she wrote for a performance in England in 1938.

> Is it worthwhile cultivating in Palestine the modern dance system which is alien to the spirit of the country's glorious past? I believe that it is not wise to do this, for the Holy Land is a unique land and its art too must harmonize with its setting.
>
> Observing Arab life, you see women on their way to the wells, walking proud and erect, a picture which invariably suggests the gait of our ancient mothers—Sarah, Rebecca, and Rachel.
>
> Looking at the Bedouins dancing the fiery passion of their movements, you believe in the ancient origin of their daring spirit. When you see and hear the ecstatic prayers of the Yemenites (the descendants of those who were exiled after the destruction of the Second Temple) who are remarkable for their faith and fortitude, and when you see our own splendid, healthy, Hebrew youth dancing the Hora, you yearn to create something new. For here you feel and think differently.
>
> In the fine eyes of my Yemenites, I find a reflection of our rich past, a source of inspiration to every artist. It will be a long time, however, before our ancient treasure is restored to the advantage of art.[62]

Like Cohen, Nikova's distinctions between high and low art follow Orientalist settings of West and East. For Nikova the modern dance system and art reside in European culture. Arab dance, in her view, represents low art, but she also esteems this form and deems it authentic. Moreover, Nikova associates Arab life with the biblical past: The movement of Arab women reflects the style of the biblical foremothers. In this way Yemenite Jews signify pious Arab Jews untainted by the European Diaspora. Nikova directly links Yishuv life to an imagined biblical past, interpreting the Yemenite Jewish community, not the European, as a living connection to that history.

For Nikova, as for Yardena Cohen, the ancient period serves as a source of authenticity. Although this invented past, drawn from Middle Eastern and biblical images, is deemed genuine, it is not considered high art. Yemenite Jews and Palestinian Arabs are extolled for their authenticity, but they are denigrated for their lack of European high culture. Thus the distinctions between high and low art, adopting Orientalist and internal Orientalist notions, remain intertwined with the distinctions between Europe and the Middle East, Jewish and Arab culture.

Dances performed by Nikova's company portray in movement the same issues highlighted in Nikova's artistic process. At the National Dance Competition, Nikova's Yemenite Company opened the performance with a piece called Dance of *the Guards,* set to music by Kugel, in which the women wore white Bedouin clothes.[63] During the evening, they also performed *At the Well*, *The Prophet's Sons*, and *Debka*.

At the Well (later called *Kookie*) was a popular movement theater piece danced to a folk tune and accompanied by song.[64] Constructed to portray traditional Eastern women at the well, this work depicts a village scene where women gather to socialize. In subsequent programs during her European tour, Nikova placed an explanatory note next to the title: "In the East the well is the only meeting-place of the women where the gossip of the village is exchanged" (Figure 34).[65]

At the Well features seven women. Each dancer has a solo segment, and all chant a song titled "Kookie" in Arabic.[66] The dance appears Middle Eastern in form. As the performers emerge in bare feet, they offer a stark contrast from the European ballet tradition. Dressed in colorful traditional dresses, the dancers balance pitchers on

Figure 34. Rina Nikova's Yemenite Ballet Company in *At the Well*, 1945. The principal dancer, Raḥel Nadav, is featured in the center. They performed this dance at the National Dance Competition. Photo: Zoltan Kluger. Israeli Government Press Office.

their heads; in addition, each performer carries a timbrel, and one dancer possesses a drum as well. The most active components of the dancer's body are the feet and the head. In contrast to the virtuoso movements featured in ballet, such as expansive jumps and leaps and high leg lifts, this dance presents small and contained motions of the feet and legs. Because the dancers do not traverse extensive space, the foot movements are intricate and complex—a feature of Yemenite dance. In keeping with Nikova's stated goal, the dancing and the scene appear Middle Eastern, but she places a European structure on the dance. Rather than featuring improvisation, typical of Middle Eastern dance practices, this piece is choreographed and rehearsed. Dance that looks Middle Eastern in fact rests on a European foundation.

Nikova and her company also performed *The Prophet's Sons*, a dance based on the biblical story of the meeting between the prophet Samuel and King Saul.[67] Staged to words by the well-known Hebrew poet Saul Tchernichovsky, "They went far away from the world that they might better understand the voice of God," the performers wore white bands around their heads and white dresses draped in a fashion thought to represent biblical dress. The work intends to evoke a spiritual scene. In photographs of the piece, the focus of the movement faces skyward, with the dancers arms positioned in a manner suggesting a readiness to listen to the heavens (Figure

Figure 35. Rina Nikova's Yemenite Ballet Company in *The Prophet's Sons*, 1945. They performed this dance at the National Dance Competition. Central Zionist Archives.

35). In other images the dancers' arms are positioned as though in a supplication, with the hands appearing to be cupped upward, a common Yemenite gesture.[68] This motion, as well as the costumes, seeks to capture a Middle Eastern character. Yet the European structure is again overlaid on the scene. Just as in the European theatrical dance tradition, the performers are positioned in an organized set fashion on the stage and their movements are clearly choreographed and assigned. In this way the two perceived cultures remain inherently meshed in the dance.

Nikova's dances, then, like Cohen's, reflect a combination of influences and elements of dance from both the Middle East and Europe. Their pieces exhibit a strong European dance technique and configuration at the same time as they appear Middle Eastern in costume, in scene, and in elements of the movement. Nikova, like Cohen, represents the aesthetic of fusion of East and West.

The Critics' Responses
Socialist Versus Bourgeois: The Event's Structure

As with the other events in this book, each aspect of the National Dance Competition was critiqued. The structure and title of the event and the form and content of the presented dances were debated. The critics addressed each aspect in a self-conscious manner.

On the one hand, the competition embodied the ideals of urban Zionism: It aimed to develop a high art dance form modeled along the lines of Europe; it took place in the urban center of Tel Aviv; and it featured skilled dancers. At the same time, the socialist Zionist ideal was embedded in the structure of having the audience choose the prizewinners, as opposed to a professional panel of judges. Everyone present at the event was equally responsible for the outcome; everyone's choice was uniformly valid; and thus everyone had an equivalent say in the building and defining of their own culture.[69]

This notion itself, however, was problematic for the critics. In their articles on the competition, almost all the reviewers emphasized the presumably autonomous and active role of the spectators by referring to them as "the judging audience" (*ha-kahal ha-shofet*). Interestingly, this phrase resembles Kesari's use of "the judging people" (*ha-am ha-shofet*) in discussions of the Queen Esther competitions. At the same time, though, the critics closely watched over and themselves judged the audience and its selections. It is as though the reviewers judged the audience itself because they could not judge the performance. By rating the audience, the critics exhibited their own sense of cultural superiority and thereby support of a cultural hierarchy. This hierarchy undercut the socialist goal.

Initially, the critics aspired to prepare the audience for the occasion. Before the competition the journalist Shriah described the dancers and the upcoming event in the Hebrew daily *Ha-Boker*.[70] He asserted that his intention was not to "influence in any way 'the audience—the judge'" but rather to introduce the performers and "to bring the audience closer to the artists."[71] Shriah's understanding of the critic's role in bridging the gap between the public and the artists echoes Ben Tzion Yedidya in the 1920s. Implicit in Shriah's statement is the notion that the general audience would not be able to understand high art without the assistance of the educated elite. Although Shriah seeks to explain matters to the spectator, at the same time he emphasizes that the task of selecting a winner lies with the public and he stresses that he will not infringe on their autonomous role: "We have not spoken at all about the principal side of this gala. We did not mention a word about the dance itself because . . . the observer alone will decide."[72]

The goal of making theatrical dance approachable to the spectators was also expressed in Shriah's article, in an excerpt from an interview with the Ornstein Sisters: "Indeed," the twins would say, if you were to speak with them, "you don't make a dance; it makes itself. But our aim is to deliver it to the audience simply, lightly, so that everyone can understand it."[73] Here as well socialist Zionist values come into view: High art should be accessible to all.

The critics monitored the audience not only before the competition but also afterward; they judged the public's choice of prizewinners and made claims about the spectators based on their decisions. In voicing her concerns about the selection capabilities of the audience, the prominent poet and critic Leah Goldberg illustrated her low opinion of them. In the following disparaging statement she assumes that the spectators will vote not on the basis of an artistic opinion but rather on the basis of relationships.

> There was another fear until we knew the results of the competition: the majority of our dancers are teachers, directors of studios; in the studios there are students, the students have aunts and uncles, relatives, and acquaintances, and they are the audience. This audience sits and melts from the movements of Chanaleh and Shoshanaleh ("I knew her when she was five years old!").[74]

Despite their disregard for the observers, however, the critics ultimately expressed some relief and satisfaction with the results. Goldberg even complimented the audience for delivering the first prize to Yardena Cohen: a choice that was, in her words, "justified."[75] The critic in the *Palestine Post*, writing under the pen name Rashi (assuming the name of a famous medieval rabbi and biblical commentator), thought that Yardena Cohen alone "succeeded in creating a purely indigenous motif" and applauded the public for its objectivity and fair-mindedness in selecting an unknown dancer: "Famed or unfamed, whatever reputation an artiste has previously achieved, here at least she can be sure of an impartial audience. This is not to say that our public lacks discrimination, but it chooses not to be influenced by the taste of others."[76] Similarly, Shriah also approved of the outcome. He thought Yardena Cohen represented "the discovery of the ball," and he interpreted her selection as a sign of the public's maturity and of their ability to understand and comprehend high art: "A very interesting aside, that the stories of 'the public that does not understand anything' were found mistaken in their foundations. An audience that did not know Yardena Cohen beforehand, handed over most of its votes to her dances. This is the certificate of the maturation of the Tel Aviv audience."[77] In addition, the editor Uri Kesari consulted with the renowned dancer Gertrud Kraus (Figure 36) about the results of the competition.

> "To whom would you give the first prize?" I asked Gertrud Kraus . . ., the one and only, the one who stands outside and above all competitions.
> —"To Yardena Cohen"—answered our wonderful Gertrud.
> And the voice of the people—this time, not only was it like the voice of the Almighty—it was also the voice of the artist who is intelligent, deep, soulful.[78]

Kesari thus esteemed the public for exhibiting the same opinion as the eminent choreographer.

In addition to placing the public under scrutiny and questioning its role, the critics challenged the structure and concept of the event. They maintained different interpretations and understandings of "competition." By definition, the act of having a contest, in which a prize will be awarded to a winner, establishes a hierarchy. The critics' concerns with the concept of competition emerged from their desire to set cultural standards and hierarchies, an objective that posed a direct affront to socialist Zionism.

Some thought that the notion of competition became inappropriately tied to the event. Leah Goldberg took issue with using the term for an occasion in which the audience, rather than a professional group, judged. She once again portrayed her low estimation of the public.

> A competition of dancers. Competition? It is customary in the world to arrange congresses of national and international dance. The judges—specialists, professionals who know how to judge not based on the "general impression" alone, who know the professional secret of movement, of the originality of an idea. The widespread public

Figure 36. Gertrud Kraus in *Night*, early 1940s. Silver print. The famous modern dancer Gertrud Kraus attended the National Dance Competition but was not a contestant in the event. Photo: A. Himmelreich. Courtesy of Igal Presler Collection, Tel Aviv.

who comes to judge the dance can at best be influenced by the temper of the dancer from their aesthetic "pleasantness." That is not enough in order to judge.[79]

In her longing for a professional group of judges, Goldberg aspired to set criteria, to uphold a social hierarchy, and to emulate a European model.

Like Goldberg, Shriah also imposed European culture as a model. By referring to the contest as a "meeting of artists," who are "common in every cultural country," he places the event in the context of activities in Europe.[80] Shriah similarly portrays a low opinion of the public. Because he also grapples with the term *competition*, the center of his concern rests on the argument that if a different name, such as "convention," were used, the public would not understand.

> It is possible that the word "competition" is not suitable to this artistic phenomenon. The artist creates from the peace of his soul, without fear; in the ears of many the word "competition" sounds like a "horse race." The word that better suits a meeting of artists is "congress." But I'm afraid that if in the advertisements they called for a "national dance congress" or a "national convention of dancers," many would not understand. I think that many would shrug their shoulders: "Again a convention that won't do anything."[81]

Shriah views the term *competition* as inappropriate, not because of the judging audience of nonprofessionals but because the occasion needed to be distinguished from a sports event. His argument, like Goldberg's, emerges from his belief in the necessity of a cultural hierarchy. His use of the term *artistic phenomenon* illustrates a desire to place this event at the top of a cultural ladder and thereby to distinguish it from activities deemed culturally inferior, such as a horse race. Shriah expresses disappointment over the presence of prizes and winners because they detract from the cultural hierarchy—from the real purpose, which is the "gathering of the artists together to show their work."[82] He favors a different title to clarify for the public that these dances represent high art.

Similarly, Rashi agreed that this dance experience should not be labeled a competition because the word connotes an insignificant or insubstantial occasion. In fact, the contest, in Rashi's estimation, proved to be the contrary: "The programme was announced as a competition, but it was something less frivolous than that. It was a full-dress parade of talent."[83]

Beyond the titles and structure of the event, Leah Goldberg posed a question addressing a central tension in the objective of creating a theatrical dance form in the Yishuv: "But one principal question still stands: the artistic dance that expresses the human being, the individual dancer, and maybe also our collective personality that is looking for expression in movement—where is it?"[84] Beyond Goldberg's clear overall dissatisfaction with the dances presented, embedded in her question is the tension between socialist and bourgeois, the collective and the individual. On the one hand, aiming to craft a high art form is an individualistic process—each choreographer offers her own vision. High art also often expresses the universal, broad issues pertaining to all of humanity. But in seeking to develop a national style for concert dance, the public and critics sought work that expressed or signified the particularity of the emerging nation. The goal of fashioning a high art form itself was an affront to socialist Zionist values. Yet, at the same time, the Yishuv wanted concert dance to express the communal and the collective, a central feature of the pioneering ethos. This tension between the individual and the communal remained at the center of the goal of creating national concert dance and of the mission of the National Dance Competition.

Establishing Cultural and Artistic Hierarchies: Rating the Dancing

The effort to establish cultural and artistic hierarchies also emerges in the critics' assessments of the dances presented at the competition. In their reviews they dispute whether or not the choreographers' works represent high or low art. These assessments are laden with cultural assumptions. They use the terms *ethnography*, *primitive*, and *folk* to describe what they considered Arab dances, which they viewed as representing low culture. In this way the divisions between high and low culture were intermingled with the distinctions between Europe and the Middle East and between Jewish and Arab.

For example, Shriah praised Nikova's piece *At the Well* but also categorized it as low art.

> I think that I will not be mistaken if I say that the most effective performance was the performance of Rina Nikova's Yemenite studio in "At the Well." Brown-skinned girls in colorful clothes singing and walking with pitchers on their heads towards the well "to give drink to the shepherds"—each girl and her clothing, each girl and her tune, a little bit loud, sometimes a little bit funny; doubtfully dance, doubtfully theater, but very effective, as aforesaid.[85]

Several critics also categorized Yardena Cohen's works as low art. The *Ha'aretz* reviewer, Batya Krofnik, criticized Yardena Cohen's dances.

> Yardena Cohen showed copies of Arab dances, maybe correct and natural copies, in very fine costumes, with a small orchestra that plays well on simple Eastern instruments. Perhaps, for her all of this is self-explanatory. But is this the right path to a new national art? What can you compare it to? It is as if they represented a perfect performance of synagogue tunes as new Hebrew music. . . . And behold there is in the case in front of us another missing thing, that the ethnography that is represented is not at all ours.[86]

Krofnik juxtaposes the dichotomies between the Middle East and Europe and between Arab and Jewish, considering Cohen's dances Arab, not Jewish, and Middle Eastern rather than European. She associates Cohen's Arab dances with low culture by referring to them as ethnography. Further, she distinguishes this ethnography from being Jewish, because it is "not at all ours" in her terms.

This review overlooks the Sephardic or Mizrahi community, which was both Jewish and Middle Eastern. Krofnik's use of the term *simple* to describe and belittle the Oriental instruments further denigrates the Middle Eastern qualities. In addition, Krofnik asserts that Cohen's work is unoriginal, because it shows copies of Arab dances. The Middle Eastern element, then, in this critic's estimation does not possess either authenticity or creativity. Krofnik associates Arab and Middle Eastern components with low culture, and for this reason she viewed Cohen's work as an inappropriate path for a new national art.

Similarly, Leah Goldberg associated Cohen's work with low art and agreed with Krofnik that it represented an imitation of Arab folk dance. Goldberg faults Cohen for using too much folk movement in her dances. In her article Goldberg invokes the Spanish dancer Argentina as an example of a theatrical dancer who used Spanish folk dances as a foundation in her work. In Goldberg's view Argentina converted these folk elements into an artistic format and served as an appropriate model for transforming folk sources into high art.[87] Goldberg uses the example of Argentina to critique Cohen, who she believed used the folk elements alone without adding artistic quality: "The basic folk primitive (and in the case of Yardena Cohen, not our folk—rather the Arab), can, should, and must be used as a foundation, but only as a foundation and not as a complete thing in and of itself."[88] Like Krofnik, Goldberg criticizes Cohen for drawing from Arab folk dances instead of Jewish ones.

Although the equating of Cohen's dances with folk or low art can be contested, the assessments continued to fall along the lines of these dichotomies. Writing in response to Goldberg in particular, Shriah promoted Cohen's work and praised it as representing high art. Shriah refutes Goldberg's assertion when he states:

> In the eyes of many they [Yardena Cohen's dances] looked like simple Arab dances.
> This is a mistake. Between the Arab dance and the creations of Yardena Cohen there is but one common stage: the Orient. And the difference between the two of them is that which differentiated between the dances of Argentina and the Spanish folk dances: the art.[89]

Shriah's assessment differs from his colleagues. He places Cohen's work in the realm of high rather than low art. However, despite this overt dissimilarity, Shriah agrees with Goldberg's and Krofnik's distinctions between high and low forms. In his claim that the only quality Cohen's dances have in common with Arab dances is the Middle Eastern landscape, Shriah, like his opponents, upholds the notion that Arab dance represents low art. He differs from them only in that he separates Cohen from that realm. To assess Cohen's dance form as high art, Shriah has to distinguish it from Arab dance.

Uri Kesari also differentiated Cohen's choreography from Arab movement.

> Her subjects will be now all of them from the life of the East. . . . Not Arab, as LG [Leah Goldberg] thinks. To know how to differentiate between Arab dance and our Oriental dance—please leave it to us! Our eyes are full until today with the figures of the dance of the Arab city and the Arab village—but Yardena Cohen's dances bring before us something entirely different.[90]

In this instance as well, Cohen's pieces, in order to be considered high art, are separated from Arab dance.

The debate about high versus low art continued beyond the National Dance Competition, especially when the dancers traveled abroad.[91] Critics discussed how Hebrew dance should be represented not only within the country itself but also in Europe.[92] After a performance in Palestine in November 1937, Nikova's company toured Europe for two years. Among their many shows the company performed at the Palestine Pavilion at the Paris Exhibition in the summer of 1938. Yardena Cohen also gave a solo performance on November 17 at Mugrabi Hall and then embarked on a European tour.

The critics wanted to ensure that only high art would be represented in Europe. Several claimed that the work of Nikova and Cohen should therefore not be performed abroad because it was not deemed suited to that category. Leah Goldberg illustrated these concerns in her discussion of Rina Nikova's dances at the competition.

> The cultivation of the basic folk element is necessary, interesting, and pleasant. But I doubt if it is permissible to show it, let's say, at international dance congresses as an Eretz Israeli dance. The issue is similar, as if Russian dance were to be represented not by Diaghilev, not by *The Red Poppy of Mesarer* [a well-known Soviet ballet], but rather by the villagers.[93]

Implicit here is Goldberg's notion that the dances at the competition were not good enough to characterize Hebrew culture; she did not consider them high art.

The critic Batya Krofnik echoed Goldberg's concerns, even using a similar analogy: "Who would the Germans have sent to a dance competition to represent Germany: mountain dancers from Bavaria, or the representatives of modern schools of dance like Wigman, Palucca, Luhaland, and others like these?"[94] These commentators fear that Hebrew dance will not receive the recognition and approval of Europe; Krofnik and Goldberg seek a concert dance form that will be viewed as high art from the European perspective.

The Aesthetic of Fusion

The reviewers' impressions of the correct path to a new national art represent the aesthetic of fusion. They thought that the best dances achieved the following three elements: (1) They successfully combined the two perceived cultural milieus of the Middle East and Europe; (2) they blended Jewish and Arab qualities; and (3) they produced high as opposed to low art.

Batya Krofnik highlights the aesthetic of fusion in her discussion of Rina Nikova's work. Krofnik praises this choreographer for the directions she takes toward blending the cultures: "Rina Nikova is doing wonders in her achievements of teaching her Yemenite girls discipline without taking their temper and their natural grace away."[95] Krofnik associates "discipline" with European dance while linking "temper" and "natural grace" to Yemenite or Arab dance. She interprets Nikova as "doing wonders" because the choreographer combines these two perceived cultural backgrounds. Krofnik criticizes her, however, not only for creating low rather than high art but also for falling short of achieving a complete mixing of the cultures.

> In the last dance, which is almost not a group dance but a kind of play with singing, she [Nikova] gives all of the participants a chance to make her character stand out. It is a pleasure to the eyes. But even here there is the same problem as with Yardena Cohen. This too is ethnography . . . indeed more Jewish than that of Yardena Cohen, because the Jews are the guards of this tradition, but even here the blending with the European culture is missing.[96]

Krofnik interprets Nikova's work along the same lines and dichotomies as that of Yardena Cohen. But this reviewer views Nikova's choreography as better than Cohen's because she considers it to be more Jewish than Arab. However, in Krofnik's final estimation, both Nikova and Cohen fail because they do not maintain an appropriate balance between East and West. They each fall too closely on the Eastern side at the expense of European culture.

Krofnik further concludes that the emphasis on folk movements is an inappropriate path for the development of theatrical dance in the country.

This doesn't mean that there isn't a right for this direction [the ethnography of Nikova] to exist as well. Of course there is a place for different directions in the nation. Except, in the quest to find art which is both new and Jewish as one, there is in this attempt to convey Oriental art as it is, a roundabout way, if not to say, chaos, not a way.[97]

In her distinction between folk and concert dance, Krofnik once again places Nikova's work in the category of folk dance rather than high art.

Leah Goldberg shares Krofnik's assessment that the new national concert dance should include more European components and fewer Middle Eastern elements. Goldberg takes issue with Yardena Cohen's dances because she finds them too Middle Eastern in character.

And even those that won the prize—and won, it would seem, justly—awaken somewhat sad thoughts. . . . Yardena Cohen dances an Eastern dance. We will say more simply: Arab dance. There is capability, rhythmic feeling, her shoulders listen to her, the Eastern music suits her dance. But—indeed this is a photograph. Are we, the Jews who resided for 2,000 years in European countries, who listened to Beethoven and saw the Russian ballet, the companies of modern dancers from Isadora Duncan and onward—is this the Eastern feeling of ours? Are we capable of reacting to our heat waves in exactly the way that a Bedouin woman reacts to them?[98]

Goldberg upholds the cultural hierarchy of high versus low art along the lines of Jewish and Arab as well as along the lines of Europe and Middle East. In addition, she overlooks the Sephardic and Mizrahi community: Goldberg views Jews as having a European background, disregarding Jews with a Middle Eastern and North African heritage. Even though Goldberg believed that Cohen presented dance that was too Middle Eastern, it seems that for this critic it was better to be on that side of the divide than on the European side.

Little was written about the performers who did not earn prizes in the competition, but it is interesting to note that they were for the most part interpreted as representing dance that was too European. The critic Shriah illustrates this impression in his statement about Tehilla Rössler, who came in fourth place but did not win any prizes.

Tehilla Rössler—I think that she has the best school of all who appeared on the same evening. This is a deep, serious school, and Tehilla is an excellent teacher. She is sometimes a little bit theatrical, especially when she performs with her group. And she is European in all that does not touch the temperament. This is possibly the reason that she received only the fourth place in the public's judgment.[99]

Similarly, Krofnik wrote: "The complete opposite from Rina Nikova in this competition was Tehilla Rössler, who led her company well but didn't find enough attention in this framework, maybe because she is too new to the country she still hasn't found the inner and spiritual path of the new developing life."[100] Dances considered too European, then, were also criticized and were not selected by the audience.

In the reviewers' estimation the best direction for the new national theatrical dance was in the middle of the established dichotomies: between Middle Eastern and European, Arab and European Jewish culture. Those dances that were considered the most successful, and the closest to an original Hebrew dance, were reviewed in this fashion. Krofnik regarded the Ornstein Sisters as best working in this direction precisely because she saw them as fusing the European and Jewish elements.

> In this sense of blending European theatrical dance with our essence the bearers of the third prize went in new directions. In the dances "Jepthah's Daughter" and "Shevet Achim" they danced modern dances on Jewish subjects that were perhaps better suited to the program of the competition in terms of the content and the successfully stylized costumes. If we are already impatient to invent our own theatrical dance immediately, indeed the Ornstein Sisters' path is the shortest path for modern theatrical dance.[101]

Krofnik claims that the Ornstein Sisters' work is high art because of its association with and form in the European modern dance tradition. The Jewish component, in Krofnik's view, rests not in the movement but rather in the costumes and content of biblical themes. Thus the movement is deemed European while the content is deemed Jewish. The combination happens on different levels, in that the movement itself is not fused, nor is the content.

The critic Shriah also praised this blending of the cultures. He considered Yardena Cohen's dances so successful precisely because he found in them a mix of East and West.

> It was a dance built beautifully that filled the whole stage, a dance that was completely Eastern in character, and together with it there was a recognizable restraint, the fruit of a European education. But foremost this was a true dance, a performance that the dancer believed in from the depth of her heart—and the audience felt this and believed her.[102]

In this instance as well, the "restraint," referring to the form of the dance, is seen as European. The character, however, is interpreted as Middle Eastern. In this way Cohen's dance mixes the two cultural qualities.

Thus the path for a national concert dance is the aesthetic of fusion. Those dances considered the best were thought to have succeeded in reaching this blend. Those dances deemed problematic or deficient were those thought to represent either too many Middle Eastern qualities at the expense of the European, or an excess of European elements at the expense of the Middle Eastern.

Conclusion

In a review of the National Dance Competition in the *Palestine Post*, the critic Rashi opens with the following prescient statement affirming the elevated place of theatrical dance: "When a history of the Palestinian Renaissance comes to be written there can be little doubt that dancing will be cited for first honors among the arts."[103] The National Dance Competition succeeded in solidifying a space for concert dance in the Yishuv.

In the process of creating theatrical dance, the Yishuv aimed to set distinctions between folk and concert dance. This goal of distinguishing between the two forms will be further addressed in Chapter 4 from the opposite vantage point: that of fashioning and defining a folk dance style.

The critics self-consciously addressed every aspect of the event, from its structure and title to the dancing, the results of the contest, and the best path to craft a national theatrical dance. Within this process they established hierarchies and made assessments based on cultural perceptions.

In seeking to create a concert dance form, the Yishuv further represented the goals of cultivating the body, because dance is a physical activity that requires strength and agility. Although tensions between urban and socialist Zionist values emerged, both sensibilities were incorporated into the event. Even though the dance contest showcased Tel Aviv and urban Zionism, it also honored egalitarian ideals through the structure of a competition, with the "judging audience" determining "high art." The aesthetic of togetherness that esteemed the collective's choice was evident.

In aiming to create authentic Hebrew concert dance, the tensions between old and new and East and West remained central. Ultimately, the aesthetic of fusion served as the dominant model. The first two prizewinners, Yardena Cohen and Rina Nikova, both aimed to blend East and West. In choosing their work, the audience—and the critics in their assessments—also advocated this aesthetic, viewing the finest dances as representing this mix.

CHAPTER 4

Creating National Folk Dance

The Dalia Dance Festivals, 1944 and 1947

In the summer of 1944 a national folk dance festival took place at Kibbutz Dalia, located in the Jezreel Valley (Figure 37).[1] Dancers and onlookers arrived from all over the Yishuv to participate in the celebration and to share in what would prove to be a defining moment in the creation of Israeli folk dance. By nationalizing and institutionalizing the Israeli folk dance movement, the festival was a watershed event that solidified a space for this form in the emerging nation.

The first Dalia Festival was organized by Gurit Kadman, considered the mother of Israeli folk dance, and was held under the auspices of the Inter-Kibbutz Music Committee, the Cultural Division of the Histadrut,[2] and Kibbutz Dalia. Not only did this dance extravaganza generate significant excitement and enthusiasm, inspiring and encouraging its participants to create and learn new Israeli folk dances, but it also resulted in important institutional developments, including the establishment in 1945 of the Israel Folk Dance Committee, which became part of the Cultural Division of the Histadrut.[3] Following this period of extensive dance activity and organization, a second folk dance festival was held at the kibbutz in 1947, also directed by Kadman. These first two Dalia Festivals during the British Mandate era set the stage for three additional Dalia Festivals after the establishment of the state: in 1951, 1958, and 1968.

The emergence of the Dalia Festival was connected to other kibbutz celebrations developed in the months preceding the event. The first festival in the summer of 1944 took place after two related occasions in the spring of that year: a festival of musical choirs at Kibbutz Ein Harod and a Shavuot festival at Kibbutz Dalia.

Figure 37. General view of Kibbutz Dalia, 1947. Photo: Zoltan Kluger. Israeli Government Press Office.

In contrast to the National Dance Competition of 1937, which searched for a theatrical dance form, the Dalia Festivals fostered a folk dance style. The creation of both a national folk dance form and festival highlights the paradoxes and dilemmas intrinsic to this process. Because folk dance generally refers to movement that develops organically over time, the notion of constructing new, original "folk" dances contains an inherent contradiction.

The 1944 and 1947 Dalia Festivals encompassed all the major tensions: old versus new, East versus West, celebration versus sorrow, socialist versus bourgeois, and religious versus secular. Unlike the other events examined thus far, the Dalia

Festivals took place in a rural rather than an urban setting and showcased socialist Zionist values. Folk dancing was a participatory activity open to everyone—no training or skills were necessary; it fostered community and represented the aesthetic of togetherness. In addition, the labor Zionist ethos calling for a physical and spiritual connection to the land was also evident in the way that folk dances were performed—outside, in nature, often with bare feet or wearing light sandals. The lack of a barrier between the dancer and the earth denoted deep roots in the land.

Although the festivals took place in a rural socialist Zionist environment, urban influences were also prevalent. The events drew participants from all over the Yishuv, including city and agricultural settings. Moreover, even though the organizer, Gurit Kadman, had formerly lived on a kibbutz, she resided in Tel Aviv at the time of the festival. As with the National Dance Competition, notions of high and low culture were used to define what constituted a folk dance.

Unlike the other festivals and competitions in this book, the Dalia Festivals occurred during and shortly after World War II and the Holocaust. Even before the 1944 proceedings, the propriety of holding a celebration at this juncture, given the overwhelming number of Jews who had perished in the Holocaust, was extensively debated. Because Kadman decided to hold these festivals in spite of the unfathomable tragedy and suffering, the events embodied defiance: They showcased the new Jewish body and epitomized Hebrew strength precisely at a time when Jews were being annihilated.

The Dalia Festivals, like the Queen Esther competitions, ignited debates about the interpretation and celebration of Judaism in the Yishuv. The creation of folk dance was an integral part of the emerging civil religion and the secular effort to find new ways of observing Judaism. Many folk dances were based on themes from the Bible and Jewish holidays, thus linking them to Judaism. The choreographers viewed dancing in a pageant to celebrate traditional Jewish holidays or dancing to music on the Sabbath as appropriate ways of interpreting and maintaining Judaism. For the Orthodox Jewish community, however, these forms challenged traditional norms.

Especially conspicuous in the relationship of dance to religion was the staging of the first two festivals on the Sabbath. By the second festival the Orthodox sector protested this timing, and a conflict between the religious and secular Jewish communities flared up. The debate focused not only on how to observe Jewish tradition but also, as with the Queen Esther competitions more than fifteen years earlier, on who had the authority to dictate public guidelines for the practice of Judaism in the public sphere. As the Yishuv came closer to the realization of a state, that question became more pressing.

Creating a Folk Dance Festival
Dalia Festival, 1944

Gurit Kadman, or Gert Kaufmann as she was then known, initiated and organized the Dalia Festivals and thereby spearheaded the Israeli folk dance movement. Kadman, a choreographer of a number of folk dances, became recognized for her vision and organizational capacities and is credited with centralizing the genre. In 1981 she was awarded the Israel Prize for her achievements and contributions.[4]

Kadman had already been active in the arena of folk dance in Palestine in the early 1940s. She was born in Leipzig, Germany, and was influenced by the Wandervogel youth association and its popular return-to-nature ideology. Begun in Germany before World War I, the movement aimed to connect youth with nature and to build antibourgeois feeling by promoting folk expressions such as song and dance. The Wandervogel movement had an influence on Zionist youth movements in Germany, and Kadman brought this sensibility with her when she immigrated to Palestine in 1920.[5] Drawing on concepts of romantic nationalism, Kadman strongly believed that Jews in Palestine needed to develop a national folk dance along the lines of national folk dances in Europe if they were to create a modern nation.

Before the first Dalia Festival, Kadman had organized two other folk dance festivals, in 1929 and 1931, at Ben Shemen, a youth village. These events showcased mostly European dances.[6] In the early 1940s Kadman taught folk dance at Hapoel, the Hebrew workers' sports association that had abstained from the first Maccabiah Games, and at the Seminar Hakibbutzim, the Kibbutz Teachers' Seminary, in Tel Aviv.[7]

In addition, Kadman, like many others working in dance in the Yishuv, was familiar with the work of Rudolf von Laban and his creations of movement choirs, in which large groups of people, often amateurs, performed together with the intention of building community through dance. The holiday pageants created in the kibbutzim from the 1920s to the 1940s, designed to celebrate the ancient Jewish agricultural festivals, were replete with folk songs and dances informed by Laban's ideas of using dance to foster community.[8] Kadman furthermore maintained a strong friendship with Gertrud Kraus. Kraus, who remained close to the Kaufmann/Kadman family,[9] choreographed a piece for the first Dalia Festival and assisted Kadman with the direction of the first three Dalia Festivals. She had also worked with Laban in the 1920s in Vienna and other parts of Austria.[10]

In early 1944 Dr. Yeshayahu Shapira, one of the leaders of the Inter-Kibbutz Music Committee, asked Gurit Kadman (then Kaufmann) if she would organize a folk dance component for the end of the festival of choirs, scheduled to take place in April of that year at Kibbutz Ein Harod during Passover. Intrigued by Shapira's suggestion, Kadman invited thirty people who were active in dance in different parts of the country to a meeting in her Tel Aviv home in February 1944. To her great amazement, all thirty invitees attended. They decided to tour the country to take an inventory of what was being danced at the time, and Kadman collected twenty-two dances, many of which came from the immigrants' different countries of origin. These findings surprised Kadman and encouraged her to move forward with the idea of creating a folk dance festival, but she decided not to plan it as part of the choir festival, mostly because of the lack of time to prepare. However, Shapira's request had instilled the idea in her, and she decided instead to organize a folk dance festival separately at another point.[11]

In the spring of 1944 Ilza Gutman (Piltz), a student of Gurit Kadman's in the Seminar Hakibbutzim in Tel Aviv and a member of Kibbutz Dalia, asked her to choreograph a dance pageant at Kibbutz Dalia for the celebration of the festival of Shavuot.[12] The kibbutz members used dance in their innovative celebration, creating new, nontraditional ways of observing the traditional Jewish holiday. Each year three kibbutzim—Dalia, Ein Hashofet, and Ramat Hashofet—would celebrate the Shavuot festival together at one location, and in 1944 it was Kibbutz Dalia's turn to host the event.[13] Like many of the kibbutzim at the time, they focused on the agricultural component of the holiday: the offering of the first fruits, or *bikkurim*.

At first, Kadman was reluctant to travel to the kibbutz. Although Dalia is geographically close to Tel Aviv, the roads leading there had not yet been paved and, as a result, it was a six-hour journey. Ultimately, she agreed and choreographed a pageant titled *Megillat Rut* (Story of Ruth), based on the biblical book traditionally read in the synagogue on Shavuot.[14]

While visiting the kibbutz, Kadman realized that the site would be an ideal venue for furthering folk dance. She recognized that the kibbutz could connect the people with the land and with nature, a key component of labor Zionist ideology. She also fell in love with the natural setting of Kibbutz Dalia. The kibbutz featured an outdoor stage with a view of the hills behind and space on the ground in front for an audience. Shaped in the form of a U by white columns adorned with vines, the stage was referred to by Kadman with the ancient Greek word, *pergola*, denoting a type of garden gazebo.[15] She was convinced that she had found the perfect place for a dance festival.

Kadman moved forward with her idea of developing a folk dance celebration, and only two months later the first Dalia Festival took place on Friday and Saturday, July 14–15, 1944. The event included dancing, singing, teaching, and discussion; it also featured opening and closing performances. About 1,000 guests participated in the full festival, and about 3,500 attended the final performance on Saturday evening.[16] The unpaved roads to the kibbutz did not seem to deter the guests and the roughly 200 dancers from coming from all over the country.[17] Like Kadman, the journalists also appreciated the beautiful natural landscape and pergola. The *Palestine Post* reported:

> The settlement of Dalia, situated in the mountains of Ephraim and overlooking the Carmel Range, provided a magnificent site for the festival. A pagoda fashioned of living stone columns was the background of the ample stage. The large audience was comfortably accommodated on chairs and hay-bales and enthusiasm did not wane although the packed programme began at 6 o'clock and finished after midnight.[18]

The guests at the first Dalia Festival included prominent composers and concert dancers, such as Gertrud Kraus, Devorah Bertonov, Yardena Cohen, Ms. Ornstein,[19] and Baruch Agadati.[20] This event set the format for future dance festivals at Kibbutz Dalia: a meeting of the dancers in which they taught their dances to one another followed by a public performance for spectators along with a pageant presented by the members of Kibbutz Dalia.[21] Kadman scheduled time for both teaching dances to the participants and discussing the project itself. Her intention was to generate a community of dancers and actively engage participants in the mission.[22]

In 1944 the festival aimed to bring together people working in folk dance as they conceived it. The goal encompassed both taking stock of what was being danced in the Yishuv at the time and showing new dances and inspiring further creations. Already in the 1920s and 1930s, many agricultural settlements had begun to develop new dances in celebration of traditional Jewish festivals. New dances were created in urban areas in these decades as well. Dancers, choreographers, and teachers, such as Yardena Cohen, Rivka Sturman, Lea Bergstein, Sara Levi-Tanai, and Gurit Kadman, had been working in this arena before the 1944 Dalia Festival.[23] This gathering, however, was the fundamental event that changed the course of folk dancing in the emerging nation.

The 1944 Dalia Festival showcased the new fledgling Israeli dances as well as dances that were already familiar in the Yishuv at the time, including some from Jewish Diaspora communities and European cultures. At the closing performance on Saturday night, thirty dances were performed by fourteen or so groups. Kadman opened and concluded the show with creations from kibbutz holiday pageants based on traditional Jewish sources. The evening opened with *Hallel*, a dance by Yardena Cohen based on her choreography for the Shavuot (*bikkurim*) pageant at Kibbutz Ein Hashofet and alluding to the songs of praise that are part of the daily and holiday liturgy.[24] *Hallel* was followed by *Megillat Rut*, the full pageant created by Kadman for Shavuot earlier that year and performed by members of Kibbutz Dalia

(Figures 38 and 39). The program closed with another pageant based on the Bible: *Shir Ha-shirim* (The Song of Songs), choreographed by Sara Levi-Tanai earlier that year for the celebration of Passover at Kibbutz Ramat Hakovesh.[25]

Between presentations based on biblical stories, Kadman organized the rest of the program in a pattern moving from old to new to international. Thus the new Israeli folk dances were presented as the center of the show. She divided the program into several sections. First came the dances created for the joint school of the kibbutzim at Ein Harod and Tel Yosef—this part included the performance of such dances as *Mahol Ha-goren* and *Rikud Habe'er*, crafted by the soon to be well-known folk dance choreographer Rivka Sturman. Another section was built around Jewish and European folk dances from the Diaspora familiar in the Yishuv, such as shereles, tcherkessias, krakoviaks, and polkas. A third part featured new creations and suggestions for novel dances, including *Mayim, Mayim*, a debka (Arab dance), and a suite in Yemenite style. Following this segment was a performance by a Yemenite troupe from Tel Aviv and Rishon Le-Tzion, directed by Saadia Damari and Raḥel Nadav, the principal dancer in Rina Nikova's Yemenite ballet troupe. Finally, the

Figure 38. The characters Ruth and Boaz in the pageant of *Megillat Rut* (Story of Ruth), Dalia Festival, 1944, performed by members of Kibbutz Dalia. Gurit Kadman choreographed this pageant for the celebration of Shavuot at Kibbutz Dalia in 1944 and presented it again at the first Dalia Festival. Central Zionist Archives.

Figure 39. Dance depicting the gathering of wheat in the pageant *Megillat Rut* (Story of Ruth), Dalia Festival, 1944. Central Zionist Archives.

section of European folk dances included Scandinavian, old English, Moldavian, and Czech dances (Figure 40).[26]

Dalia Festival, 1947: Dancing Beyond Politics

In addition to occurring in the aftermath of the Holocaust, two years after the Allied forces defeated Hitler, the 1947 Dalia Festival took place on the eve of what would shortly become statehood, when the Jewish community in Palestine was ardently seeking to gain independence from the British. In February 1947 the British announced that they were relinquishing the Mandate, and the U.N. Special Committee on Palestine (UNSCOP) was appointed to determine a political solution for the country. The second Dalia Festival took place in the summer of that year.

During this time of great political uncertainty and despite a British-imposed curfew under which no one could travel after sunset, 25,000 people from both villages and cities[27] (approximately 5 percent of the Jewish population of Palestine) traveled on unpaved roads to take part in the event.[28] The 1947 Dalia Festival was

Figure 40.
Czech dance,
The Beseda,
on the pergola
stage, Dalia
Festival, 1944,
choreographed
by Gurit Kadman
and performed
by the Seminar
Hakibbutzim
from Tel Aviv.
Central Zionist
Archives.

a defining moment in the development of Hebrew culture; it illustrated how folk dance was already becoming central to the public expression of national sentiment in the Yishuv.

Held under the auspices of the Cultural Division of the Histadrut and Kibbutz Dalia, the second Dalia Festival received extensive press coverage. The *Palestine Post* reported: "For a week in advance a 'Dalia Dance' madness seemed to infect Tel Aviv as well as the other towns and villages. Nobody remembered anything quite like it. From noon on Friday the little village in the Ephraim mountains became a Mecca, vehicles streaming up the mountain road in an orderly unbroken ribbon."[29] There were roughly 500 dancers from 18 different groups, and even representatives of the UNSCOP were present as guests at the event. Some neighboring Arab communities took part as well (Figure 41).[30]

Gurit Kadman remained astounded that people were undeterred by the British-imposed curfew. She described the scene at the public performance.

This was the time of the curfew imposed by the British Mandate authorities in 1947. There were incidents of gunfire and with all our asking for one night free of the curfew,

Figure 41. Crowds at the 1947 Dalia Festival, including Arab participants. Central Zionist Archives.

it didn't come. We were not allowed to be on the roads from sunset to sunrise. What would we do with the thousands who would surely come to Dalia? We decided to enlarge the facilities—there was a natural amphitheater on the land of the kibbutz formed by the hills. . . . We were prepared for about 8,000 spectators. Before the public performance 500 folk dancers from all over the country came to participate in two days and two nights of continuous dancing. On the third night, despite the curfew, we had the public performance, attended by more than three times as many people as we had expected. The 25,000 were squeezed into the hillside for the nonstop program that had to last all the night long. There was no place for them all to move to, nor was there the possibility of making an intermission in the program, for I had gotten a note backstage from the kibbutz that they feared a landslide if such a large group left their seats.[31]

Because the curfew was not lifted for the night, people were forced to stay, and the closing performance had to last the whole night, instead of until midnight or 1 a.m., as had been planned. Thus a new tradition was invented at the dance festival thanks to the political circumstances in 1947. In subsequent years participants stayed awake and danced through the night, even though they no longer needed the marathon, perhaps because staying awake all night ritually bonded later participants to this defiant moment and to the importance of continuing to celebrate Jewish strength.[32]

Another significant feature of the 1947 Dalia Festival was that Arabs and Jews danced together. Because the performance had to continue throughout the night, Kadman needed to have a much longer program than she had anticipated. She was pleased, relieved, and moved by the participation of Arab dancers in the program.

> Despite the tension in the country, which the British used in order to impose the curfew, three groups of Arabs and Druze came and performed on the stage one after the other. And once they start they cannot stop, that is the character of Arab dances. They warmed up and performed for a full hour, and I was so happy because this filled a full hour of this dangerous program. And our people were standing about and clapped and danced along with them. And this was a picture of peace and tranquility that did not match the picture of tension that the British spoke of.[33]

Shimon Piltz, a member of Kibbutz Dalia, also commented on the unusual occurrence of Arabs and Jews dancing together at this political moment.

> Here we also mention the performance of our neighbors. . . . More than the influence of the "debka" was the influence of the performance by Arabs. In my opinion, there were many dances that had great artistic value. But the participation of Arabs in this scene, at this time, and in this place, isn't this worthy of special attention beyond all the artistic points? Indeed, it was the performance of the Arabs that was so central and not the dances.[34]

The combined horas of Arabs and Jews at this event, as well as the debka performances of the neighboring Arab communities, were viewed by the press at the time as significant and memorable components of the 1947 festival.[35] At such a politically tense juncture, the notion of Arabs and Jews dancing together presented an image of peace and coexistence.

Creating a National Folk Dance Form
The Paradox of Creating Folk Dance

The idea of "creating" a folk dance form presents a paradox and raises the immediate question of authenticity: How does a people "create" folk dance, when the very concept implies its gradual development among the "folk." Just as with the aim to find the "most beautiful and the most typical" woman in the Queen Esther contest, the goal of constructing folk dance in and of itself reveals an inherent contradiction.

Participants, organizers, and critics at the Dalia Festivals addressed these issues in a forthright and self-conscious manner. They wrestled with the paradox, questioned the best path for attaining a national folk dance, and argued over who should develop the new dance form. In this process they also grappled with definitions of high and low culture and, as with the National Dance Competition, aimed to set distinctions between folk and theatrical dance. Leah Goldberg addressed the central contradiction in her article about the first Dalia Festival in 1944: "They showed the dances and with them the basic question was also shown: the question of the dance—of a nation in particular, and the question of folklore in general—is it possible to create folk art not in the natural-historical path, but out of a wish and direct cultivation?"[36]

The festival also raised the question of who constituted the "folk." One concern was that the Jews in Palestine, even those who lived in agricultural settlements, were not the typical uneducated folk from whom folk culture presumably emerged but were instead educated people who often viewed themselves as members of the intelligentsia. Y. M. Naiman, a writer for the *Davar* newspaper, noted the problem: "The village folklore in the world was created from the enclosed and conservative village. Our villagers are not closed and are not conservative; they are intelligentsia. They go to the theater and to dance recitals."[37] His comments also reflect the intermingling of urban and rural sensibilities in the Yishuv.

Similarly, Leah Goldberg thought that the Jews of Europe were neither a village nor a dancing people.

> In our discussion of the folk dance we refer in general, and principally, to dances of village people who are rooted in the ground. . . . But we are a nation that is hurried in movement and uprooted. We are not only not "a dancing people" by nature, but more than that: we are a people who have lacked the earthly and village happiness, . . . that healthy eroticism and the dance from which it arises.[38]

These comments illustrate the concerns that Israeli folk dances were not only emerging out of a conscious process rather than "naturally" but also arising from a community that did not constitute a "classic" folk community. Implicit in Goldberg's observations stands the notion that Jews were too urban to create true folk dance.

Moreover, according to its classic definition, folk dance should be created by the people, not by an individual choreographer. Yet the choreographers of the dances were noted at the time (and continue to be recognized today). Unlike many other folk dance forms that feature a repertoire of particular steps and movements that can be danced to a variety of tunes, Israeli folk dance is choreographed primarily with specific steps and patterns for particular songs. Each dance has a set structure intended to be danced to its designated music, raising the question of whether an organized or formalized tradition can contain the kind of variation and spontaneity associated with folk culture.

The notion of choreographing folk dances established another tension: the issue of distinguishing between folk and concert dance. The lines between folk and theatrical dance were meshed not only through the actual choreography of folk dances but also through the influence and participation of concert dancers at the Dalia Festivals. Just as questions arose in the National Dance Competition over the influence of folk elements in concert dance, concerns arose at Dalia over the effect of theatrical dance on the budding folk form. Because these discussions formed a component of the larger issue of what constituted high and low art, they were connected to the tensions between socialist and bourgeois values as well.

Many believed in the necessity of maintaining a link between skilled dancers and the folk. Theatrical dancers such as Yardena Cohen participated in and choreographed for the 1944 Dalia Festival. Gertrud Kraus directed the public performance at this event and choreographed a dance called *Davka* that was performed at the opening.[39] In addition, Yemenite Jewish women from Rina Nikova's dance troupe performed at the event.[40] Y. M. Naiman advocated for these connections.

> One thing is clear: there are mutual relations between the professional artist and the folk creation. . . . Reciprocity. Stating this fact is very important. When we aim for folk art in the land, we do not need to give up . . . on the influence of the professional artists. . . .
>
> . . . The only solution is: reciprocal relations so that the professional artists will not be cut off from the masses.[41]

For Naiman the appropriate way to create folk dance is to combine the talents of the artists and the public.

Yet others contended that the Dalia Festivals featured too much participation from concert dancers. The journalist Menahem Aloni expressed disappointment in the festival dancing in 1947 precisely because he believed that it stood closer to theatrical dance than to folk dance. He thought the dances had not captured the "heart of the folk."

> And indeed it is true, that we are lacking folk dances and forced to use mostly "imports" from outside. . . .
>
> . . . I will admit the truth, what I hoped to see—dances of "our people" (not dances from specialists)—I didn't see. . . .
>
> . . . And with all of this despite the organizers' good intentions, they did not succeed in giving the audience true folk dances. It seems that we have not yet acquired enough in this area and it is upon us to work on it a great deal.[42]

The participation and impact of trained dancers in the process were too extensive for Aloni.

This divergence of opinions about the appropriate extent of participation of concert dancers crystallized in the discussions about Gertrud Kraus's level of involvement in 1947. Some wondered why Kraus herself and theatrical dancers in general were not more prominent. Naiman questioned the lack of Kraus's contribution.

> How did it happen that they gave up on the part of Gertrud Kraus? . . . Are we valuing all of the worth of Gertrud Kraus for the dance culture in the country? She is a blessing of talent, taste, . . . artistic image. They will say: the intention is for folk dance and not for ballet—but in music they have not been satisfied with folk tunes, and with the tunes of the recorder.[43]

The conversations over Kraus's involvement also led to the question of the purpose of the festival itself: Was it to develop theatrical dance or folk dance? The debate over Kraus became a symbol of what type of dance was being created and how that dance was to be developed. *Ha'aretz* stated, "If we intended for the art of dance, wouldn't it have been good and right to place the achievements that the country has already achieved in this art in the center of the gathering—Gertrud Kraus and her company at the head?"[44]

In contrast to those who wanted Kraus to be more involved, Shimon Piltz thought it would have been inappropriate to enlist Kraus and emphasized that the festival's objective was fostering folk dance, not concert dance.

> And I doubt if it would have been possible to enlist the help of professional dancers

from the beginning. And indeed the intention was truly for a demonstration of the specific achievements mainly in the village: both you and others took steps to mention the name of Gertrud Kraus. Indeed, she was also present, and as I heard from her lips, she was very deeply impressed. I know that during the years she accompanies Gert Kaufmann [Gurit Kadman], the main organizer of the gathering, with approval and with advice. I doubt, though, if a performance of her company here would have been appropriate.[45]

Piltz stressed the rural character of the event and the importance of low culture.

The Dalia Festivals also confronted another paradox: the folk dance performance. The opening show (and in 1947 the closing performance as well) presented folk dance on stage. These dances were not only choreographed but also performed. In fact, as noted, part of Gurit Kadman's attraction to Kibbutz Dalia stemmed from its natural outdoor stage. These folk dance performances, in which many of the dances of the festival were presented to the participants, crossed the line between theatrical and folk dance. These shows also established a tradition of a staged event for folk dance. Indeed, the folk performance has remained an integral component of contemporary Israeli folk dance.

According to Gurit Kadman, the intention of the festival was always to generate folk, not theatrical, dance: "As to the crux of the program—we did not aim to show high art or a performance of something perfect—we aimed for exactly what we announced: a closing evening of a gathering of folk dance."[46] Yet Kadman's inclination toward the pergola—the stage to which she was so drawn—inevitably produced a mixing of the dance genres. Once the dances were presented on stage, they were critiqued as a performance. When Kadman as the organizer had to clarify the intention and purpose of the event, it indicated that the boundaries between folk dance and concert dance had become permeable. Because folk and theatrical dance were created at the same time by many of the same people, who also shared several notions about sources of authenticity, these two arenas overlapped. Yet each form simultaneously aimed to distinguish itself from the other and to establish its own unique character.

Influences from Jewish Tradition: Old Versus New

In their efforts to connect to Jewish tradition, the folk dance creators, like the theatrical dance choreographers, turned to the Bible and Jewish holidays as key sources of inspiration. Just as with theatrical dance, folk choreographers incorporated biblical stories and influences into the new dances to assert that their creations encompassed ancient times and thereby represented "genuine" compositions.

Developing a "Hebrew-style" dance was one of the most significant questions with which the festival organizers grappled. The dancers, choreographers, and commentators considered the Dalia Festivals the beginning of the project of fashioning a new style and repertory and of integrating folk dance into Hebrew culture in the Yishuv. The *Palestine Post* likewise discerned the launching of a search for a Hebrew mode and assessed its progress: "It is too early to say that we have found the style, but there is a beginning. The future generation will dance—dance without questions or problems or searching. Today we are building the foundation of the Hebrew dance."[47]

Similarly, Leah Goldberg noted the difficulties of the project, in particular, the challenges of creating a unique form.

> And from here is the beginning of the path to the second aim, the very difficult one, the very problematic one, an aim, that if it will be achieved—will not be achieved until after many years, and it is possible that only the children after us will enjoy its fruits: the creation of a style of the dance of the country. Style is not created in an arbitrary way, style is dependent not on the wishes of individuals, and not on the desirable aims of entire groups—it is always and forever the result of historical development.[48]

Goldberg's comments echoed those of Margalit Ornstein regarding the creation of theatrical dance in the 1920s. Goldberg grappled with the same issues regarding the folk arena; she also thought a Hebrew style needed to develop over time, out of the experience of the youth and the life in the country.

Although both folk and theatrical dance choreographers turned to the Bible for inspiration, folk dance choreographers attempted to actually recreate biblical dances. They investigated biblical references to dance, searching for its role in ancient Jewish life. In the biblical period dance had been connected to life cycle events and festivals. The ancient Israelites danced in victory celebrations, in prayer, and in mourning. For example, Moses's sister Miriam danced with timbrels at the Sea of Reeds to celebrate the exodus from Egypt (Exodus 15:20) and King David danced before the Ark of the Covenant (2 Samuel 6:14, 16).

The Yishuv choreographers tried to incorporate biblical stories and influences into the new dances to assert their ancient and therefore perceived genuine nature (Figure 42). They borrowed not only content but also the concept of dance as ritual from biblical times. Although they attempted to revive actual ancient Israelite dances, no records exist that depict what these dances looked like. Avraham Levinsohn, the director of the Cultural Division of the Histadrut, addressed this problem when he said, "While there is a tradition for literature, painting, sculpture, architecture, music and other forms of art, there are no signposts yet regarding the ancient Hebrew dance."[49] Dr. Haim Gamzu, director of the Tel Aviv Museum and art and theater critic for *Ha'aretz*, also spoke of the difficulty of attempting to revive something for which there were no records. Addressing "the renaissance of the dance," he claimed: "And indeed we have hardly any memory, any document, any record or witness to how our forefathers danced. And here we can ask a question: how can we revive something for whose material reality we have no recognizable signs?"[50]

This question of how to recreate and reimagine the ancient dances was a significant issue discussed and debated at the Dalia Festivals. Despite the lack of knowledge of Israelite dance in biblical times, leaders of the folk dance movement sought nonetheless to recapture its symbolic nature. The *Palestine Post* reported:

It must be remembered that this was far more than just a night's entertainment. In

Figure 42. Performance of a biblical-style dance, *Dance of the Well*, presented by students from the Mikveh Israel Agricultural School, Dalia Festival, 1947. Photo: Zoltan Kluger. Israeli Government Press Office.

the field of dancing there is a definite search for national expression. The question is primarily, "Exactly how did Miriam dance with her timbrels in biblical days?" and on the basis of that, to build the modern dance with roots in the past and branches developing into the future.[51]

The journalist Sh. Shriah also remarked that the dancers themselves participated in the debates about how to create a Hebrew dance: "And all day they took part in arguments . . . on the subject: what is the folk dance, and what is the original Hebrew dance?"[52]

Leah Goldberg addressed the issue of generating a new form from what she considered a blank slate, signifying her view that Jews did not constitute a dancing people. "It is not easy to revive a folklore that is dying because of historical developments, but it is much more difficult . . . to create something new from nothing. And it is mainly us, the Jews, who stand before this question."[53]

In their efforts to connect to an imagined Jewish past, the creators of Israeli folk dance also looked to ancient biblical agricultural festivals and to the land for inspiration. In addition to turning to the Bible to fashion "Jewish" dance, they also looked to design dances specifically for Jewish holiday celebrations. As with the Queen Esther contest and the renewed Purim festivities in Tel Aviv, these new creations offered secular Jews a different way to celebrate the traditional Jewish festivals, representing the secular Zionist goal of finding new meaning in the Jewish holidays without adhering strictly to Jewish law.

The dances produced for the 1947 Dalia Festival were divided into two categories: folk dances and holiday dances, which were to be performed at divergent Jewish holiday celebrations. In contrast to the numerous international dances at the 1944 Dalia Festival, a concerted effort materialized to show only Hebrew dances in 1947. The closing performance consisted of two sections of folk dance and two of festive dance. The folk dances included *Hora Agadati*, by Baruch Agadati; *Hey Harmonika*, by Rivka Sturman; *The Dance of Ovadia* and a fisherman's dance, both by Yardena Cohen; and a hora by Gurit Kadman. The section devoted to holiday dances included works for a variety of festivities: for Jewish celebrations, such as Tu b'Shevat, Shavuot, and Sukkot; and for Talmudic celebrations, such as the festival of the vineyards and Tu b'Av. The choreographers of the dances included Yardena Cohen, Tova Cymbal, Rivka Sturman, Lea Bergstein, and Gurit Kadman. The well-known dance *Mayim, Mayim* also appeared; it celebrated finding water at a specific kibbutz, although some connected it to the ancient Simchat Beit Hasho'eva ceremony, or the "joy of the water-drawing," a celebration held in Temple times during the festival of Sukkot. This section of holiday dances even included a new dance choreographed for the socialist holiday of May Day.[54]

Many believed that the effort to create holiday dances was crucial. At the Histadrut's Cultural Division meeting in 1947, Baruch Shwartz voiced his opinion of the importance of generating this new form of expression for the Jewish holidays: "I especially appreciate dance that is connected to a holiday. We are searching for a form for our holidays, and this is one of the fine forms. We will shorten our solemn speeches and will gradually include a festive ceremony that speaks more to the heart and also better educates the masses."[55] At this same meeting, Ya'akov Uri, another member of the Histadrut, also expressed his conviction that holiday dances needed to be developed: "There needs to be more and more emphasis on holiday dances. This is what is essential for us. Folk dances—how fine. But our holiday is missing dance and this is what needs to be filled."[56]

To link the Dalia Festival more closely with the Jewish holidays, some wanted to hold the event in conjunction with a specific Jewish festival. At an internal meeting of the Histadrut's Cultural Division, Nahum Benari (Brodsky) described the efforts to connect the 1947 Dalia Festival to a Jewish festival: "To the heart of the matter—we had the idea in the beginning to connect the dance festival to a date that matched the Hebrew calendar, either Lag b'Omer [a minor holiday that falls between Passover and Shavuot in the spring] or Tu b'Av [a minor holiday in the summer].[57] It's good to have a set date for gatherings like this, so that it will turn into a folk tradition."[58]

Yom-Tov Levinski, editor of the festival anthology, thought that Tu b'Av, the ancient holiday of love, would be the most appropriate time for convening the dance festival.

> If only the custom of our forefathers were known to the organizers of the folk dancing gathering at Dalia, . . . they would organize the great and lofty gathering at Tu b'Av. . . . They would bring back from antiquity the crown of the folk holiday. . . . They would have revived our ancient holiday of dances, the holiday of equality and love, unity and brotherhood. . . .
>
> The gathering of folk dances at Dalia would have become a national new-old holiday.[59]

The commentator Dan B. Amos also thought that the value of the dance festival would increase if it were connected to a traditional holiday. In a statement reflecting the dual value system of socialist Zionism, Amos pronounced: "But also in a big artistic assembly like this, it would be better to put it into the framework of a holiday—like the Bikkurim [celebration of the first fruits on Shavuot] or May 1 [a socialist holiday], or connected to a day of remembrance of the events in our renewed lives in the land."[60]

Initially, the 1947 Dalia Festival was scheduled for July 1946. The date had to be changed because of the political circumstances: Two weeks before the festival was expected to take place, on June 29, 1946, the British launched a two-week search for Jewish underground leaders and arms in response to the Jewish underground's (Haganah) blowing up of ten of the eleven bridges connecting Palestine to surrounding countries. At this time the Haganah aimed to thwart British immigration restrictions directed at Jews. In retaliation the British established a curfew for the entire population and began their most intensive search operation to date among the Jews in Palestine on the day referred to by the Yishuv as the Black Sabbath. They arrested about 3,000 people, including many of the youth who would have participated in the festival.[61] As a result of the postponement, the festival was rescheduled for Lag b'Omer in May 1947, but it ultimately took place on June 20–21, 1947.[62] Thus the occasion did not in the end coincide with a Jewish festival.

The efforts to connect both the dances themselves and the timing of the event to a Jewish holiday represent the secular community's desire to find appropriate ways to celebrate Jewish traditions in an emerging modern Jewish state. In their search to create "authentic" Hebrew dance, they intended to connect to an imagined ancient Jewish past.

East Versus West: The Aesthetic of Fusion

As in the development of theatrical dance shown in the National Dance Competition and in the development of beauty deliberations in the Queen Esther contest, the aesthetic of fusion likewise was prevalent in the creation of folk dance.

As part of their search for connection with Jewish tradition, the choreographers and dancers examined the dances of two religious Jewish communities: the Hasidic Jews of Eastern Europe and the Yemenite Jews. Both Leah Goldberg and the renowned dancer Devorah Bertonov noted that Hasidic dance was absent from the 1944 Dalia Festival program. Goldberg thought that Hasidic dancing was "in its essence closer to the type of mystical ecstatic dancing than to folk dancing in its general structure" and concluded that it therefore was an inappropriate source for folk dances.[63] Bertonov, on the other hand, thought that the emerging Israeli dance should represent a mix of Hasidic and Yemenite dances.

> Our folk dance is still in its formation. . . . Let's say: it won't be a bridge between Russian dance and Arab dance, but the blending of Hasidic dance (it's a great shame that this dance was not shown at the gathering) and Yemenite dance. From the Yemenite it will receive the burning syncopation, from the Hasidic—the "craziness,"

the drunkenness of the dance; and it will be Eretz Israeli because the builders and their children will dance it.[64]

Like Bertonov, Nahum Benari thought that the dances of the Hasidim and of the Yemenite Jews should serve as an essential source of inspiration for Israeli folk dances. He made his point at an internal meeting of the Histadrut's Cultural Division.

> With the widening of the activity in this area we need to ensure one more thing: more Eastern-Jewish color. Most of the people who work among us in this area are from the schools of Western Europe. They grasp Jewish dance from hearing and from artistic intuition, but it is not in their blood. Therefore we need to bring in more and more people from the East, who, if they feel the rhythm more, will express the Eastern movement that lives in their blood, that they know still from the home, from dances of the Hasidim and from weddings. We need to learn Yemenite movement.[65]

Benari's and Bertonov's comments represent the aesthetic of fusion, the widely held opinion, as with the creation of theatrical dance, that the best solution was developing a mix between East and West. Gurit Kadman likewise wanted to find folk dance that represented such an amalgamation.[66]

The creators of Israeli folk dance also drew influence from Arab dances in Palestine that they viewed as rooted in the experience of living on the land. Because connection to the land was a central tenet of Zionist ideology, Arab dance suited the aspiration to create a form that would be Middle Eastern with a strong connection to the local environment. Incorporated into many Israeli dances were elements of the Arab debka, a line dance in which men stand shoulder to shoulder, stomping on the earth in varied rhythms.[67]

Although both Yemenite Jewish and Arab movements were encouraged—and indeed became important sources for and an integral part of Israeli folk dances—they were also questioned.[68] These discussions represented the broader and continuing question of what constituted a folk dance and what therefore formed the best source for it. On one level, as mentioned earlier in my discussions about the Yemenite Purim queen Tsipora Tsabari and Rina Nikova's Yemenite Company, Yemenite Jews were approached with an internal Orientalism and viewed as possessing authentic Hebrew qualities. Yet at the same time leaders and critics still cast doubt on the suitability of Yemenite Jewish movement for folk dance inspiration. Leah Goldberg believed that Yemenite dance constituted true folklore, but she remained uncertain whether it could serve as an appropriate basis for Israeli folk dance: "But between this [Yemenite] dance and us . . . lies a chasm, and even if it were possible to use these Yemenite dances . . . for the revival of our dances—most of us are not able to dance them in their essence, in a natural way, simple, as a folk dance would be danced in general."[69] Goldberg ultimately concluded that Yemenite dance did not constitute a fitting starting place for folk dance but was rather a suitable source of inspiration for concert dance. She continued, "A difficult and complicated question is if this pure folklore will be used as a basis for our folk dances. It appears to me not—but . . . it can be used to enrich without limits the artistic choreography in our country and to make it original, interesting, special."[70] Of course, in her critiques of concert dance Goldberg advocated for this movement to be transformed into a "higher" form.

Yishuv members also debated the incorporation of Arab dances, especially because they aspired to create a Jewish folk dance form. Benari believed that the influence of the Eastern Jewish communities had to be greater in the new dances; in his view the non-Jewish Arab dances did not appropriately represent the emerging Israeli dance.[71] At an internal Histadrut Cultural Division meeting, he claimed: "I don't know if the movement and the rhythm of the Arab debka fits our dances. It has a particular nature, more desert-like; even though it looks good on the dancing Arab, indeed when our youth dance it, it loses its originality and there is some kind of an imitation in it that is inconsistent with our nature."[72]

These discussions reflect the self-conscious deliberations around the development of a folk dance form. Also embedded in them are conceptions of the definition of a folk dance genre, namely, dances that could be performed naturally or spontaneously. This delineation was tied to notions of East and West and reflected the Ashkenazic hegemony. Interesting differences between these assessments regarding folk and theatrical dance emerged. In evaluations of theatrical dance, Middle Eastern influences were viewed as authentic because they evoked the new locale and diverged from European dance. Yet in folk dance these same influences were at times construed as inauthentic because they seemed foreign and unfamiliar to the majority Ashkenazic population. Thus a folk dance came to be identified as a dance that should be inherent to the popular experience, and that form of movement was viewed as distinctly Ashkenazic.[73]

Dancing the Nation

Dancing During the Holocaust and Its Aftermath: The Aesthetic of Defiance

Just as questions had been raised about the propriety of holding the Maccabiah Games and the Purim carnivals in the early 1930s because of the 1929 Arab riots, even greater conflicts emerged over the appropriateness of holding a celebration during World War II and the Holocaust. Gurit Kadman believed in the importance of convening a dance festival even during the Holocaust. Of course, not everyone agreed with the wisdom of holding festivities at this time.[74] Although Kadman received much criticism for planning the events, which were considered disrespectful to the memory of the dead, she believed that, despite the tragedy, it was necessary to celebrate. Regarding the 1944 Dalia Festival, Kadman stated: "It was during World War II and I was told I was crazy to plan something like that, but my opinion has always been that people need time to be joyous so I went ahead with the plans."[75]

The title for the first festival encapsulated the atmosphere and Kadman's intention: It was nicknamed the *davka* event. Talking about her decision to hold the Dalia Festival, Kadman recalled:

> Many warned us about the action that we were about to do, that indeed these were the days of the Second World War (1944), when the terrible scope of the Holocaust of European Jewry was beginning to be revealed. They asked us: how is it possible to arrange a gathering of dances at a time like this? But our answer was: "*Davka* now," and the word *davka* was chosen as the symbol of the gathering, according to the words of A. D. Gordon [Zionist philosopher, considered to be the father of labor Zionism]: "If the whole world hits me and attacks me—I will *davka* burst out in dance."[76]

In addition, Gertrud Kraus choreographed a piece titled *Davka* that influenced Kadman and was performed at the closing show of the festival.[77] The 1944 gathering represented the defiant nature of the Jews of the Yishuv, affirming life in the face of tragedy; it conveyed a message that *davka* in these times it was essential to rejoice.

In the daily newspaper *Mishmar* in 1944, Mordechai Amitai, one of the editors of *Mishmar li'Yeladim* (Guard for Children), agreed with the suitability of convening a dance festival at this moment.

> Dance in these days—can it be? No—not a play of dances for display, not a celebration that bursts forth in days of mourning, but a piece of the unforgettable experiences of a people that includes the wishes of generations, sorrow and grief, happiness and rebellion. And the gathering did not come but to serve as a guide to all who strive to develop the movements of the body into a precious human expression. These hours will serve us as hours that renew our existence and renew our strengths.[78]

Folk dancing was not viewed as peripheral but was rather envisioned as a form of resistance and even as generating the renewal of the Jewish people. Those who saw the importance of holding a dance festival in this period also considered the dance festivals at Kibbutz Dalia as an exhibition of vitality and as a symbol of the new society. As writer and poet Shlomo Tenai stated in *Ha'aretz*, it was a "demonstration of the strength of the renewed Hebrew life."[79]

The different perspectives concerning the propriety of convening a dance festival at such a time were also expressed about the second Dalia Festival in 1947. After that event Uri Kesari published an article in the daily newspaper *Yedi'ot Aharonot* titled "Dalia Danced at Dalia...," which captured the divergence of opinions. Kesari addressed the divided attitudes toward this issue between the older and younger generations. In his typical ironic style Kesari wrote of a young girl named Dalia, returning from the dance festival at Kibbutz Dalia, expressing the wonderful and exciting quality of the event that was so far removed from all the worries of the Yishuv. Of course the young girl's name, just as that of the kibbutz, was a reference to nature (the dahlia flower), thereby giving importance to the land and its growth. In contrast to those who opposed the festival, young Dalia stood strongly in favor. She tried to convince Kesari of the importance of the festival, and he responded in a patronizing tone.

> Of course, of course—I said to her—you are right, Dalia. We need to continue! All of the loudspeakers, all of them, in chorus, announce the need, this necessity, and therefore there is no reason to convince you. You're going to Dalia—to dance. This is a historical event.... No. You are correct and not me. We need to continue ... to continue! To shout in such a loud voice that we are continuing, that maybe, in the end, the world will also believe us that we are continuing ... to burst—but to continue. ... It is incumbent upon us to continue.[80]

For young Dalia the dance festival maintained an important *davka* quality, showing the world that the Jews were alive and were building a new life. She further responded to Kesari's concerns over holding a dance event at this time.

> Yes, yes! I know... the Yishuv is always worried... but would we help it if we sat shiva [Jewish mourning custom] and said lamentations? ... Do we need to wear sackcloth and be alone? Surely it is impossible to mourn for twelve months. True, we were exterminated, we were hit; true, to this day, they hate us, they are hostile to us, they torture and chase after us, but a demonstration of strength like that shown at Dalia amplifies our strength, emphasizes our strength, our will to live. We are continuing and will continue.[81]

The young Dalia emphasized the need to demonstrate Jewish strength and to celebrate even in these hard times. Kesari did not oppose the event, but he questioned the timing in his response to Dalia's defiant comments.

Figure 43. Lighting the eternal flame in *Vayehi Or* (And There Was Light), Dalia Festival, 1947. Central Zionist Archives.

And then I said:—all of this is well and nice. Dalia was a celebratory project, nice and charming. It is possible that a great Hebrew art will develop from Dalia. . . . I would only be happier if the Yishuv danced at Dalia after the commission left [a reference to UNSCOP, which arrived in May 1947 to help determine the future of Palestine once the British announced they would end the Mandate], after the aliyah [immigration] of those held in Cyprus [a reference to Jewish refugees prevented from entering Palestine by the British and held in British detention camps in Cyprus] . . . [and] after the elimination of the camps in Europe [the Displaced Persons camps after World War II] . . . because I would want the people of Israel to dance not before it exists, but rather after it is revived. . . .

Dalia didn't agree:

—You wouldn't understand this—she said.

—And I saw in her the face of a reckless youth, without patience, but so dear![82]

For Kesari, holding the Dalia Festival during such a tense political period was problematic. His debate with the symbolic young Dalia illustrates the difference of opinion not only between the generations but also between the view that it was inappropriate to hold a festival at the time and the notion that it was critical to celebrate and to demonstrate Hebrew strength precisely at this juncture.

Although Kadman moved forward with the event plans despite the timing, she incorporated Holocaust remembrance into the 1947 festival: The closing ceremony began with a memorial to the Holocaust victims in a pageant called *Vayehi Or* (And There Was Light), a title from Genesis 1:3, performed by members of Kibbutz Dalia and directed by Gurit Kadman and Yehuda Ehrenkranz. They recited Hebrew poetry (by Abraham Shlonsky), spoke about remembrance, marched onto a hill carrying torches, and lit a large memorial flame, an eternal light that burned throughout the night (Figure 43).[83] This commemoration—considered a focal point of the evening—was followed by the entrance of groups of dancers; it was one of the earliest instances of a Holocaust memorial ceremony in a country that would later come to develop a multitude of commemorative practices and institutions in remembrance of the tragedy.[84]

Dancing the New Jewish Body: The Aesthetic of Toughness

The folk dancers presented an image that was fundamentally different from the stereotyped Zionist image of Diaspora Jews. The very notion of developing a national folk dance form stood as a challenge to the anti-Semitic image of the European Jew as devoid of vigor and lacking a folk tradition, central features of romantic nationalism. The dancing bodies at Dalia—just like the Maccabiah athletes—were seen as signs that the new Jew was breaking away from Diaspora life.[85] Representing socialist Zionist ideals of equality, women and men danced together in contrast to the separation of sexes in Orthodox Judaism. As one commentator proclaimed after the second Dalia Festival: "Indeed the collective folk dance and the free whistling—are loyal evidence that a new generation is rising in the homeland, disconnected and free from the chains of the old Diaspora."[86]

As with the Maccabiah athletes, the dancing bodies at Kibbutz Dalia projected the aesthetic of toughness. They also epitomized the ideals of labor Zionism: connected to—and presumably transformed by—the earth. Photographs of the festival in newspapers, posters, and pamphlets celebrated the "new Jewish body," depicting vibrant, upright youth dancing exuberantly on the outdoor stage at Dalia amid a sunny and beautiful scene. The smiling dancers appeared jubilant; they were energetic and buoyant. They were connected to the land, often adorned with flowers in their hair and on their costumes, or carrying flowers or leaves (Figures 44–46). Drawing on the labor Zionist notion that living and working the land would transform the Jews, Y.

M. Naiman remarked on the appearance of the dancers, illustrating his assumption that growing up in Palestine had changed their bodies: "The human material was excellent. It was simply a joy to see the young generation that had grown up in the land. Straight bodies, tall, flexible, filled with tension and expression. The joy of life is stirring in them."[87] Healthy, youthful, robust, and cheerful, they stood as a symbol of the new Jew fashioned by life in the Yishuv.

These dancing bodies were also interpreted as a signal that the Jews were capable of creating a new state and a new society. The dancing Jewish body represented an expression of nationalism and a symbol of defiance: It demonstrated—both to themselves and to the world—that Jews were alive and were resilient. Defending the importance of representing Jewish strength precisely at this juncture and in part through a strong body, a commentator proclaimed: "*Davka* in front of the members of the research commission [of the U.N.] we will show that we are strong in our spirits, in our bodies and strong in our decisions."[88] The whole idea of dancing together cultivated a new image; it also fostered community.

Figure 44. Folk dancing during the 1947 Dalia Festival, featuring vigorous and energetic movement in these various circles of the hora. Photo: Zoltan Kluger. Israeli Government Press Office.

Figure 45. Folk dance group performing at the 1947 Dalia Festival appearing healthy and robust. Photo: Zoltan Kluger. Israeli Government Press Office.

Figure 46. Folk Dancers in the vineyard of Kibbutz Dalia during the 1947 Dalia Festival. In the front stands Ayalah Kaufmann (now Goren-Kadman), daughter of Gert Kaufmann (Gurit Kadman), who was later to become a noted Israeli folk and ethnic dance expert. Photo: Zoltan Kluger. Israeli Government Press Office.

Creating a Nation of Dancers: The Aesthetic of Togetherness

The Dalia Festivals also represented the aesthetic of togetherness: They both promoted unity and expressed nationalism. Just as the Maccabiah Games encouraged cohesion through athletics, Kadman sought to establish a community of dancers through the Dalia Festivals.

The importance of gathering together remained a central facet of the Dalia Festivals, self-consciously addressed by the critics and participants.[89] Dancers and journalists alike commented on the formation of community at Dalia out of dance. Gurit Kadman claimed that the "25,000 people of Israel were as a family for one night,"[90] and the writer Sh. Nosa thought that those who attended, even if not dancing, felt as though they stood "among a big family of dancers."[91] Similarly, in a description evoking the responses of those who participated in the closing ceremony of the 1932 Maccabiah Games, the journalist Y. M. Naiman cited a biblical reference when he wrote: "The great experience at the gathering was not the program but the audience. . . . 'Mah tov umah na'im shevet achim gam yachad' [how good and how pleasant it is that brothers dwell together (Psalm 133:1)]. The masses that participated in the gathering will never forget it."[92]

The collective singing of "Hatikvah" further enhanced the goal of nation building. Starting off the opening performance, "Hatikvah" was a central component of the communal experience according to news accounts.[93] *Yedi'ot Aharonot* noted that 30,000 people sang the anthem together.[94] Likewise, *Ha'aretz* emphasized the importance of "Hatikvah" and its place in the national experience.[95]

In addition to bringing people together and expressing the collective, dance was viewed as a means of building both social and political bonds. At the second Dalia Festival, Avraham Levinsohn, the director of the Cultural Division of the Histadrut, proclaimed in a memorable phrase that rhymed in Hebrew: "There is no unity without dance" (*ein likud beli rikud*).[96] Similarly, at an internal meeting of the Histadrut's Cultural Division, Nahum Benari addressed the ways in which folk dance fostered social cohesion.

> This is an important tool for social unity. . . . What [sports] lacks is found in folk dance, which unites, and still contains movement and pleasant rhythm, bringing aesthetic enjoyment both to the participant and to the viewer. It also has an element of enthusiasm that is connected to lovely music. It is not by chance that the Hasidic movement elevated dance to a high level, as it connected the great masses to the teaching of Hasidism, without their knowing the depth of its teaching.[97]

In the Hasidic movement dance is used for spiritual purposes: to bring people closer to God. Benari here suggests that dance maintains a profound ritual power, because it can provide unique social benefits, and should be used to foster unity.

Commentators also noted the diversity of groups dancing and the fact that many political rivals, such as socialist and revisionist Jews, danced side by side. Shriah remarked on the ability of dance to unify the people.

> The answer was given, at the end of the evening, by the public itself. When the program was over, people from the audience went up on the stage and danced. And the excitement was so great that Lipa Livyatan, the ardent revisionist, danced until he lost consciousness on the stage of a *"Hashomer Hatzair"* kibbutz.[98]

Thus folk dance served as a bridge for a variety of sectors in the Yishuv. It built community, expressed the collective, embodied the pioneering ethos, and represented a public evocation of nationalism.

Religious Versus Secular: The Sabbath Controversy

Although the Dalia Festivals brought together many diverse sectors of the Yishuv, one segment remained opposed: the religious community. These festivals celebrated the new society, but they also unleashed bitter debates between the religious and secular populations. The secular public expressed satisfaction with the success of the event, and for them a Jewish dance festival that occurred on the Sabbath was in accordance with Jewish tradition. However, in the aftermath of the 1947 festival, the religious community protested that the event transpired on the Sabbath and used this occasion, as with the contention over the Queen Esther beauty competitions at the end of the 1920s, to once again express its concern over the future of the role of Judaism and the development of Hebrew culture in the Yishuv.[99]

The Sabbath controversy in 1947 reflected the internal politics of building a new state in which each party and political view sought to claim its own place. As the society solidified, the Orthodox community's insistence on the public abiding by the rules of Jewish law intensified. In the aftermath of the second Dalia Festival, the Orthodox leadership attacked the very nature of the evolving Hebrew secular culture.

Members of the religious community insisted that the issue of the Sabbath and Judaism be addressed and constitute an essential concern, even though the Yishuv's primary focus in 1947 centered on forming a political state. Their views were published in the daily newspaper *Ha-zofeh*, established in 1937 as the organ of the religious Zionist political party, Mizrahi (an abbreviation for *merkaz ruhani*, meaning "spiritual center"). Expressing this attitude, one critique declared: "We are concerned today with the political question. But this concern does not give us permission to delay the question of the Sabbath to a more comfortable time."[100]

The 1947 festival took place on Friday and Saturday, June 20 and 21. The day before the event, the religious community sent a letter to the Histadrut requesting that the celebration be changed to a different time to preserve the sanctity of the Sabbath. However, the Dalia organizers decided to proceed as planned because they received the letter close to the start of the festival, when many of the dance troupes had already arrived at the kibbutz.

The next day *Ha-zofeh* printed several pieces that described its dismay over the festival and the distress of both the Mizrahi political party and the religious labor party, Hapoel Hamizrahi (the Mizrahi Worker). They reported that they had written to David Ben-Gurion, head of the Jewish Agency, and David Remez, head of the National Committee (Va'ad Leumi), asking that "for the sake of the Sabbath they move the program to a different day."[101] At the request of Rabbi Yehuda Leib Fishman (Maimon), the representative of religious Zionism in the Jewish Agency, Ben-Gurion went to the Histadrut headquarters in Tel Aviv to try to delay the Dalia Festival until after the Sabbath. Representatives of Mapai (the labor political party founded in 1930) in the leadership of the Jewish Agency accompanied him.[102]

The Dalia organizers, however, stood by their initial response: They did not want to delay the festival at the last minute. They instead promised that the preparations would be completed by Friday at 6 p.m., before the onset of the Sabbath, so that they could comply with the Jewish law that forbids work on that day.[103]

After the festival, on Sunday June 22, 1947, the religious party Mizrahi began a vociferous protest in *Ha-zofeh* against the nonadherence to Jewish Sabbath laws at Dalia. Rabbi Fishman threatened to resign from the administration of the Jewish Agency over this matter and, not wanting to lose their support, Ben-Gurion condemned the event at Dalia. He, as head of the Jewish Agency, and Yitzhak Greenboim, one of the Agency's administrators, sent a letter of reprimand to the Cultural Division of the Histadrut.[104] The notice sounded as though it had been written by the Orthodox protestors.

> Rabbi Fishman directed our attention to the gala of dances that took place on Sabbath eve at Dalia and expressed his protest against this act, which constitutes a mass public desecration of the Sabbath and damages the religious sensibilities of many in the Yishuv. It would not be possible for the entire directorate to not take part in the anguish of many who were hurt, especially when this matter took place during a troubled time for Israel.

We express our wish and our hope that in the future they will find an appropriate way to avoid such matters that cause anguish and anger for many in the Yishuv.[105]

In response, the Cultural Division of the Histadrut sent a letter of apology to Rabbi Fishman. Copies of this letter also reached the Council for the Sabbath and Dr. Hirschberg, the representative. An excerpt reads:

Regarding the risk of desecrating the Sabbath, we made sure to avoid it with the following arrangements: 1. the transportation to Dalia takes place on Friday by public vehicles from 2–4 in the afternoon only; thereafter there is no transportation to Dalia. 2. We banned all selling of tickets on site. And we announced this in all of the newspapers. 3. The main part of the performance began at 4:30 in the afternoon. 4. We clung to every means to prevent the desecration of the Sabbath in public.

We are sorry that your letter reached us on the day of the gathering itself, when we did not have the option to delay. Since the announcements for the gathering were published in all of the newspapers two weeks before, if we had received the letter in time we would have looked for a different way to organize the gathering.[106]

Apparently, this response did not arrive in time to lessen the Orthodox furor. In the aftermath of the event, Nahum Benari explained:

A response letter was sent from the cultural division to Rabbi Fishman (as was printed in the newspapers). It was written on Friday, and its intention was to mitigate the scandal that the members of Mizrahi had started. And in this particular instance a technical-administrative error occurred, that this letter that was written on Friday was sent only after the gathering on Sunday. What happened around this after the gathering is known from the newspapers.[107]

The Jewish National Fund (JNF) also became involved in the dispute and expressed its dismay over the violation of Sabbath laws at Dalia, held on land that the JNF owned. It joined the fray by looking into the foundation of the tenancy contract between the JNF and Kibbutz Dalia and considered prosecuting the kibbutz for its actions.[108] The dispute over the appropriateness of holding a dance festival on the Sabbath extended into different organizations within the Yishuv. The religious and secular communities, competing for power in the Yishuv, viewed the issue from their diverging perspectives of how to develop Jewish culture in an emerging Jewish state.

The Orthodox Protest

For the Orthodox community the need to ensure that the incipient state would be appropriately Jewish was paramount. They fought persistently against the nonadherence to Jewish Sabbath laws at Dalia. The titles of their newspaper articles featured the same hyperbolic quality evidenced in their reactions to the Queen Esther competitions in the 1920s. In an editorial in *Ha-zofeh* titled "In Malice and Wickedness," the writers complained that the event took place despite their attempts to stop it. In another piece titled "A Horrible Act at Dalia," the writers referred to the festival as "discerning of heavy crime" and blamed the Jewish Agency, the National Committee, and the Histadrut.

> Many days they begged them to postpone the "holiday of dances" to another day. . . .
> But it does not matter to them. The members of the Jewish Agency and the National Committee and the Histadrut do not care. They have no G-d in their heart, they are not respectful of the tradition and they have no respect for the many Jews in the land [of Israel] and in the Diaspora.[109]

Members of the Orthodox community worried about Jewish observance in the Yishuv: "The dances that took place on the Sabbath eve at Dalia were a wicked and crude desecration of the Sabbath, that had never before taken place in the country in this measure, on such a broad and public scale. Here it hurt the sacredness of the Sabbath."[110] Believing the event damaged the "soul of the nation,"[111] another writer claimed:

> There are no words to express the feelings of pain, the protest and fury over this terrible desecration. Because the pain is very great and great is the shame, that in this way it is possible in our land and in this time of our revival, that in this way they strike on everything that is sacred to us against all of the people.
> We are shamed and are ashamed![112]

This language also resembled the debate over Queen Esther.

After the Dalia event the chief rabbinate organized a protest, which was planned to take place in synagogues throughout the Yishuv on the following Sabbath. On Tuesday, June 24, an announcement emerged in *Ha-zofeh* titled "On the Scandal at Dalia"; it was signed by Ashkenazic Chief Rabbi Yitzhak HaLevi Herzog (he succeeded Rabbi Kook) and Sephardic chief Rabbi Ben-Zion Meir Hai Uziel (the former Sephardic chief rabbi of Tel Aviv–Jaffa who became the Sephardic chief rabbi of the Yishuv in 1939). The chief rabbis called for all rabbis and other synagogue officials, as well as the public, to delay taking the Torah scrolls from the ark and subsequently reading from them on that day until after they gave speeches of protest "against this threatening blow to the national soul."[113]

Ashkenazic Chief Rabbi Herzog's speech at Yeshurun synagogue on this Sabbath of protest appeared in *Ha-zofeh*. Emphasizing the importance of the observance of the Sabbath in the public sphere, he declared:

> There have been public desecrations of the Sabbath . . . but these are different as they are individual. . . . This was tons of people publicly together. . . .
>
> . . . They are abandoning the source of their own tradition and are creating an incorrect version of a day of rest based on the modern gentile outlook. . . .
>
> We have heard that there are signs of awakening within the federation of workers of Eretz Israel [Histadrut] to promise that shameful acts such as these will not be repeated . . . And not only that heaven forbid the actions at Dalia will not recur, but we will all awaken together to strengthen our holy of holies, the Sabbath.[114]

In addition to its concern over the Sabbath specifically, the Orthodox community more broadly opposed the character of the new Hebrew culture. Rabbi Meir Berlin, the editor of *Ha-zofeh*, conveyed his deep disapproval of the entire event, beyond even its timing: "And we should see light in the light of the Torah and we will continue to follow the pure ways of the prophets and . . . the great enlightened teachers—and here is Dalia dancing and dancing and destroying all that we have wished and longed for. . . . Oy, what has happened to us!"[115] A further article in *Ha-zofeh* expressed the same concerns in similar language.

> The cultural division of the General Workers' Histadrut organized the celebration. And the head of the division stood amidst the massive desecration of the Sabbath and he spoke without shame: "The dance is not a game for us, but a vital necessity and with it we will shape our lives."
>
> "A vital necessity"—on the trampled body of the holy Sabbath.
>
> . . . 30,000 desecrators demonstrate their wish to end the soul of the nation, to destroy the values of generations, to change the nation of G-d's Torah from Sinai to a nation whose cultural baggage will be dances—and these—these are the demonstrators of the "strength of the Hebrew life."[116]

Similarly, another writer in *Ha-zofeh* took issue with the definition of the demonstration of Hebrew strength in the secular community.

And all this was described . . . as a demonstration of the life force of the renewed Hebrew!

This is how the dancing-desecrators desecrated the precious and holy day of Israel in the hills of Ephraim. This is how they renew the life force of the Hebrew! If there had been any sense of the tradition of generations . . . the organizers and the desecrators would have at least understood the great calamity that they are committing to their people and to themselves by destroying our own foundations with this foreignness, with this alien culture .[117]

An article titled "How Did This Happen?" again raised the concerns about the future of Hebrew culture. Just as with the Tel Aviv Purim festivities, the question of who had the authority to control and determine how to observe Jewish tradition emerged.

In the face of the wild dances at Dalia, the clear question is: to the G-d of Israel—or to "Ba'al" [an ancient Babylonian god]. To the continuation of the tradition of Sinai—or for idol worship [*avodah zarah*]. For Jewish life in thought or in action—or to the way of life taken from all other based and despised nations.

This is the choice. If thousands of Jews will recognize the danger that is before them, then the celebrations at Dalia will be a passing episode in the Hebrew Eretz Israel.[118]

The religious community believed that the dancing on the Sabbath at Dalia represented pagan, foreign practices and thus was forbidden by Jewish tradition and custom. Its members contended that the dance festival at Dalia gave evidence of a threat to Jewish observance in an emerging Jewish state and bolstered their resolve to make sure that this kind of infringement did not recur.

The Response

Despite the vociferous protests of the Orthodox community, for the most part the non-Orthodox Jewish public remained indifferent to the matter. The secular Hebrew press, primarily concerned with the content of the festival at Dalia, expressed satisfaction with the overall success of the event. Because the Sabbath issue stayed outside their focus, they did not allocate extensive coverage to it; nonetheless, they published announcements in *Ha'aretz* and *Ha-Boker* about developments in the religious protest.[119]

For the Orthodox community the lack of adherence to Jewish law was the principal reason for alarm; they advocated addressing the matter even before tackling other issues standing in the way of statehood. In contrast, the secular community involved itself primarily with other political matters; its greater concern focused on conserving the unity of the population deemed necessary for statehood. Despite their fury with the political-religious party Mizrahi, secular leaders ultimately ceded the issue of Sabbath observance in the public sphere to them.

However, secular leaders remained exasperated with the Mizrahi party for inciting the protest and, in their view, disproportionately politicizing the situation. Many interpreted these objections as attempts by the religious segment of the population to gain more support for their party politics. Benari wrote in *Davar*:

> With the Dalia gathering on the Sabbath, members of Mizrahi began to put out excommunications against the workers' movement.
>
> If the things printed in *Ha-zofeh* had a real sense of religion, they would certainly be said in a completely different tone, and it would have been possible to discuss the matter in a different way.... But there was no such will. All of the controversy around Dalia was turned into a religious political matter. And we are not willingly complying with this controversy.
>
> ... I know that for the sake of peace the gathering should have taken place on a weekday. For different random reasons it took place on Sabbath eve. After the fact—it is incumbent upon us in any case not to use the matter for party politics.[120]

Ya'akov Uri also expressed frustration with the political strategies of the Mizrahi party in this matter.[121] At an internal meeting of the Histadrut's Cultural Division, he argued: "They started a scandal against us that already has the smell of elections in it. We have to emphasize in particular: in all of this there is an incitement against the Histadrut.... The people of Mizrahi heralded a political war against us."[122]

In addition to their irritation over party politics, secular leaders were also upset by Mizrahi's assumption that they alone had the authority to decide the appropriate foundation for Jewish culture. As with their responses to the rabbinate's efforts to control the celebration of Purim, here again members of the secular community asserted their right to observe in ways they deemed suitable. Benari published a full article in *Davar* against the Orthodox protest, claiming that the religious hierarchy did not represent the sole authority on Judaism. He argued that the Mizrahi party did not own the Sabbath; rather, in his view, the secular public sanctified the Sabbath in its own way.

> First of all, the sense of all of the masses who participated in this gathering—and

thousands of others who wanted to come and couldn't—there was a sense of the sanctity of the Sabbath and not of the desecration of the Sabbath. The members of Mizrahi can refer to this experience of all of these people however they want, but this is the truth. And it is not possible to eliminate the controversy. Something has changed in the sense of the vast majority of the people of Israel regarding the way to sanctify the Sabbath. As it is also among the members of Mizrahi themselves, many concepts of the religion and tradition have changed. Among my people, I sit and I know that they are missing their beards and their earlocks and many of them are trampling on many commandments and customs that were accepted by our fathers for generations. To whom then was the permission given to speak on behalf of millions of Jews and on behalf of the Jewish tradition in general?

The Sabbath is dear for the Hebrew worker in Eretz Israel, and he sees it as one of the most precious assets. . . .

The worker's movement in the country is a movement of conscience and it is Jewish according to a deep internal character, and it looks for ways to materialize these both in the building of the nation and the land and also in the laws of ethics and Judaism. It will find the right path; this will be the way of Judaism in the coming generations.[123]

Ya'akov Uri advocated the same position at an internal meeting of the Histadrut's Cultural Division.

I claim my rights for the Sabbath, as I grasp it. . . . It was not the Mizrahi that brought the Sabbath from the heavens. It is the heritage of the whole people. And I keep the rest of the Sabbath. I will also always be for not impinging upon the feelings of religion of others in their homes. But I will not agree that others will come to my home and will force me to desecrate the Sabbath, against my recognition of what is rest on the Sabbath. My Sabbath pleasure is trips, music, and so on. I admit, this is not according to the Shulchan Aruch [Jewish law code]. But this is the Sabbath, that of our generation.[124]

Not only did members of the secular community seek to celebrate the Sabbath according to their own approach, but they also wanted the Mizrahi movement to tolerate their interpretation of the festivity. Whereas secularists asserted that they were ready to respect the religious community, they wanted the Orthodox population to accept them as well. Zev Bloch reiterated Uri's position.

I will not go to Jerusalem to desecrate the Sabbath of Jerusalem, but I do not want the Mizrahi to come to me to desecrate my Sabbath. I am not in favor of fighting heresy, but I want them to honor our way of life, as we honor other people's way of life. To call our way of life an "outrage" indeed is an outrage the likes of which have not been heard. There is holiness in our lives that may be much greater than what is to be found among many of the religious politicians.[125]

Yet even as secular leaders remained adamant over their attitude toward the Sabbath, they also aspired to achieve national unity. Embracing the aesthetic of togetherness, some members of the secular contingent maintained that for the sake of public accord, it would be best to refrain from holding future events on the Sabbath. Alongside his extensive article in *Davar*, Naiman included a postscript in which he advocated that the secular community should avoid upsetting the religious sector and alienating a part of the Yishuv.

I forgot one principal matter: after these things were written, the protests against the desecration of the Sabbath at Dalia arrived. There is no need to argue with the secular ones [referring to the members of Mizrahi] who want to use the arms of religion for political aims. But the folk culture in the country needs to reach a broader front, to the majority of the masses, and it is best not to distance a large portion of them. If you ask a secular person who loves to dance, he will say and will admit that for the sake of the dance it is even worthwhile not to desecrate the Sabbath.[126]

The ambivalence of secular leaders toward the Sabbath issue was evidenced by Baruch Shwartz's comments; he recognized that from the religious perspective, the gathering at Dalia represented a desecration of the Sabbath.

We have to admit that in the traditional-religious understanding there was an organized desecration of the Sabbath here. But we don't have another day for large folk celebrations, and we have to ensure the culture of our generation. It is possible that if we knew what a storm would arise around this—we would need to take this into consideration from the political side. But for our internal attitude—it wouldn't have mattered. In any case in this time of political tension, and the need to unite our strength inward, we need to take things like this into account.[127]

Shwartz, like Naiman, who also advocated the aesthetic of togetherness, called for more sensitivity to the Orthodox perspective for the sake of national unity. Angry as they may have been about the religious community's unwillingness to see any different forms of observance as legitimate, they were still ready to acknowledge the power of the religious leadership.

The Orthodox Call Prevails

The controversy over the timing of the Dalia Festival arose because of the lack of another time during the week for holding such events. At the internal meeting of the Histadrut's Cultural Division following the event, Nahum Benari explained that they had tried to convene the festival at another time, but it was not possible because of logistical and technical reasons, since the farmers could not take off on a workday.[128] Because the Sabbath served as the only day they did not work in the fields, it became, by default, the time for a festival.

In the months following the Orthodox sector's outrage over Dalia, religious and secular leaders held discussions to try to find a date for events of this nature. They considered instituting a half-day of rest during the week to avoid the Sabbath issue. In July 1947 *Ha'aretz* reported on the suggestion of Ashkenazic Chief Rabbi Herzog at the discussions of the Council for the Sabbath to set up a committee to look into the possibility of instituting a half-day of rest during the week; this break would give workers time to arrange sports competitions, trips, and gatherings without violating Sabbath laws.[129]

Weeks later, the chief rabbinate and the Council for the Sabbath were still upset about and troubled by the festival at Dalia.[130] *Ha'aretz* reported:

> The Chief Rabbinate published an announcement in which it said that the extended council of the Chief Rabbinate does not find satisfaction in the excuses of the cultural division that the warning did not arrive in enough time, and condemns the incident at Dalia, which will not be forgiven, except by showing remorse about the past, and taking upon itself the task of preventing such things in the future. The council calls to the public institutions and organizations: do not let a hole arise in our walls and do not continue to undermine the unity of our people and bring about a situation in which the House of Israel is torn apart.[131]

Whether for political reasons, as claimed by secularists, or from a purely religious motivation, the Orthodox protest over Dalia created a deep fissure between the secular and religious communities. Whereas the rabbinate highlighted its dissatisfaction with the administrators' excuse that they did not receive the objection letter in time to delay the event, the organizers remained defiant in their belief that the rabbinic leadership was trying to impose its own view of how the Sabbath should be observed.

Although attempts to find a compromise solution were unsuccessful in this instance, it is significant to note that the next Dalia Festival, which took place in 1951, was not held on the Sabbath: It took place on Tuesday, August 21, 1951. Subsequent

Dalia Festivals also convened at alternative times. Thus the contestation over the celebration of Judaism in the budding state directly affected the timing of future folk dance festivals. Unwittingly, a custom developed based on the religious-secular debate.

Conclusion

The Dalia Festivals of 1944 and especially 1947 occurred in a different political environment from the earlier events in this book. By 1944 Zionist leaders had declared their intention to create a Jewish commonwealth in Palestine, and the celebration took place despite the British curfew. By mid-1947 it was clear that the British Mandate was going to end, and the British had turned to the U.N. to produce a new solution. Therefore the Dalia Festival itself had political overtones.

The creation of an Israeli folk dance form accepted as authentic meant, implicitly, the confirmation of another element in the Jewish claim to a state, especially as it was connected to romantic nationalist conceptions directly linking a folk dance form to a nation-state.

The goal of crafting a folk culture remained inherently paradoxical. There were debates over whether the dances should be designed by professionals or by amateurs, representing the conflicts between theatrical and folk dance. These disputes were also prevalent in the discussions surrounding the National Dance Competition of 1937. Here as well, questions of what constituted high art versus low art and concert dance versus folk dance emerged. Because of the importance of folk dance to the nationalist goals, the paradox, although addressed, was ultimately overlooked.

Some of the other cultural contestations in the Dalia Festivals achieved resolution. The struggle between East and West in 1947 resembled that evidenced in the beauty competitions for Queen Esther in Tel Aviv of the 1920s and the National Dance Competition of 1937. As in those venues, it gave way to the aesthetic of fusion.

The folk dances themselves solidified the aesthetic of togetherness. Dancers from a wide variety of Jewish immigrant communities participated, and influences from different countries of origin became part of the new dances. Women and men, Ashkenazim and Sephardim, all danced together, their bodies linked.

However, the religious-secular conflict, evident in an incipient form in the conflict over the Queen Esther contest at the end of the 1920s, became even more apparent by the 1947 Dalia Festival and was aggravated further after the festival. As the society solidified, the religious sector's insistence on abiding by the rules of Jewish law intensified.

At this juncture, close to statehood, the internal politics of building a Jewish state became an even more central element of the debate. The second Dalia Festival took place in a period of fervent discussions about the future of religion in the budding society. An agreement between the Jewish Agency, the formal body representing the Jews in Palestine, and Agudat Yisrael, the anti-Zionist ultra-Orthodox political party, was signed in the summer of 1947. The document, which became the basis of the status quo agreement on religion in the State of Israel, was sent to the world headquarters of Agudat Yisrael on June 19, 1947, the day before the second Dalia Festival opened. The agreement was vague but delineated the Sabbath as the formal day of rest in the emerging state.[32]

In the aftermath of the 1947 Dalia Festival, the Orthodox Jewish leadership attacked the very nature of Hebrew culture. The secular sector aspired to create a Hebrew culture connected to Jewish traditions, whereas the religious sector assumed that the Jewish religion constituted the culture. These disputes between the religious and secular communities continued into statehood and remain unresolved.

The Enduring Legacy

The Yishuv's Embodied Public Culture

Building an embodied Hebrew national public culture was one of the primary goals of the Yishuv. The secular majority believed that developing a Hebrew and corporeal way of life was an essential prerequisite for establishing a modern nation. All the events in this book were formative in creating a new Jew, with a new Jewish body, who would be ready to build a state.

Because the emphasis on the corporeal became prevalent, investigating the process of embodiment serves as a window into the various defining characteristics of Hebrew culture. Each of the activities examined in this book demonstrates how culture and politics were intertwined in the Yishuv.

The heated disputes illustrate that every aspect of the new public was up for discussion, self-consciously examined, and viewed as imperative. In all four cases the old-new dichotomy was recognized and welcomed as the founders aspired to create a new society connected to its ancient roots.

The socialist-bourgeois tension was also woven through all the events, because socialist and urban Zionist sensibilities frequently had different priorities. Ultimately, the need to affirm unity prevailed, and the aesthetic of togetherness developed. Although unity was not fully achieved in the Maccabiah Games because of Hapoel's abstention from the games, it nonetheless stood as the pursued goal.

The East-West tension was central in three of the examples: the beauty competitions for Queen Esther, the National Dance Competition, and the Dalia Festivals.

The Maccabiah Games, based fully on a European sports model, did not struggle with the dichotomy. In each of the three other events the resolution became the aesthetic of fusion: a cultural model that sought to blend components of East and West.

Debates over the appropriateness of celebrating in a time of sorrow took place on three of the occasions: the Purim carnival in 1930, the Maccabiah Games, and the Dalia Festivals. Except for the Purim celebrations of 1930, shortly after the 1929 Arab riots, the festivities convened despite opposition. An aesthetic of defiance prevailed, affirming the importance of celebrating life even in the midst of grief and distress. Happiness and sadness were held together in a delicate balance.

The undisputed goal of the aesthetic of toughness was most highly apparent in two cases: the Maccabiah Games and the Dalia Festivals. Both sought to represent a tough and masculine image and to prove the successful construction of a new Jew. The Maccabiah Games were based on the desire to show the world muscular Jewish bodies, capable of forming a nation. Similarly, the Dalia Festivals sought to portray strong Jews who could maintain their desire to survive and to dance *davka* during, and in the aftermath of, World War II and the Holocaust.

The religious-secular dispute materialized in two events: the Queen Esther competitions and the second Dalia Festival. At the Maccabiah Games leaders and members of the Orthodox community both supported and participated in the event. However, the religious sector opposed both the Queen Esther contests and the timing of the second Dalia Festival, protesting in angry and emotional language and thus threatening the unity of the Yishuv. Ultimate authority over the observance of Judaism in the public sphere was granted to the Orthodox sector in both instances. The religious and secular communities failed to agree in the Mandate era, and their opposing visions for the role of Judaism in the public arena remain.

Tensions and Aesthetics in Contemporary Israeli Culture

The nature of what would later become Israeli culture was solidified in the British Mandate era. Although contemporary Israeli society has undergone dramatic shifts since this period, the tensions and the cultural aesthetics have had a lasting impact.

The models developed in the British Mandate era still endure; the same patterns, processes, and resolutions persist. Indeed, almost every aspect of Israeli life presents some combination of these qualities and oppositions. Although the Holocaust and the ongoing Israeli-Palestinian conflict have also played important roles in the development of Israeli culture, the cultural aesthetics consolidated during the Mandate era continue to serve as a means of interpreting Israeli society.

Old Versus New

The old-new dichotomy is an ongoing component of contemporary Israeli life. From advertisements to popular songs to architecture, the paradox of portraying the ancient and modern is present and welcomed. The national emblem of the modern state is the menorah, the seven-branched candelabra from the ancient Jewish temple. The Chords Bridge in Jerusalem, inaugurated in 2008, also called the Bridge of Strings, was created in the modernist style but references King David's harp. Israeli soldiers in the Armored Corps take an oath of allegiance to the modern state at Masada, the mountain that has come to signify the active resistance of Jews to the Romans in ancient times.[1] Various state ceremonies, including the official opening for Yom Hazikaron, the national memorial day, take place at the Western Wall in Jerusalem, the remaining outer wall from the second ancient Jewish temple. Nearly every major speech at national events incorporates references to the mix of old and new.

Socialist Versus Bourgeois: The Aesthetic of Togetherness

Israeli society has undergone dramatic shifts since the British Mandate period. These shifts are heavily influenced by commercialization, consumerism, mass media, and Americanization.[2] All these changes have led to a loosening of community and have encouraged a trend toward individualism and privatization. The pioneering ethos, focusing on an ascetic and communal lifestyle, has been replaced by a desire for individual and material gain. These developments appear in a variety of arenas. The kibbutz, the quintessential socialist Zionist institution, has weakened. At folk dance sessions participants no longer hold hands during circle dances, and the togetherness that had been formed by dancing shoulder to shoulder has not been sustained. At military cemeteries a trend to write personal notes on tombstones, once seen as taboo, has emerged. This new custom is part of a larger process that focuses on "articulating private mourning and personal pain" rather than on the collective loss.[3]

Yet, at the same time, the aesthetic of togetherness is nevertheless significant. In her examination of speech metaphors, Tamar Katriel found that certain images used in Israeli society stress the importance of the group. In the course of her study, Katriel noted that the term *community* is never used in a negative way. "The focus on the positive aura of the collective, on the weaving of shared communal bonds in both casual and formal encounters is a central aspect of the Israeli experience."[4] In her examination of the use of the term *gibush*, or social cohesiveness, Katriel found that it is viewed as positive and as a goal toward which to work.[5]

Moreover, a strong sense of nationalism and group commitment endures. On the closing night of the 2008 Karmiel Dance Festival, about 30,000 people assembled on a packed outdoor hill to view the final performance. Toward the end of the show, many started to leave early in order to get to their cars before the crowds. In the last moments a surge of audience members began climbing up the hill to exit. Yet, when the first notes of "Hatikvah" sounded, everyone stopped, stood in place, and sang along, holding their hands over their hearts. The expression of nationalism trumped the individual desire to beat the traffic. Singing "Hatikvah" still binds the participants in a public event just as it did before the establishment of the state.

East Versus West: The Aesthetic of Fusion

The tension between East and West and the ambivalence about these different cultures persist. Israel continues to wrestle with its desire to be accepted as a Western culture while aspiring to be recognized as a legitimate Middle Eastern country.

In the early years of statehood Israel focused its attention on unifying the nation. In that process it failed to recognize the diversity of its subcultures and, in particular, belittled Sephardic and Mizrahi Jewish traditions. In the 1970s Sephardic ethnic groups, by then a majority of the Jewish population, started to object to their position as second-class citizens. The repercussions of the Ashkenazic hegemony still permeate Israeli society, and an ongoing battle for greater recognition of Sephardim and Mizrahim persists.[6]

In the 1980s Andre Elbaz, a Moroccan-born artist and filmmaker, claimed that the nation's attitudes toward Ashkenazic and Sephardic artistic forms illustrated a debasement of Sephardic culture. "When people speak about the Ashkenazim," he was quoted as saying, "they use the word *culture*, while when they speak about the Sephardim they use only [the term] *heritage*."[7] His comments resemble the discussions after the National Dance Competition about whether dance containing Middle Eastern influences could be considered high art.

Tensions between Ashkenazim and Sephardim or Mizrahim endure in the cultural sphere. With increasing Americanization and Westernization, Middle Eastern influences are often overlooked as Israel continues to turn its gaze toward acceptance in the West. Nonetheless the aesthetic of fusion remains one of the enduring resolutions.

For example, in the concert dance arena, the work of the Inbal Dance Company and independent choreographer Barak Marshall embodies this aesthetic. Established in 1949, the Inbal Dance Company was created by Yemenite Israeli Sara Levi-Tanai to present Yemenite movement on stage in a Westernized framework.[8] In many respects this troupe is a direct successor to Rina Nikova's Yemenite Company, the second-prize recipient of the National Dance Competition. Contemporary choreographer Barak Marshall, son of Margalit Oved, the Yemen-born Israeli star and former director of the Inbal Dance Company, aims to bridge Western and Middle Eastern influences in his work. Present-day Israeli folk dance also continues to incorporate this aesthetic.

Similarly, in music the work of renowned Israeli singer Noa (Ahinoam Nini) has gained acclaim for embracing this fusion. At a concert Noa presented in San Francisco in the late 1990s, the cultural attaché of Israel introduced her as the best that Israel has to offer because she successfully mixes the cultures and styles of the Middle East and the West. The rise to fame of Moroccan Israeli singer Zehava Ben also embodies the blending of these backgrounds. She sings in both Arabic and Hebrew, embracing the songs of legendary Egyptian singer Umm Kulthum alongside Israeli classics.[9]

The Aesthetic of Toughness

Just as during the British Mandate period, the aesthetic of toughness maintains a central place in contemporary Israel. The still used label sabra, used to denote native-born Israelis, encapsulates this characteristic. The sabra, a cactus fruit grown on the land, prickly on the surface but sweet on the inside, was viewed as a fitting term for expressing the Israeli character, seen as tough and strong on the outside but kind and soft in the interior. The tough exterior was, and is, continually extolled in Israeli society.

The emphasis on masculinity remains deeply tied to this aesthetic. In a country regularly at war, military strength is highly valued. The significant role that the armed forces play in Israeli society has served to strengthen, solidify, and even intensify the importance for Israelis of presenting a strong, masculine front. As Tamar Mayer states, "In a culture like the one that has developed in Israel—as a result of its struggles to survive—national strength and heroism have become deeply coupled with masculinity."[10]

The "ethos of the warrior" and the emphasis on security or the "security framework" pervade all of Israeli society.[11] The importance of maintaining a tough image is continually stressed. This goal is also emphasized in the army and its approach to soldiers. For example, when the question of employing therapists in army units was addressed, the response reflected the aesthetic of toughness. "A major in the reserves who served as a mental health officer [a general term denoting psychologists or social workers] in combat units explains the resistance of field commanders to the use of therapists in their units: 'If you allow the use of mental health officers, it is perceived to be a sort of admission of weakness. It's part of Israeli machismo that maintains that one is not allowed to cry, to talk, to say one is frightened.'"[12]

The aesthetic of toughness appears in all facets of daily life, from aggressive driving (the country has a relatively large number of road accidents)[13] to speech patterns. The term *dugri* means speaking straight to the point and was used in the early days of the state to symbolize the sabra character.[14] As sociologist Oz Almog notes, *dugri* represents "the courage to speak boldly."[15]

This aesthetic has also been integrated into the artistic sphere. Contemporary Israeli dance embraces this model: Unlike some dance styles that aim to be beautiful and dainty (such as classical ballet), contemporary Israeli dance is tough and aggressive. Choreographer Niv Sheinfeld says, "In Israel, you need to be strong and vital to survive, and I think choreographers bring this kind of energy to their work. It's a kind of urgency."[16]

Celebration Versus Sorrow: The Aesthetic of Defiance

The continued resonance of the permeability of the boundary between celebration and sorrow is illustrated in the placement of Yom Hazikaron, the national memorial day, and Yom Ha'atzmaut, Independence Day. In the Israeli national calendar these two holidays are linked: Yom Hazikaron precedes and is immediately followed by Yom Ha'atzmaut. The deep mourning of Yom Hazikaron moves instantly into the celebration of independence at sundown; the nation moves from sadness to joy in a matter of moments.

This permeability is an integral component of the Israeli sensibility. In the summer of 2008, while attending Israel's annual three-day dance festival in the northern development town of Karmiel, I spoke with an Israeli woman who once performed regularly at the Karmiel Dance Festival and now attends the event yearly. As we discussed the festival and dance in Israel more broadly, she noted, "In Israel, dancing isn't just dancing. It's always more: it's always tied to the country and it's always on the edge, the border between celebration and sorrow, just like the crossover, that edge, from Yom Hazikaron to Yom Ha'atzmaut."

As Israeli journalist Yossi Melman further reflects, "Israel is a nation of extremes: the moods of its population swing widely and nervously between a sense of catastrophe and intense enjoyment of celebrations and festivals."[17] Melman also describes the juxtaposition of war and celebration in the 1990s.

In their desperate pursuit of fun and entertainment, the new Israelis have turned the long Middle Eastern summer into one protracted festival, apparently shrugging off, or perhaps sublimating, the acute existential problems of political violence, terrorism, and military tension that constantly face them. To a foreign observer this mania for culture may seem appalling or even perverse: Are cultural pursuits and war compatible? But to most of the new Israelis, this peculiar coexistence of combat and culture does not pose any serious contradictions. Israelis are used to having wars while also enjoying music, theater, and other kinds of entertainment.[18]

The aesthetic of defiance appears in the ways in which Jewish Israelis responded to the second intifada—viewing themselves as defiantly choosing life by riding buses and frequenting cafes. The Karmiel dancer also illustrated this defiance when she reflected that dancing always take place on "the edge."

Religious Versus Secular

The religious-secular debate was unresolved during the British Mandate era and continues to be so to this day. This rift regularly emerges in almost every arena of Israeli life, such as the exemption of most ultra-Orthodox Jews from serving in the army, the absence of civil marriage and divorce, the delineation of how Jews are permitted to pray at the Western Wall in Jerusalem, the evaluation of the flying routes of the national airline, El Al, and the prohibition against El Al operating on the Sabbath.[19] Indeed, the debate over Sabbath observance in the public sphere, contested so vociferously after the 1947 Dalia Festival, remains one of Israel's central and enduring disputes, consisting of ongoing questions over the use of public transportation and the opening of businesses on the Sabbath.

When developing the status quo agreement in 1947, Ben-Gurion believed that he was witnessing the last generation of religious Jews, and he did not realize the impact that this agreement would have in years to come. The religious community still has ultimate authority over many questions of Jewish observance in such areas as weddings and burial and matters of personal status (who is a Jew). The Orthodox sector, roughly 20 percent of the Jewish population, has been growing and playing an increasingly greater role in the public arena. And the animosity of the rest of the population, particularly toward the ultra-Orthodox community, has intensified in response.

Among the numerous examples are the controversies over two public celebrations in 1998 and 2008: a scheduled performance by the Batsheva Dance Company for Israel's fiftieth anniversary and a performance by members of the Mehola Dance Company for the dedication of the Chords Bridge. These examples revisit the same issues that developed in the cultural sphere during the British Mandate era.

At celebrations in Jerusalem for the fiftieth anniversary of the establishment of the state in 1998, the Batsheva Dance Company was scheduled to perform in a three-hour event intended to display the country's history in song and dance.[20] This contemporary troupe, considered one of the premiere Israeli dance companies, receives state subsidies.

The program for the anniversary celebration featured the piece *Anaphaza*, created by artistic director Ohad Naharin. In a section of the work choreographed to the traditional Passover song "Echad mi yodea" (Who Knows One), dancers wearing black suits and hats strip off their outer garb and remain only in their underwear. Their outer clothing could be interpreted as the attire of the ultra-Orthodox (Figure 47). When the company performed this piece in New York, however, many thought that the dancers were portraying stockbrokers!

Shortly before the anniversary celebration, the ultra-Orthodox deputy mayor of Jerusalem, Haim Miller, and two religious parties raised protests against its performance.[21] They not only objected to the "Echad mi yodea" section of Naharin's piece but also threatened to start a demonstration to interrupt it. Echoing Prime Minister Ben-Gurion's call to the organizers of the second Dalia Festival, asking them to postpone their festival to placate the Orthodox community, Prime Minister Benjamin Netanyahu's office urged Naharin to change the underlying clothing to long underwear. "Even President Ezer Weizman summoned 45-year-old Mr. Naharin and, using the Yiddish word for long underwear, urged him not to make waves. 'He told me, so let them wear *gatkes*,' Mr. Naharin said."[22] The choreographer at first agreed to mollify the Orthodox sector with the requested change, but upon further thought, he resigned from his position before the program. In solidarity with Naharin, the company did not perform in the jubilee show. Shortly after this affair, Naharin was reinstated in his position.

Batsheva's abstention from the program—and the reasons behind it—stirred a national controversy that also garnered international press coverage. The pitch and tenor of the debate sounded just like the discussions during the British Mandate period. The language used by the religious community resembled the language in the Queen Esther and Dalia controversies—dramatic and hyperbolic. "The Chief Rabbi of Israel warned that those who did not condemn Batsheva's 'forbidden act' would bring upon themselves 'suffering, and even death.'"[23] At the same time, the anger in the secular community soared.

That incident unleashed a torrent of fury among secular Israelis. Several days later,

Figure 47. *Anaphaza*, by Ohad Naharin, performed by the Batsheva Dance Company, c. 2006. Photo: Gadi Dagon. Courtesy of the photographer and Batsheva Dance Company.

at a packed outdoor arena in Tel Aviv, the company staged a retaliatory performance in which a dancer dressed as an ultra-Orthodox Jew stripped to her underwear. The Tel Aviv audience cheered as if their team had scored a touchdown and had retaken the lead.[24]

The dispute, as in the Mandate era, centered on the character of the Jewish public sphere.

Ten years later, in June 2008, a similar occurrence took place over the celebrations of the inauguration of the Chords Bridge in Jerusalem, designed by architect Santiago Calatrava. Female teenage dancers in the Mehola dance troupe were scheduled to perform as part of the festivities, which also included fireworks and a speech by Prime Minister Ehud Olmert. Hours before the ceremony the dancers were pressured to change their costumes and their performance was reduced from three segments to one. Just as with the Batsheva controversy a decade earlier, the ultra-Orthodox community threatened to stage a large protest at the ceremony. "Jerusalem Mayor Uri Lupolianski was reportedly under pressure to cancel the performance altogether, but a compromise was reached."[25] Instead of their original costumes, the female dancers wore black woolen caps and brown cloaks. Likewise, they did not dance extensively. As Yaniv Hoffman, the artistic director, noted, "They stood like statues."[26] Just as with the Batsheva case, the politicians did not want to risk offending the ultra-Orthodox community, whose demands were therefore met.

In the Mehola case as well, the tenor of the debates was similar to that in the Mandate era. Almost repeating the Orthodox position during the debates about modesty that took place over Queen Esther in the 1920s, the ultra-Orthodox deputy mayor of Jerusalem stated, "Their short-sleeve shirts and ankle-length white trousers were simply too revealing. And their dances—involving tambourines and balloons-were downright 'promiscuous.'"[27] He further lauded the results, stating that the girls "had been dressed offensively and would have interfered with residents' enjoyment of the show. Because of their more modest attire and toned-down moves, ... everyone was able to have a good time."[28] But, again, the more secular community was outraged and incensed and viewed this decision as caving in to the Orthodox community and as a personal affront.

Between the Edges: Contemporary Israel's Embodied Public Culture

Contemporary Israeli society features a deep-seated embodied public culture. On the annual Independence Day holiday, just as in 1948, crowds flock to the streets and parade and dance en masse in celebration. On Holocaust Martyrs and Heroes Remembrance Day (Yom Hashoah Ve-Hagevurah) and Memorial Day (Yom Hazikaron), citizens stop in the middle of streets and highways to stand upright in silence to a piercing siren for two minutes as an embodied memorial.[29] When Prime Minister Yitzhak Rabin was assassinated in 1995, crowds flocked to the streets, marching in unison with candles. Throughout the year parades take place in celebration of a variety of events and holidays; crowds gather weekly to dance in public spaces, such as the promenade in Tel Aviv; and numerous athletic, dance, and beauty activities are avidly fostered. The importance of the army in Israeli society, as discussed earlier, also upholds and reinforces the value of the corporeal.

As in the British Mandate era, this embodiment serves as a window into present-day Israeli society. Contemporary Israeli culture continues to be a culture of debate. Every aspect of life offers a potential source of contention. And the tenor of the debates has not changed from the period before statehood. The disputes possess the same pitch and intensity—and express many of the same points—as they did in their foundations in the Mandate era.

Cultural activities maintain the equivalent significance that they held during the time of British rule. Film director Amos Gitai stated in 1999:

Culture here has held a powerful role. . . . In the Western world, both the visual arts and the cinema suffer from a lack of context. But in the Middle East, we are anachronistic: things still count. Until very recently, every work of art that tried to be something was treated as something defining, something that strove to express what it is to be Israeli.[30]

The country regularly aims to define what is Israeli and who is appropriate to signify it. Israelis persist in debating who should be a symbol for their society. In 1998 a controversy arose over sending Dana International, a Yemenite Jewish transsexual singer, to represent Israel in the Eurovision contest. The reality show *The Ambassador*, which premiered in 2005 and aired a second season in 2006, appears to have replaced the search for "the most typical Eretz Israeli woman" as Queen Esther and the National Dance Competition's attempt to find the most authentic Hebrew dance. *The Ambassador* developed specifically for the purpose of finding someone who could appropriately serve as a symbol of and an advocate for the country.

And Israeli culture continues to be intertwined with politics. The Karmiel dancer had it right when she stated, "Everything is more." In Israel, culture is "more"; it is heightened and political.

Although it has undergone extensive changes since the British Mandate era, Israeli culture persists in existing on the edge. The country remains embroiled in an ongoing political conflict, and people live with a high level of intensity. Choreographer Idan Cohen stated it well in 2008, "My work keeps getting dirtier and rougher." Asked how living in the Jewish state contributed to the challenges in his work, he said, "Israel has depth, controversy, intensity and warmth—and you are a part of this no matter what."[31]

Contemporary Israelis keep on with the struggle to define their national character, what is "authentically" Israeli, and how they should be represented. Indeed, it is difficult to comprehend the politics of Israel without understanding its culture.

The embodied national public culture, solidified and crystallized during the British Mandate era, remains a place where meanings and values are confronted and negotiated.

Notes

Introduction

1. The dancing in the streets in celebration of the Declaration of the State of Israel can be seen in the film *The Day Came*, directed by Shmuel Schweig.

2. Regarding terms for the area, Palestine is the official name for the region in the Mandate era. The Jewish community used the term Eretz Israel, which literally means the "Land of Israel" and stems from Jewish tradition, connoting sacredness without defining specific borders. In adjectival form, Eretz Israeli is a term the Jewish community used to describe itself at this time. See Shapira, *Land and Power, ix.*

3. Arieh Bruce Saposnik's seminal work on the development of Hebrew culture in the Ottoman era uncovers critical foundations set during the decade before World War I. Nonetheless, Hebrew culture solidified during the British Mandate era. Saposnik, *Becoming Hebrew.*

4. For further discussion on the significance of—and debates over—creating national communities in European nationalism, see, for instance, Anderson, *Imagined Communities*; Gellner, *Nations and Nationalism*; and Hobsbawm, *Nations.*

5. For a further discussion of Herzl's attention to symbols, see Mosse, *Confronting the Nation*, 124–25. Herzl's wishes were also expressed in his diary when he wrote about his desires for folk and national festivals throughout the country. Y. Shavit and Sitton, *Staging and Stagers,* 21–22.

6. For instance, the Fifth Zionist Congress in Basel in 1901 featured the first visual arts exhibition. Concerts and communal singing were important components of the congresses,

including the singing of "Hatikvah" (The Hope), which was to become the national anthem of the state. Jewish sports presentations were also a significant feature. At the Sixth Zionist Congress in Basel in 1903 there was an international Jewish Gymnastics Day. Cultural components continued to expand at the congresses and incorporated new activities, such as a movie and a play by the Eleventh Zionist Congress in 1913. See Berkowitz, *Zionist Culture*, 20–23; Presner, *Muscle Judaism*, 122; and Schmidt, *Art and Artists*, 2, 7.

7. Mosse, *Confronting the Nation*, 7; and Mosse, *Nationalization*. See also Ozouf, *Festivals*; and Roshwald, *Endurance of Nationalism*.

8. Geldern, *Bolshevik Festivals*, 5–6; Petrone, *Life*.

9. See, for instance, Saposnik, *Becoming Hebrew*; Helman, *Or ve-yam hikifuha*; Helman, *Young Tel Aviv*; Mann, *A Place in History*; and Y. Shavit and Sitton, *Staging and Stagers*. Although there have been some important studies investigating the role of the body in both contemporary Israel and the Yishuv, they have focused primarily on literature and health. See, for instance, Gluzman, *Ha-guf ha-tsiyoni*; Sered, *What Makes Women Sick?*; and Weiss, *The Chosen Body*.

10. See, for instance, S. Almog, *Zionism and History*; Boyarin, *Unheroic Conduct*; Mosse, *Confronting the Nation*; and Presner, *Muscle Judaism*.

11. For an important new study on Jewish lives during the Mandate era, see Divine, *Exiled in the Homeland*.

12. Shaffer, *Public Culture*, xiv. For a further discussion on public culture in a variety of societies, see Walkowitz and Knauer, *Contested Histories*.

13. For a discussion on the relationship between the urban landscape, the natural environment, and the moving body in the development of Tel Aviv and its culture, see Spiegel, "Constructing the City of Tel Aviv."

14. Although I am dealing with the concept of socialist Zionism here as a unified whole, I want to clarify that there were different competing strains within this broad grouping.

15. O. Almog, *The Sabra*.

16. See, for instance, Bernstein, *Pioneers and Homemakers*; and Fuchs, *Israeli Women's Studies*.

17. See, for instance, Chapter 4 and the case of Gurit Kadman. Many choreographers lived in urban areas but choreographed in the kibbutzim, such as Yardena Cohen, who is discussed in Chapter 3.

18. The National Dance Competition has not been addressed before. The first Maccabiah Games have been largely overlooked. Some studies have mentioned the first Maccabiah Games in passing or have mostly focused on the second Maccabiah Games. See, for instance, Helman, *Or ve-yam hikifuha*; and Helman, *Young Tel Aviv*. A doctoral dissertation by George Eisen and a piece by Chaim Wein contain data on the first Maccabiah Games but do not provide the detailed and extensive analysis or context provided here. See Eisen, "The Maccabiah Games"; and Wein, *The Maccabiah Games*. Although there has been some material on the first two Dalia

Festivals in 1944 and 1947, most of it has focused on the later Dalia Festivals after statehood. For instance, Ruth Ashkenazi's book has comparatively little material on the first two Dalia Festivals. See Ashkenazi, *Sipur maholot ha'am b'daliah*. An exception is Tzvi Friedhaber's work. He provides some important historical data but does not offer analysis. Moreover, none of these works provide material on the religious-secular conflict ignited by the Dalia Festivals, a critical component of the story. See Friedhaber, "First Folk Dance Festival"; and Friedhaber, *Hava netze b'meholot*. There has been recent interest in Purim in Tel Aviv. Several studies have addressed the Purim carnivals in Tel Aviv briefly but have not examined the Queen Esther competitions. See, for instance, Helman, *Or ve-yam hikifuha*; Helman, *Young Tel Aviv*; and Mann, *A Place in History*. There are also articles on Purim in Tel Aviv by Aryeh-Sapir, "Karnaval Betel Aviv"; and Shoham, "A Huge National Assemblage." Shoham's dissertation examines Purim in Tel Aviv extensively and has addressed aspects of Queen Esther, but from an anthropological vantage point, overlooking the issues that I investigate. See Shoham, "Purim Celebrations." An important exhibit at the Eretz Israel Museum and accompanying catalog contained important data on Purim and Queen Esther but without the analysis I provide. See Carmiel, *Tel Aviv*. An article by Bat-Sheva Margalit Stern addresses aspects of Queen Esther, but also from an entirely different perspective and without the extensive data and analysis I provide. See Stern, "Who's the Fairest." Last, Nili Aryeh-Sapir and Michal Held discuss the experience of the 1928 Purim Queen, Tsipora Tsabari, based on an interview they conducted with her. See Aryeh-Sapir and Held, "Vatilbash Malkhut." In sum, although a few aspects of some of these events have been previously examined, they have been investigated either individually or in brief and thus have remained peripheral to the history of the era. None have been integrated into the broader history of the Yishuv or placed within the context of the building of an embodied national public culture.

19. Shoham, "A Huge National Assemblage."

20. See Chapter 1. In addition, Adriana Brodsky investigates the spread of the Queen Esther custom in Argentina. See Brodsky, "Contours of Identity." Although it was not connected to Queen Esther, the concept of Jewish beauty pageants spread to Europe with a Miss Judea beauty pageant held in Warsaw in 1929 to select Poland's most beautiful Jewess. See Portnoy, "Move Over Miss Polonia."

21. Both Mizrahi and Ashkenazic Jewish women have been selected as winners of the Miss Israel pageant in recent years, and Rana Raslan was the first Israeli Arab Miss Israel, crowned in 1999.

22. *Ha'aretz*, 30 March 2009.

23. Although it was before the establishment of the State of Israel, the Yishuv referred to its folk dance creations as Israeli folk dance: *rikudei am yisrael*, literally "dances of the people of Israel." Thus, although I use the term *Hebrew culture* for all other forms, I use the term *Israeli folk dance* in this case.

24. Although it has several differences from its predecessor at Dalia, the Karmiel Dance

Festival, held in the summer, maintains the tradition of outdoor performances and dancing throughout the night. For a further discussion of how traditions developed at Dalia became instilled at Karmiel, see Spiegel, "New Israeli Rituals."

25. Berkowitz, *Western Jewry*, esp. ch. 6 and p. 134.

26. Ingber, "Vilified or Glorified? Nazi Versus Zionist Views."

27. See, for instance, Greenblatt, "Recreational Israeli Dance"; Kaschl, "Beyond Israel"; and Roginsky, "Israeli Folk Dance Movement."

28. Tom Segev's work provides a textured account of this era. See Segev, *One Palestine*.

29. Jordan, *Daughter of the Waves*, 11.

30. As Barbara Kirshenblatt-Gimblett states, "Performance Studies starts from the premise that its objects of study are not to be divided up and parceled out, medium by medium, to various other disciplines—music, dance, dramatic literature, art history. The prevailing division of the arts by medium is arbitrary, as is the creation of fields and departments devoted to each. Most of the world's artistic expression has always synthesized or otherwise integrated movement, sound, speech, narrative, and objects." Kirshenblatt-Gimblett, "Performance Studies," 43.

31. For a more detailed discussion of Max Nordau's thought, see Stanislawski, *Zionism*. In addition to Nordau, other theorists called for the development of the Jewish physique, such as Dr. Max Mandelstamm, but Nordau became the symbol of this ideological position. See Eisen, "Zionism," 249, 253.

32. Excerpt of the speech by Max Nordau at the Second Zionist Congress, printed in the brochure of the First Maccabiah Games, Joseph Yekutieli Maccabi Archive (Ramat Gan, Israel).

33. Mosse, *Confronting the Nation*, 126–28.

34. In 1811 the first gymnastics arena opened in Berlin. According to Michael Krüger, "Turnen developed as a synonym of German body culture and physical education." M. Krüger, "Body Culture," 410.

35. M. Krüger, "Body Culture," 411.

36. Wedemeyer, "Body-Building," 477.

37. See Mosse, *Confronting the Nation*, ch. 11. This notion that a healthy body was the place to begin regeneration was also evidenced in Western European Jewish attitudes toward North African and Middle Eastern Jews. In the Alliance Israèlite Universelle (AIU), Western European Jews viewed North African and Middle Eastern Jews as in need of regeneration. There was an emphasis in the AIU on the body and on physical education as part of the moral regeneration of the "natives." See Rodrigue, *Images*.

38. Presner, *Muscle Judaism*. These notions were also connected to social Darwinism. According to Peter Baldwin, Nordau viewed Zionism as a "remedy for degeneration." Baldwin, "Liberalism," 112. See also Mosse's discussion on Nordau and degeneration in *Confronting the Nation*, ch. 11; and Söder, "Dr. Jekyll and Mr. Hyde."

39. Gilman, *The Jew's Body*, 53.

40. Presner, *Muscle Judaism*, 120–21.

41. Presner, *Muscle Judaism*, 106.

42. For a further discussion of the image of the new Jewish body and how it would be cultivated through gymnastics, see Mosse, *Confronting the Nation*, 165–67. For a further discussion of the negative stereotypes of the Jewish body in European society, see Gilman's extensive studies: *The Jew's Body*; *Difference and Pathology*; and *Visibility of the Jew*. Gilman also addresses the feminization of the male Jew in European society in "Salome." For additional material on images of Jews in European society, especially as connected to health and medicine, see J. Efron, *Defenders of the Race*; J. Efron, *Medicine and the German Jews*; and Hart, *The Healthy Jew*.

43. Butler, "Performative Acts." For an additional discourse on gender theory and history, see, among others, Butler, *Gender Trouble*; Riley, *Am I That Name?*; and Scott, *Gender and the Politics of History*. For relevant discussions of gender and masculinity in European society, see, for instance, Engelstein, *Keys to Happiness*; Nye, *Masculinity*; and Roberts, *Civilization Without Sexes*.

44. T. Mayer, "From Zero to Hero," 99.

45. Shmuel Almog addresses the importance of the cultivation of the body across different Zionist factions. See S. Almog, *Zionism and History*, 108–18. See also David Biale's chapter "Zionism as an Erotic Revolution," in Biale, *Eros and the Jews*, 176–203.

46. Rabbi Abraham Isaac Kook, "Lights for Rebirth," in Hertzberg, *The Zionist Idea*, 431.

47. See, for instance, Deslandes, "The Male Body"; Mosse, *Image of Man*; and Zweiniger-Bargielowska, "Building a British Superman."

48. See Ladd and Mathiesen, *Muscular Christianity*; and Putney, *Muscular Christianity*.

49. The phrase *aesthetic of toughness* stems from an article by Jan Nederveen Pieterse in which he claims that in Israel "the aesthetic of toughness was driven by a collective memory of loss and defeat." Although this phrase referred to the post-state period, the notion of toughness was also prevalent in the Mandate era. See Pieterse, "Aesthetics of Power," 39.

50. For a further discussion of the negation of the Diaspora in Zionist thought, see, for instance, Ratzaby, "Polemic"; and Schweid, "Rejection of the Diaspora."

51. Eric Hobsbawm, "Introduction: Inventing Traditions," in Hobsbawm and Ranger, *Invention of Tradition*, 14.

52. For additional visual images of Zionism, see Arbel, *Blue and White*; Berkowitz, *Zionist Culture*; and Schmidt, *Art and Artists*.

53. As Yael Zerubavel notes, in their reconstruction of the past, Zionists ignored Diaspora Jewish history, focusing instead on ancient Jewish life. Zerubavel, *Recovered Roots*, 26.

54. Saposnik, *Becoming Hebrew*, 108–13; and Y. Shavit and Sitton, *Staging and Stagers*.

55. Azaryahu, "Tel-Aviv's Birthdays."

56. For a discussion of additional public funerals, see Helman, *Young Tel Aviv*, 47–51.

57. A statue of a roaring lion was erected in Tel Hai; it was the first modern monument

in the country, and the location itself also became an important pilgrimage site. Zerubavel, *Recovered Roots*.

58. In this book I use the terms *religious* and *secular* according to groupings, visions, and differentiations in the Yishuv era that have continued into the present. Although I refer to these sectors as a whole, they were varied and complex, embracing a range of Zionist—as well as non-Zionist and anti-Zionist—visions. In contemporary Israeli society the religious sector encompasses Orthodox and ultra-Orthodox Jews, including those who identify as Zionist, non-Zionist, and anti-Zionist. The secular sector encompasses a wide variety of relationships to Judaism and Jewish practice, ranging from none to extensive. For a more complete discussion of these terms and categories and their development, see Sobel and Beit-Hallahmi, "Introduction." See also Liebman and Don-Yehiya, *Civil Religion*.

59. A religious-secular rift was already apparent at the early Zionist Congresses. Creating a new culture was debated early in the movement, threatening to tear the Zionist movement apart early on. For Orthodox Jews cultural creation was one of the most threatening aspects of modern Zionism, because for them Judaism itself provided a culture of its own. A separate secular Zionist culture, according to this view, was not necessary and was indeed dangerous, because it threatened Jewish observance. As the chair of the early Zionist Congresses, Theodor Herzl tried to avoid the culture question in order to maintain unity within the Zionist movement and to focus on what he viewed as the primary issues of the day: the political ones. But the issue of culture continued to be contentious at the Zionist Congresses in Europe, setting the stage for further controversies. See Berkowitz, *Zionist Culture*, 66, 89–91; Halpern and Reinharz, *Zionism*, 122–26; Rinott, "Religion and Education," 4–6; and Saposnik, *Becoming Hebrew*, 192.

60. Liebman and Don-Yehiya, *Civil Religion*, 48.

61. For a more detailed discussion of the role of Hanukkah in the Yishuv, see Aryeh-Sapir, "Tahalukhat ha'or"; Liebman and Don-Yehiya, *Civil Religion*; and Zerubavel, *Recovered Roots*. Liebman and Don-Yehiya explore the transformation of a number of traditional Jewish holidays in the Yishuv, but interestingly they do not investigate Purim.

62. Israel Bartal discusses the Zionist transformation of Jewish holidays through the anthology project's *Sefer hamo'adim* (Book of Festivals). Although this series was published mostly in the 1950s, after the establishment of the state, it was, according to Bartal, inspired by Hayyim Nahman Bialik's *Sefer hashabbat* (Sabbath Book), published in the 1930s in Tel Aviv. These anthologies are one more example of the ways in which Zionists appropriated traditional Judaism. See Bartal, "Ingathering."

63. Liebman and Don-Yehiya, *Civil Religion*.

64. Mosse, *Confronting the Nation*, 1–10.

65. Liebman and Don-Yehiya, *Civil Religion*.

66. For a discussion on the role of outdoor festivals in Tel Aviv, see Y. Shavit and Sitton, *Staging and Stagers*, 85.

67. Mosse, *Confronting the Nation*, 1–26. For a discussion on the role of social and cultural myths in the shaping of the Yishuv and later Israeli society, see Aronoff, "Myths, Symbols, and Rituals"; Gertz, *Myths in Israeli Culture*; Shapira, *Land and Power*; Shapira, "Origins of the Myth"; and Zerubavel, *Recovered Roots*.

68. For an additional discussion of the relationship of the kibbutzim to Jewish tradition in the 1920s, see Zeira, *Keru'im anu*.

69. Penslar, *Israel in History*, 192–93. On the formation of Tu b'Shevat celebrations and their importance in the Ottoman era, see Saposnik, *Becoming Hebrew*, 60–61.

70. In addition, for Passover, Haggadot were created that connected the traditional Passover story to Yishuv life; many versions were an important form of satire. For an additional discussion, see Penslar, *Israel in History*; and Y. Shavit and Sitton, *Staging and Stagers*.

71. Liebman and Don-Yehiya, *Civil Religion*, 48.

72. For an important discussion of rifts between religious and secular worldviews in the public sphere both during the Mandate period and later in the state, see Marmorstein, *Heaven at Bay*, especially chaps. 6 and 7. For a discussion of clashes between secular Zionists and ultra-Orthodox Jews in the Mandate era, especially regarding the Western Wall, see Segev, *One Palestine*, 70–73.

73. For a political and institutional discussion of the rabbinic role and status in the Yishuv during these years, see Kolatt, "Religion."

74. Saposnik, *Becoming Hebrew*, 165.

75. There have been extensive studies on the development of Hebrew literature. For some classic examples, see Alter, *Invention of Hebrew Prose*; Band, *Nostalgia and Nightmare*; Brinker, *Ad ha-simtah ha-teveryanit*; Gertz, *Sifrut ve-ideologyah*; Miron, *Bodedim be-moadam*; Hever, "Our Poetry"; Hever, *Paytanim u-viryonim*; Shaked, *Panim aherot bi-yetsirato*; and Z. Shavit, *Ha-hayyim ha-sifrutyiyim*. For important articles on Hebrew literature, language, and publishing, see Lissak and Shavit, *Toldot ha-yishuv*. On language and culture, see also Helman, "Even the Dogs"; and Hirschfeld, "Locus and Language."

76. For a more detailed description of the inauguration of Hebrew University, see Segev, *One Palestine*, 202–20.

77. For more material on the development of radio, see Katriel, *Soul Talks*; Penslar, "Broadcast Orientalism"; Penslar, *Israel in History*; and Penslar, "Transmitting Jewish Culture." On the development of the Hebrew press, see Kressel, *Toldot ha-itonut ha-ivrit*.

78. Hirshberg, *Music*, 61, 129, 141–45. See also Bohlman, *World Centre for Jewish Music*; Gai, *Hanna Rovina*; Even-Zohar, "Emergence of a Native Hebrew Culture"; Ofrat, *One Hundred Years of Art*; Lissak and Shavit, *Toldot ha-Yishuv*; D. Manor, *Art in Zion*; Rokem, "Ha-dybbuk"; Rokem, "Hebrew Theater"; and Zakim, "Missing Representation."

79. In 1935 *The Land of Promise* was the first sound film to be produced in Palestine; it was designed to encourage Jewish immigration to Palestine. That same year, *Zot hi ha'aretz* (This Is the Land) was the first Hebrew talking film; it celebrated fifty years of Zionist settlement

in Palestine. According to Hillel Tryster, these two films were among the five most important sound films produced in Palestine in the 1930s. Tryster, "Land of Promise," 214–17. For a discussion of the development of silent film, see Tryster, *Israel Before Israel*. See also Feldestein, "Filming the Homeland"; and Gross, *Ya'akov Ben Dov*.

80. See, for instance, Shahar, "Eretz Israeli Song."

81. After the establishment of the state and especially since the 1980s, the West has also come to include cultural influence from the United States. The use of the term *European culture* overlooks the differences between Eastern and Western European Jewish communities and is often used to denote the high culture of Western and Central Europe, which is identified with dominance and hegemony. For a more detailed discussion of these issues in other societies, see Levine, *Highbrow/Lowbrow*; and De Grazia, *How Fascism Ruled Women*, 208–209.

82. Kalmar and Penslar, "Introduction," xix. In his seminal work, Edward Said argues that Westerners made a binary distinction between East and West. See Said, *Orientalism*. Additional works on Jews and Orientalism have further complicated these concepts in the case of Jews, especially with regard to Zionism. See, for instance, Kalmar and Penslar, *Orientalism*; Peleg, *Orientalism*; and Piterberg, "Domestic Orientalism."

83. The term *Sephardim* refers to the descendants of the Jews who fled or were expelled from Spain in 1492, many of whom settled in Middle Eastern countries as well as in North Africa, the Levant, and various European centers. *Mizrahi* literally means "Eastern" and refers largely to Jews who settled in North Africa and the Middle East who do not necessarily trace their ancestry to the expulsion from Spain. Jews from Arab countries or Persian Jews from Iran are also known as Oriental Jews. As is evident from these definitions, there is an overlap between the groups. Jews from other areas, such as the Caucasus, are also often referred to as Mizrahim. The use of the term and its categorization bear political connotations in contemporary Israeli society. This issue is addressed from a cultural standpoint in the Conclusion. For a further discussion of these matters and the development of the term, see, for instance, Kalmar and Penslar, *Orientalism*; Raz-Krakotzkin, "Zionist Return"; Shohat, "Invention of the Mizrahim"; and Shohat, "Mizrahim in Israel."

84. See Raz-Krakotzkin, "Zionist Return," esp. 171 and 180. In addition, an exhibit at the Israel Museum in the summer of 1998 addressed the conversation about Israeli attitudes toward the Arab and Jewish "East" through an examination of this issue in Israel's visual arts and multimedia history. See the exhibition catalog, *Kadimah: ha-mizrah be-omanut yisrael*.

85. D. Manor, "Orientalism," 158.

86. See Druyan, *Be-ein marvad kesamim*; Guilat, "Yemeni Ideal"; D. Manor, "Orientalism"; and Saposnik, *Becoming Hebrew*.

87. Kalmar and Penslar, "Introduction." See also Raz-Krakotzkin, "Zionist Return," 167.

88. When political parties were founded, Labor Zionism gained political dominance, including but not exclusively limited to the socialist Zionist Labor Party, Ahdut Ha'avoda, in 1919; and the long-standing followers of A. D. Gordon, Hapoel Hatzair. These two parties

merged in 1930 into Mapai (Mifleget Poalei Eretz Yisrael, the Land of Israel Workers' Party), led by David Ben-Gurion.

89. For an additional discussion of different forms of Zionism, see, for instance, S. Almog, *Zionism and History*; S. Almog et al., *Zionism and Religion*; Avineri, *Modern Zionism*; Reinharz and Shapira, *Essential Papers on Zionism*; and Zipperstein, *Elusive Prophet*.

90. See, for instance, Helman, *Or ve-yam hikifuha*; Shoham, "A Huge National Assemblage"; and Troen, *Imagining Zion*.

91. For an important discussion of the role of land in Israeli culture, see Eric Zakim's book, the title of which stems from these lyrics. Zakim, *To Build and Be Built*.

92. O. Almog, *The Sabra*, 160–76; Zerubavel, *Recovered Roots*, 28. For a discussion of the role of *tiyulim* (hikes) in contemporary Israeli society, see Ben-David, "Tiyul"; and Katriel, "Trips."

93. Recently several studies on Tel Aviv and urban development have been published. See, for instance, Azaryahu, *Tel Aviv*; Azaryahu and Troen, *Tel Aviv*; Helman, *Or ve-yam hikifuha*; Helman, *Young Tel Aviv*; Mann, *A Place in History*; and Schlör, *Tel Aviv*. For a detailed discussion of the relationship between Tel Aviv and Jaffa, see LeVine, *Overthrowing Geography*.

94. Helman, "Was There Anything," 126; Y. Shavit and Sitton, *Staging and Stagers*, 86; Troen, *Imagining Zion*, 102–103.

95. Naor, *Tel Aviv*, 58. For an additional discussion of the development of literature and culture in Tel Aviv in the 1920s, see Yoffe, *Esrim ha-shanim ha-rishonot*.

96. For visual images of Tel Aviv's cafes, see Carmiel, *Bate ha-kafe*. For additional images of Tel Aviv during the Mandate period, see Carmiel, *Korbman*. For images of posters and illustrations, see Donner, *To Live with the Dream*.

97. For a more detailed and descriptive depiction of the relationship between Jews and Arabs during the Mandate period, see Segev, *One Palestine*. For important analyses, see, among others, Gorny, *Zionism and the Arabs*; and Stein, *The Land Question*. For a discussion of economic and political relations in the pre–World War I era, see, for instance, Penslar, *Zionism and Technocracy*; and Shafir, *Land*.

98. For historical debates on this issue, see, for instance, Ofer, "Fifty Years After"; Porat, *Blue and Yellow Stars of David*; and Segev, *The Seventh Million*.

99. O. Almog, *The Sabra*, 114.

Chapter 1

1. Harris, "Purim," 167.

2. I. H. Rubin, secretary of the Jewish National Fund, 2 March 1928, Central Zionist Archives (Jerusalem, Israel), KKL5 2452.

3. For a description of the connection between Purim and Tel Aviv, see Avi-Shulamit, "Purim b'eretz yisrael," 36.

4. For a greater discussion of the connection between Purim and Tel Aviv's urban space, see Helman, *Or ve-yam hikifuha*; Helman, "Two Urban Celebrations"; and Mann, *A Place in History*. For a greater discussion of the organization of the festivities, see Y. Shavit and Sitton, *Staging and Stagers*.

5. Helman, "Two Urban Celebrations," 388–89. Hizky Shoham and Yaakov Shavit and Shoshana Sitton also discuss the economic ramifications. See Shoham, "A Huge National Assemblage," 9–10; and Y. Shavit and Sitton, *Staging and Stagers*, 103.

6. Press reports often noted Arab participation in the carnival. See, for instance, *Palestine Bulletin*, 1 February 1926, 3; *Do'ar ha-Yom*, 8 March 1928, 4; *Do'ar ha-Yom*, 25 March 1932, 4.

7. Shoham, "A Huge National Assemblage," 1–20.

8. Helman, "Two Urban Celebrations," 390.

9. For instance, Nahum Gutmann was involved with decorations for the city. Poems were printed in the Hebrew press in honor of the event; rhyming ads for the different evening galas appeared as well.

10. In many years prizes were distributed for the best decorations on houses. Carmiel, *Tel Aviv*, 234. For a further discussion of the role of balconies in Tel Aviv's urban space, see Aronis, "Balconies of Tel Aviv."

11. Each year, as the festival celebration changed and grew, the floats represented different themes: political satires, biblical motifs, advertisements, and so on. For more detailed descriptions and illustrations of the floats, see Carmiel, *Tel Aviv*, 238–49.

12. The comedy was directed by Chaim Halachmi. Steven Spielberg Jewish Film Archive, R0008.

13. S. Sharnopolsky provided a detailed and significant account of the Purim festivities in 1928, addressing the crowds, the parade, the children's events, the hora, and Queen Esther. See Sharnopolsky, *Guide to Palestine*.

14. At first, the only galas were those organized by Baruch Agadati, often with the support of the Jewish National Fund. Later, galas were organized by other organizations as well, such as the theater companies. For a more detailed discussion of these various galas, see Carmiel, *Tel Aviv*, 156–73.

15. Costumes ranged in themes from commentaries on the political, social, cultural, and financial situation, to characters from the Scroll of Esther, to representations of Eretz Israeli products and the building of the Yishuv, to European fashion, and to the local way of life of the "East." For more detailed descriptions of these various themes and illustrations of the costumes, see Carmiel, *Tel Aviv*, 21–93. See an additional illustration in Silver-Brody, *Documentors of the Dream*.

16. Several newspaper accounts of the period refer to the stormy hora danced in the streets.

See, for instance, *Ha'aretz*, 27 March 1929 and 5 March 1931. See also M. Cohen, "Tel Aviv," 76. The horas took place both in the streets and at the galas, particularly at the popular galas. In 1933 two new horas were introduced at the Ohel-Agadati galas: *Kan* (Here), which was created by Agadati; and *Ha-goren*, which was created by Rivka Sturman. Other folk dances included the debka, tcherkessia, krakoviak, Polish mazurka, polka, and rondo. Carmiel, *Tel Aviv*, 95.

17. Carmiel, *Tel Aviv*, 101–102.

18. Each year, as Shavit and Sitton describe, the Tel Aviv Municipality became more involved in the preparations and officially took them over in 1929. Y. Shavit and Sitton, *Staging and Stagers*, 92, 98.

19. *Do'ar ha-Yom*, 4 March 1928, 1; *Do'ar ha-Yom*, 2 March 1931, 1. At the bottom of the March 2 article is a photograph from Europe of people wearing large masks and parading, with the caption, "For the parade of our celebrations: An example of 'Carnival' in a European city." The European carnival, then, is clearly the goal and the model.

20. *Do'ar ha-Yom*, 1 March 1931, 1.

21. Aryeh-Sapir, *Itsuvam shel tarbut ve-chinukh ironiyim*. Aryeh-Sapir discusses the concept of joy in a variety of celebrations in Tel Aviv in these years.

22. Ta'anit 29a.

23. A committee was first established by the initiative of the Jewish National Fund in 1926 to arrange the carnival. In 1928 a special office was opened to deal with it. In the early 1930s the Tel Aviv Municipality prepared an organizational and artistic committee that included Reuben Reuben, Arye Lubin, Menashe Ravina, Moshe Halevi, Baruch Agadati, and Yaakov Shifman. For more information, see Carmiel, *Tel Aviv*, 233.

24. See, for instance, *Ha'aretz*, 27 March 1929, 1; and 6 March 1928, 1.

25. Lotta Levensohn, "In Carnival Mood," Central Zionist Archives (Jerusalem, Israel), KKL5 2452.

26. The suggestions of these street names from the Megillah (Scroll of Esther) were from the writer A. Z. Ben-Yishai. For a more complete listing of all the street name changes, see *Ha'aretz*, 17 March 1932, 1.

27. For a more detailed discussion of the children's festivities and costumes, see Carmiel, *Tel Aviv*, 174–229.

28. Carmiel, *Tel Aviv*, 246; Halperin and Sagiv, *Me-agvaniyah ad simfonyah*, 247. See also Ailon Schori, "There Was Almost 'Chinga Pur' Here," undated, Zila Agadati personal collection (Tel Aviv, Israel).

29. For a complete list of all the suggested names, see Halperin and Sagiv, *Me-agvaniyah ad simfonyah*, 279.

30. Abraham Shlonsky suggested *Tzhaloula* and *Chingpur*, and these two names are mentioned in his articles and songs. For a further discussion of Shlonsky's work, see Halperin and Sagiv, *Me-agvaniyah ad simfonyah*, 247.

31. Tractate Megillah 7b.

32. *Tor Esther* (Age of Esther) was the name that one of the linguists recommended instead of *carnival*. See Avi-Shulamit, "Yemei ha-purim b'eretz yisrael," 36.

33. For more information on Baruch Agadati, see G. Manor, *Agadati*; *Agadati: Arba panim*; and Tryster, *Agadati*.

34. These Queen Esther competitions were often held on the holiday of Tu b'Shevat. For a discussion of the significance of holding this contest on Tu b'Shevat, see Stern, "Who's the Fairest," 144.

35. These galas were later held at Mugrabi Hall, beginning in 1930.

36. The first year, 365 people participated in the elections for Queen Esther. The second year, 456 people participated in the elections. *Ha'aretz*, 1 February 1926, 4; and 19 January 1927, 4.

37. The carnival and masquerade balls were also restricted to the middle class, artists, intelligentsia, and the cultural elite. In 1927 Agadati started a popular ball that was open to everyone and to which the workers came. These popular balls represented the different social and economic strata, because the tickets for them were one-third the price of those for the carnival ball. See Carmiel, *Tel Aviv*, 14.

38. Flower wars and the throwing of confetti at the carnival itself were additional influences from Europe. See Carmiel, *Tel Aviv*, 101–102.

39. Stern, "Who's the Fairest," 146–47.

40. The camel was noted as being decorated in "an Eastern style." This mix of a camel with motorcycles represents a blend of East and West, which I discuss more fully later in this chapter. *Do'ar ha-Yom*, 26 March 1929, 3.

41. *Do'ar ha-Yom*, 26 March 1929, 3.

42. Batia Carmiel also interprets Agadati's choice of a jar as connecting to biblical stories, such as that of Rebecca next to the well. Carmiel, *Tel Aviv*, 117.

43. For a further discussion of the role of the symbol of the Star of David, see, for instance, Berkowitz, *Zionist Culture*, 121; and D. Manor, *Art in Zion*, 44.

44. The inscription on the tablets read, "To Esther the Queen, Tsipora Tsabari, from Dizengoff, T"A [Tel Aviv], 1928." It is interesting to note that Dizengoff gave Tsabari, a Yemenite woman, a Polish Hanukkah menorah, representing the East-West split that I discuss later in this chapter.

45. Carmiel, *Tel Aviv*, 132.

46. Bashan, *Yesh li reayon*, 297. M. Cohen, "Tel Aviv," 78–79. The declaration of this ruling as from "this Purim evening until the Purim evening to come" is listed in the schedule of the carnival gala in the *Pamphlet of Agadati's Traditional Masquerade Balls*, Purim 1929.

47. See, for instance, Wu, "Loveliest Daughter." The first beauty contest in the United States was held in Atlantic City in 1921. For a fuller discussion of beauty pageants in the United States, see Banner, *American Beauty*.

48. C. Cohen et al., *Beauty Queens*, 2.

49. This call appeared in an announcement in *Do'ar ha-Yom* (28 January 1926, 2) as well as in other newspapers at the time. For instance, further information about the selection process was described in *Ha'aretz*: "At this gala 'Queen Esther' will be chosen—the most beautiful and typical Jewess [*ha-yehudia ha-yaffa ve ha-tipusit be-yoter*] who will fill the place of Esther of the Megillah. See *Ha'aretz*, 22 January 1926. It is interesting to note here that the Hebrew term *yehudia* (Jewess) is used in this announcement. However, in the other ads in that year, such as the one cited in *Do'ar ha-Yom*, as well as in the following years, the term *ivria* (Hebrew woman) is used instead, indicating that the search is for the most typical Hebrew, rather than Jewish, woman. This represents the ambivalence between the concept of Jewish and Hebrew that was part of the larger dilemma of what these terms meant to whom. I more fully address the conflicts that emerged between the religious and secular components of Yishuv society later in this chapter.

50. *Ha'aretz*, 27 March 1929, 1; *Do'ar ha-Yom*, 26 March 1929, 2.

51. Carmiel, *Tel Aviv*, 20.

52. Kesari founded the weekly *Tesha ba-Erev* in 1937.

53. *Kol-noa* was published in Tel Aviv from 1931 to 1935.

54. Lilia Tcherkov was a married woman, Mrs. Rosenthal-Tcherkov. The other candidates in 1926 were Mme. Leah Levun, Mme. Weinshal, and Mme. Grayeva. *Palestine Bulletin*, 1 February 1926, 3.

55. Kesari, "Mi-esther ad esther," 6.

56. For a more detailed description of the Chelouche family, see Pomrock, *Chelouche*.

57. This phrase, "the judging people" (*ha'am ha-shofet*), is similar to one that was used in conjunction with the National Dance Competition in 1937, "the judging audience" (*ha-kahal ha-shofet*), which I discuss in Chapter 3.

58. Kesari, "Mi-esther ad esther," 6–7.

59. Kesari, "Mi-esther ad esther," 7.

60. The other Queen Esther contestants in 1929 were Yaffa Lederman, Bila Kaplan, Chana Meindlin, and Batia Komarov. *Ha'aretz*, 27 January 1929, 4.

61. *Ha'aretz*, 27 January 1929, 4.

62. Kesari, "Mi-esther ad esther," 7.

63. In 1929 four other queens were also chosen from different parts of the country. They were Bathia Aisenstein for Haifa, Zemira Many for Jerusalem, Dinah Abramov for Rishon Le-Tzion, and Sarah Tchelebi-Lazar for Petach-Tikva. Chana Meyuhas-Polani was seen as the queen of Tel Aviv and of all Eretz Israel. The other queens had darker hair than Meyuhas-Polani, although they also appear fair in the photographs. See Carmiel, *Tel Aviv*, 128.

64. Carmiel, *Tel Aviv*, 140; Y. Shavit et al., *Leksikon, 290*.

65. *Ha'aretz*, 26 March 1929, 2.

66. Kesari, "Mi-esther ad esther," 7.

67. It is unclear who exactly was included on the invitation list to the election gala and

what percentage of the city was considered the middle- to upper-class segment. In a period of great financial hardship at times, it is unclear how the voters had the money to afford the elaborate celebrations and costumes that were involved in the Purim festivities in general.

68. Evening attire was required. See the poster for the selection gala, undated, Jewish National and University Library (Jerusalem, Israel), V1969/5.

69. *Ha'aretz*, 1 February 1926, 4.

70. *Ha'aretz*, 26 March 1929, 2. The second to last line of this excerpt is a play on words from a well-known saying in the Passover Haggadah: "kol ha-marbeh le-saper be-yetsiat Mitsrayim harei zeh meshubah" (Anyone who increases the telling of the Exodus from Egypt is praiseworthy).

71. The use of the term *dayenu* (enough) in the title is a reference to Passover. In the Passover Haggadah, "Dayenu" is a song in which Jews praise God for a series of miracles, after each one saying that it would have been enough.

72. *Davar*, 2 February 1930, 3.

73. M. Cohen, "Tel Aviv," 78–79.

74. Carmiel, *Tel Aviv*, vii.

75. Carmiel, *Tel Aviv*, vii. For additional photographs of the Purim queens, see Carmiel, *Tel Aviv*.

76. *Ha'aretz*, 7 March 1928; and "Purim in Tel Aviv," in *Programme for Purim*, 9, Central Zionist Archives (Jerusalem, Israel), 15223. Although this program booklet is undated, it appears to be from Purim 1930.

77. Avi-Shulamit, "Purim b'eretz yisrael," 36.

78. Tsabari went to Europe, to Prague in particular, and represented herself as the beauty queen of Eretz Israel and as Miss Palestine. This trip raised the issue of the representation of the Yishuv's beauty queen in Europe, which is beyond the scope of this chapter. A full article in *Ha'aretz* about Tsipora Tsabari's fame in Prague as the Hebrew queen also discussed how Tsabari brought fame to Tel Aviv. *Ha'aretz*, 21 February 1929.

79. *Kerobez* was a pamphlet of the Purim festivities issued by the city of Tel Aviv from 1933 to 1935. It is an acronym for the Hebrew words *Kol rinah vi-yeshuah be-ohale zadikim* (The voice of rejoicing and salvation is in the tents of the righteous) (Psalm 118:15). M. Cohen, "Tel Aviv," 74.

80. M. Cohen, "Tel Aviv," 78–79.

81. *Hefker*, 1928, 8, Diaspora Research Institute, Tel Aviv University (Ramat Aviv, Israel), A-30/403.

82. For an important discussion on the complex relationship between Jews and horses, see Hoberman, "How Fiercely."

83. *Ha'aretz*, 7 March 1928; and "Purim in Tel Aviv," in *Programme for Purim*, 9. Although this program booklet is undated, it appears to be from Purim 1930.

84. *Ha'aretz*, 7 March 1928; and "Purim in Tel Aviv," in *Programme for Purim*, 9.

85. The other seven candidates were selected to be the "ladies" of the queen. *Do'ar ha-Yom*, 21 March 1929, 6.

86. *Do'ar ha-Yom*, 28 March 1929, 1.

87. This gala was described in *Ha'aretz*. Mayor Dizengoff was invited to the event. There were five candidates, and two of them received the majority of the votes. *Ha'aretz*, 23 March 1929.

88. The Yemenite community selected its own queen until at least 1934. Posters announced the gala for selecting a Yemenite Purim queen in 1931 and 1934. In addition, a separate gala was held to select a Bukharan Queen Esther in 1931. Jewish National and University Library (Jerusalem, Israel), V1969/11. For a greater discussion of the Yemenite queens, see Stern, "Who's the Fairest," 142–63.

89. Confidential letter of Mayor Dizengoff to the Zionist Executive, the Jewish National Fund, Va'ad Leumi, and Keren Hayesod, 23 January 1930, Tel Aviv–Jaffa Municipality Archives (Tel Aviv, Israel), 4-3218a.

90. Letter of the Zionist Executive to Mayor Dizengoff, 29 January 1930, Tel Aviv–Jaffa Municipality Archives (Tel Aviv, Israel), 4-3218a.

91. Letters of Mayor Dizengoff to the Jewish National Fund headquarters in Jerusalem and to the Zionist Executive in Jerusalem, 3 February 1930, Tel Aviv–Jaffa Municipality Archives (Tel Aviv, Israel), 4-3218a.

92. Letters of Mayor Dizengoff to Chief Rabbi Kook and to the Chief Rabbinate of Tel Aviv–Jaffa, 3 February 1930, Tel Aviv–Jaffa Municipality Archives (Tel Aviv, Israel), 4-3218a.

93. In 1922 there was a dispute over a statue in front of Hotel Ben Nahum. Although the rabbinate urged the Town Committee to intervene, the Town Committee stated that it would not, precisely because it was private. The Town Committee had this same response to a variety of issues. See Mann, *A Place in History*, 110–11.

94. This hope that the Queen Esther competition would be renewed in future years is expressed in A. Z. Ben-Yishai's, "Purim 1930 bifnei va-adat ha-chakira," in *Program Booklet for Agadati's Traditional Masquerade Balls*, Purim 1930, 12.

95. As mentioned in the Introduction, the Purim queen phenomenon spread around the world and lasted longer in the Diaspora than it did in Palestine. Purim queens were selected in the United States, Canada, and Europe for several years. In 1929 the Yishuv invited Purim queens from other locations to join them in their Purim festivities. *Ha'aretz* reported on the upcoming visit of Queen Esther of America to Palestine after Purim (*Ha'aretz*, 8 May 1929, 4). The *Palestine Bulletin* announced the Jewish beauty contest in New York (*Palestine Bulletin*, 6 February 1929, 1). In 1931, when the Purim queen competition had been canceled in the Yishuv, a queen was chosen in Australia (*Ha'aretz*, 5 March 1931, 1; and *Do'ar ha-Yom*, 8 March 1931, 4). This phenomenon—that a custom gained popularity and credence in the Diaspora when it was banned in the Yishuv—raises important issues about Eretz Israeli-Diaspora relations that are beyond the scope of this chapter.

96. A. Z. Rabinovitz, known as Azar, was born in Belorussia and settled in Palestine in 1906. He was an important and prolific Hebrew writer of stories, articles, and pamphlets and was also a popular figure in the Yishuv. He was "inclined" to religious observance. See the *Jewish Encyclopedia* entry on him as well as Kressel, *Leksikon*, v. 2, 814–15; and Y. Shavit et al., *Leksikon*, 453. A gala in honor of Rabinovitz's 75th birthday was held in 1929 (*Davar*, 5 February 1929, 1). Rabinovitz was popular among the workers for supporting their cause (*Palestine Bulletin*, 4 February 1929).

97. *Davar*, 5 March 1929, 3

98. *Ha'aretz*, 1 April 1929, 3.

99. The rabbis further warned Ussishkin that the continuation of JNF support could distance a great part of the public, both in Palestine and in the Diaspora, from supporting the JNF. Letter of Chief Rabbinate of Jaffa and Tel Aviv District to Menahem Ussishkin, 16 January 1929, Central Zionist Archives (Jerusalem, Israel), KKL5 2904. The rabbis also sent a letter in protest of beauty competitions to the Tel Aviv Municipality, 28 January 1930, Tel Aviv–Jaffa Municipality Archives (Tel Aviv, Israel), 4-3218a.

100. *Ha'aretz*, 6 March 1928, 1.

101. It is unclear whether the rabbis presented with this question were Yemenite or Ashkenazic.

102. Tsabari wore a black ribbon underneath her crown as a sign of mourning. Tsipora Tsabari, interview by Nili Aryeh-Sapir.

103. The Queen Esther competition that was to take place in 1930 but was canceled was going to occur for the first time at Mugrabi Hall, the site of the National Dance Competition discussed in Chapter 3. Advertisements for the competition appeared in *Ha'aretz*, 24 January 1930, 4; *Do'ar ha-Yom*, 24 January 1930, 4; and *Davar*, 26 January 1930, 4.

104. Letter of Rabbi Kook to Mayor Dizengoff, 27 January 1930, Tel Aviv–Jaffa Municipality Archives (Tel Aviv, Israel), 4-3218a. See also Carmiel, *Tel Aviv*, 141.

105. *Davar* published a brief statement about the sermon delivered in a Mea Shearim synagogue against the "custom" of selecting a Queen Esther. *Davar*, 29 January 1930, 4.

106. This announcement, from January 1930, is in the collection of the National and University Library (Jerusalem, Israel). Reprinted in Carmiel, *Tel Aviv*, 142.

107. Avigdor Hameiri was a prolific Hebrew writer, translator, and journalist. He came to Palestine in 1921 and worked for different newspapers, including *Ha'aretz* and *Do'ar ha-Yom*. He was close to the Revisionist movement only until the beginning of the 1930s. He was also a pioneer of the satiric theater and founded the company Hakumkum. See Kressel, *Leksikon*, v. 2, 310–12.

108. Y. Shavit and Sitton, *Staging and Stagers*, 94.

109. Avigdor Hameiri, "Shilton ha-Ziknah," in *Pamphlet of Agadati's Traditional Masquerade Balls*, Purim 1929, 16.

110. Carmiel, *Tel Aviv*, 145.

111. *Ketuvim*, 14 March 1930, 6. An article with similar themes was printed in the *Program Booklet for Agadati's Traditional Masquerade Balls*, Purim 1930, 4–5.

112. Rabbi Tarfon, one of the rabbis in the academy at Yavneh who lived from about 50 to 130 C.E., appears in the Passover Haggadah, so his name would have been familiar to many of the readers. He was with Rabbi Akiba in Bnei Brak and spoke about the Exodus from Egypt on that night. For a more complete description of his life and teachings, see Neusner, *History and Torah*, 76–102.

113. *Ha'aretz*, 14 March 1930, 2. The poem was also printed in the *Program Booklet for Agadati's Traditional Masquerade Balls*, Purim 1930, 15.

114. *Davar*, 5 February 1930, 4; *Do'ar ha-Yom*, 5 February 1930, 4.

115. *Ha'aretz*, 16 March 1930, 4.

116. Manifesto written by Baruch Agadati, Purim 1930. Reprinted in Carmiel, *Tel Aviv*, 146–47.

117. A competition at this gala, sponsored by Aga Film, was held to select people who represented "the natural laugh and happy face." This contest was continued at the carnival ball during Purim. At the pre-Purim gala, 118 people participated in the competition, of which 10 men and 4 women were left for the final competition. *Ha'aretz*, 26 January 1931, 4; *Ha'aretz*, 25 February 1931, 4; gala poster, 1 January 1931, Jewish National and University Library (Jerusalem, Israel), V1969/6.

118. According to Batia Carmiel, Rachel Blumenfeld, the queen in 1931, was chosen in a hurry by Agadati because the ball had been canceled for that year. Carmiel, *Tel Aviv*, 151.

119. The appearance of the queen at the carnival ball was hinted at in an announcement printed in *Ha'aretz* for the carnival ball during Purim. The announcement said: "At this gala will be the welcoming reception for 'Queen Esther.' (The details will come.)" *Ha'aretz*, 24 February 1931, 4.

120. *Ha'aretz*, 3 March 1931, 1; *Ha'aretz*, 5 March 1931, 1; and Jewish National and University Library, V1969/6.

121. Manifesto written by Baruch Agadati, Purim 1931. Reprinted in Carmiel, *Tel Aviv*, 150.

122. Avi-Shulamit, "Yemei ha-purim b'eretz yisrael," 36.

123. After the Esther competition was canceled, the religious community next initiated an attack on the many evening galas during Purim. Posters in Tel Aviv called for the cancellation of the galas. *Ha'aretz* reported: "An announcement against the dance and masquerade balls (signed by Rabinovitz and company)" (26 January 1931, 4). Despite this opposition, approximately 4,000 people attended Agadati's masquerade gala that year. *Ha'aretz*, 6 March 1931, 1.

Chapter 2

1. A swimming pool had not yet been built in Haifa. It was built for the second Maccabiah Games in 1935.

2. Different accounts report a varying number of delegations at the first Maccabiah Games. For instance, the *Palestine Bulletin* reported twenty-five groups, and the report in Reuters, printed in the *Palestine Bulletin*, referred to thirty delegations. The "twenty-seven delegations" number stems from the accounts in both *Ha'aretz* and *Davar* as well as *Do'ar ha-Yom*. *Do'ar ha-Yom* reported twenty-eight delegations but actually listed twenty-seven. See *Davar*, 28 March 1932, 1; *Do'ar ha-Yom*, 29 March 1932, 3; *Ha'aretz*, 29 March 1932, 1; *Palestine Bulletin*, 20 March 1932, 2; and *Palestine Bulletin*, 18 March 1932, 4.

3. Mosse, *Confronting the Nation*; Mosse, *Nationalization*. See also Hoberman, *Sport*.

4. The Levant Fair (*yerid ha-mizrah*) emerged in the 1920s and grew in the early 1930s. By 1934 permanent buildings were built for the fair in the International Style, showing off this modernist aesthetic. See Kunda and Oxman, "Flight of the Camel," 54.

5. *Ma'ariv*, 20 August 1965. Yekutieli was inspired by the summer Olympic Games held in Stockholm, Sweden, in 1912.

6. Memorandum of the First Maccabiah Games, 1 May 1931, Joseph Yekutieli Maccabi Archive (Ramat Gan, Israel), 2-1-18.

7. These articles discussed different aspects of the ancient games, such as the connection to religion, the prizes, the mythology, the rules of the games, and ancient Greece's stadium. *Palestine Bulletin*, 16–27 March 1932.

8. *Davar*, 28 March 1932; *Ha'aretz*, 28 March 1932, 1.

9. For the second Maccabiah Games, Yekutieli suggested a Maccabiah torch brought from Modi'in, the birthplace of the historical Maccabees, to the opening ceremony. This idea was rejected, however. Eisen, "The Maccabiah Games," 231.

10. Zerubavel, *Recovered Roots*.

11. *Do'ar ha-Yom*, 29 March 1932. Translation from Wein, *The Maccabiah Games*, 45.

12. *Davar*, 7 February 1932, 4; *Do'ar ha-Yom*, 3 February 1932, 3; *Do'ar ha-Yom*, 4 February 1932, 3; *Do'ar ha-Yom*, 25 February 1932, 3.

13. Wein, *The Maccabiah Games*, 16; and document by Yehoshua Alouf, Wingate Institute (Netanya, Israel), 4.01/24.

14. *Do'ar ha-Yom*, 3 February 1932, 2.

15. In the same article, Silman wrote about the selection of the name Adloyada for Purim. *Ha'aretz*, 3 February 1932.

16. *Ha'aretz*, 3 February 1932, 3. Translation from Wein, *The Maccabiah Games*, 42.

17. Memorandum of the First Maccabiah Games, 1 May 1931, Joseph Yekutieli Maccabi Archive (Ramat Gan, Israel), 2-1-18.

18. *Do'ar ha-Yom*, 28 February 1932, 2.

19. A schedule of different trips throughout the country was printed in *Do'ar ha-Yom*, 3 April 1932, 1.

20. *Palestine Bulletin*, 31 March 1932, 3.

21. *Do'ar ha-Yom*, 15 February 1932.

22. Chaim Wein immigrated to Palestine in 1921 and served in a variety of leadership roles during the Yishuv era as well as after statehood. He was a physical education teacher and one of the founders of the Eretz Israeli Sports Federation. From 1944 to 1960, he served as director of the Physical Education Teachers College. He was also leader of the organizing committees for the Maccabiah Games held in 1973 and 1977. See Wein, *The Maccabiah Games*; and Y. Shavit et al., *Leksikon, 186*.

23. Because only a small number of hotel rooms were available, the residents of Tel Aviv were asked to host guests in their homes by offering one of the following three options: full accommodation (lodging and food); bed and breakfast only; or bed only. Hosts also took their guests to the different events. In addition, immigrant organizations were asked to arrange accommodations for visitors from their country of origin. Schools and public halls were used to host Maccabi groups from the Galilee and other parts of Palestine. Wein, *The Maccabiah Games*, 26.

24. Interestingly, Lilian Milwitzki Koplewitz was among those who attended the Maccabiah Games and remained in the country. She was the winner of a contest for the prettiest Jewess in Berlin, and her prize consisted of a trip to the Maccabiah Games. Joseph Yekutieli Maccabi Archive (Ramat Gan, Israel), A101-45.1.

25. The second Maccabiah Games in 1935 was considered the Aliyah Maccabiah, but many participants remained in the country after the first Maccabiah Games as well. For instance, a large portion of the Bulgarian contingent stayed in the country after the first Maccabiah Games, but the entire delegation remained after the second Maccabiah Games. Wein, *The Maccabiah Games*, 68.

26. *Davar*, 1 December 1931.

27. *Do'ar ha-Yom*, 3 December 1931, 2.

28. *Ha'aretz*, 29 March 1932, 1.

29. *Davar*, 28 March 1932, 1; *Do'ar ha-Yom*, 29 March 1932, 3.

30. *Palestine Bulletin*, 29 March 1932, 1.

31. *Ha'aretz*, 29 March 1932, 1.

32. A. Z. Ben-Yishai, in *Moreh Derech: The Second Maccabiah*, 8–9. Joseph Yekutieli Maccabi Archive (Ramat Gan, Israel).

33. The Yishuv had been looking for contributions for the building of the stadium for months. The Maccabi administration representative Dr. Alexander Rosenfeld had collected about $2,000 in New York. Mayor Dizengoff gave 100 lira of his own private funds. The Bank

Ophek, Keren Hayesod, and the Jewish National Fund also gave money. Untitled and undated article, Wingate Institute (Netanya, Israel).

34. Untitled, undated article, Wingate Institute (Netanya, Israel).

35. *Sefer hamaccabiah*, 53. Translation from Wein, *The Maccabiah Games*, 28.

36. *Palestine Bulletin*, 28 March 1932.

37. *Davar*, 1 April 1932, 5. For a discussion of how the hora was considered the emerging national dance already by the 1930s, see Spiegel, "Sporting a Nation."

38. *Palestine Bulletin*, 29 March 1932, 1.

39. Joseph Yekutieli Maccabi Archive (Ramat Gan, Israel); Eliasaf Robinson Collection, Department of Special Collections and University Archives, Stanford University Libraries, M1522.

40. *Do'ar ha-Yom*, 29 November 1931, 3.

41. Because of Mayor Dizengoff's ride, these games are often referred to as the White Horse Maccabiah.

42. These included Dr. Hermann Lelewer, the president of the Maccabi World Union; H. Kaminski, head of Maccabi in Berlin; Dr. Rozenfeld; and Dr. Bloch.

43. *Ha'aretz*, 30 March 1932, 1; *New York Times*, 30 March 1932, 22.

44. Maccabi delegations marched in alphabetical order according to the Hebrew alphabet. *Davar* and *Do'ar ha-Yom* provided a full list of the twenty-seven national delegations participating in the first Maccabiah Games, but according to press reports following the parade, it does not appear that every delegation marched in the opening parade. These reports list the following delegations as participating in the Games: Austria, Australia, England, Estonia, the United States, Bulgaria, Belgium, Germany, Denmark, Danzig, Holland, Hungary, Tunisia, Yugoslavia, Greece, Egypt, Lebanon, Latvia, Lithuania, Syria, Poland, Czechoslovakia, France, Canada, Rumania, Switzerland, and Palestine. See *Davar*, 28 March 1932, 1; *Do'ar ha-Yom*, 29 March 1932, 3; *Davar*, 30 March 1932; and *Do'ar ha-Yom*, 30 March 1932, 1.

45. *Do'ar ha-Yom*, 30 March 1932.

46. *New York Times*, 30 March 1932, 22. To view original film footage of the parade and opening of the first Maccabiah Games, see Agadati, *The First Maccabiah*; Gross, *Agadah b'holot*; and Shalit, "Film Clips of the First Maccabiah Games."

47. *Davar*, 29 March 1932, 1.

48. *Davar*, 30 March 1932.

49. *New York Times*, 30 March 1932, 22.

50. *Ha'aretz*, 30 March 1932, 1; *Do'ar ha-Yom*, 30 March 1932.

51. Rabbi Uziel arrived late. See *Davar*, 30 March 1932.

52. *Ha'aretz*, 30 March 1932, 4; *Davar*, 30 March 1932; *Davar*, 1 April 1932. The lyrics to "Hatikvah" were written by Hebrew poet Naftali Herz Imber around 1878 and sung to the tune of a Romanian folk song. The song was popular with different Jewish organizations and between the first and second Zionist Congresses, Herzl and Nordau had a contest to select

an anthem. Imber had lived in Palestine for a short period of time, and his song was selected. See Berkowitz, *Zionist Culture*, 21–23.

53. *Palestine Bulletin*, 30 March 1932, 2; Lionel Shalit, "Film Clips of the First Maccabiah Games," Joseph Yekutieli Maccabi Archive (Ramat Gan, Israel), 228, video 29.

54. *Davar*, 31 March 1932; *New York Times*, 2 April 1932, 21.

55. *Palestine Bulletin*, 7 April 1932, 1.

56. For a further discussion of the development of Jewish sports groups in Europe, see, for instance, Eisen, "Zionism"; Kugelmass, *Jews, Sports;* P. Y. Mayer, "Equality—Egality"; and Schoeps, "Modern Heirs."

57. These issues were especially prevalent surrounding the Olympic Games in Berlin in 1936. See, for instance, Large, *Nazi Games*; Guttmann, "Berlin 1936"; and A. Krüger and Murray, *Nazi Olympics*.

58. Michael Brenner, "Introduction," in M. Brenner and Reuveni, *Emancipation Through Muscles*, 2.

59. See, for instance, Norwood, "American Jewish Muscle"; Reiss, "Tough Jews"; and Taylor, "Round the London Ring."

60. See, for instance, Borut, "Jews in German Sports"; Gillerman, "Strongman"; and Jacobs, "Politics." For some visual images, see *Yahadut ha-sheririm.*

61. Bunzl, "Hakoah Vienna."

62. Pamphlet of the Maccabi Movement, London, undated, Central Zionist Archives (Jerusalem, Israel), 22714. This pamphlet was clearly from between 1932 and 1935 because it was published after the first Maccabiah Games but before the second games.

63. For additional material on the development of sports in the Yishuv, see Alouf, "Beginning of Physical Education"; Sherman, "Physical Education"; Simri and Benayahu, *Ha-hinuh ha-gufani ve ha-sport*; and Simri, *Ha-hinuh ha-gufani ve ha-sport.*

64. *Palestine Bulletin*, 31 December 1931.

65. Memorandum of the First Maccabiah Games, 1 May 1931, Joseph Yekutieli Maccabi Archive (Ramat Gan, Israel), 2-1-18.

66. The Constantinople organization was founded in response to the local German sports association (the house of Tavtonia), which decided not to accept Jewish exercisers in its ranks. *Meah B'tnuah*, 5.

67. The Maccabi clubs took their name from Judas Maccabeus. Some of the early clubs had other names that incorporated Jewish symbolism, such as Hakoah, Hagibor, and Bar Kokba.

68. The Maccabi World Union was spearheaded by the Berlin Maccabi club when the German-Jewish sports association Juedische Turnerschaft was reorganized under this name.

69. M. Brenner and Reuveni, *Emancipation Through Muscles.*

70. Memorandum of the First Maccabiah Games, 1 May 1931, Joseph Yekutieli Maccabi Archive (Ramat Gan, Israel), 2-1-18.

71. For a more detailed description of the politicization of sports in the Yishuv and later in the State of Israel, see Kaufman, "Jewish Sports."

72. In *Ha'aretz* for 29 March 1932, the opening day of the first Maccabiah Games, there was a reprint of an article of Nordau's that was written in 1900, in which he calls for the cultivation of a "Jewry of muscles." This article also appeared in several booklets and pamphlets published for the Maccabiah Games or in its aftermath. Also, on the same page of *Ha'aretz* as the Nordau article, there was an article by A. Rozenfeld titled "Ba-yom ha-hagshama" (On the Day of the Realization), which is about the realization of a Jewry of muscles. *Ha'aretz*, 29 March 1932, 2.

73. *Palestine Bulletin*, 5 April 1932, 2.

74. *Palestine Bulletin*, 3 April 1932, 3.

75. *Do'ar ha-Yom*, 3 December 1931, 2.

76. *Haitztadion*, October 1931, Wingate Institute (Netanya, Israel), 4.01/30.

77. Avigdor Hameiri, "Himnon Hamaccabim," in *First Maccabiah Song Book*, Wingate Institute (Netanya, Israel), 4.01/29.

78. *Palestine Bulletin*, 31 March 1932, 3. Excerpts from this address were also printed in *Do'ar ha-Yom*, 29 March 1932, 3; and *Ha'aretz*, 30 March 1932, 2. The welcoming reception took place at the cultural center, Beit Ha'am, in Tel Aviv.

79. During the Maccabiah Games, a physical culture exhibit that focused on physical hygiene was presented at the Hadassah Health Center in Jerusalem. The exhibit showed different types of gymnastics and sports exercises and their effects on the body. *Palestine Bulletin*, 7 April 1932, 3.

80. *Do'ar ha-Yom*, 24 February 1932, 2.

81. Reuveni, "Sports and Militarization," 56 and also 45.

82. Memorandum of the First Maccabiah Games, 1 May 1931, Joseph Yekutieli Maccabi Archive (Ramat Gan, Israel), 2-1-18.

83. *Do'ar ha-Yom*, 24 February 1932, 2.

84. *Do'ar ha-Yom*, 20 November 1931, 3.

85. For further discussion of Rabbi Benjamin, see Segev, *One Palestine*, 408, 410.

86. *Hazit ha-Am*, 15 January 1932.

87. *Hazit ha-Am*, 15 January 1932.

88. Printed announcement from the secretariat of the Maccabiah Games to the Yishuv, Wingate Institute (Netanya, Israel), 4.01/29; Joseph Yekutieli Maccabi Archive (Ramat Gan, Israel), 2-1-23.

89. *Do'ar ha-Yom*, 16 November 1931, 3. Translation by author and in Wein, *The Maccabiah Games*, 62.

90. Yosef Yekutieli, "Echoes After the First Maccabiah," undated, Joseph Yekutieli Maccabi Archive (Ramat Gan, Israel), 2-1-18.

91. Eisen, "The Maccabiah Games," 161; Wein, *The Maccabiah Games*, 16–17.

92. *Palestine Bulletin*, 3 April 1932, 3.

93. *Palestine Bulletin*, 1 April 1932, 1.

94. *Do'ar ha-Yom*, 3 April 1932, 2.

95. Kaufman, "Hapoel," 8. See also Kaufman, "Yesoda"; and Yahav, "'Hapoel'-'Maccabi.'"

96. See Helman, "Zionism"; and Kaufman, "Jewish Sports."

97. *Ha'aretz*, 28 February 1932; *Davar*, 28 February 1932. Some of these demands were, according to Hapoel, agreed on at a meeting in Berlin in July 1931.

98. *Ha'aretz*, 28 February 1932; *Davar*, 28 February 1932.

99. *Davar*, 8 March 1932.

100. *Do'ar ha-Yom*, 20 November 1931, 3.

101. *Do'ar ha-Yom*, 20 November 1931, 3.

102. *Do'ar ha-Yom*, 20 November 1931, 3.

103. *Do'ar ha-Yom*, 3 February 1932, 2.

104. *Do'ar ha-Yom*, 28 February 1932, 2. Translation by author and in Wein, *The Maccabiah Games*, 17–18.

105. *Ha'aretz*, 1 April 1932, 4. Rabbi Uziel also blessed the Maccabiah Games in the *Sefer hamaccabiah*, which was published in conjunction with the second Maccabiah Games in 1935. In that book Uziel discussed the need to celebrate the Sabbath, to understand that the participants were on holy ground, and that they were coming to Palestine with the flag and name of Mattityahu the Maccabi. Rabbi Meir Hai Uziel, "Hamaccabiah b'eretz hakodesh," in *Sefer hamaccabiah*, 27.

106. Helman, "Sport on the Sabbath," 47–48, 50–54.

107. *Ha'aretz*, 11 January 1932, 4. Translation from Wein, *The Maccabiah Games*, 41.

108. *Do'ar ha-Yom*, 10 February 1932, 3. Translation from Wein, *The Maccabiah Games*, 42; and *Ha'aretz*, 26 February 1932, 6.

109. *Sefer hamaccabiah*, 46. Translation from Wein, *The Maccabiah Games*, 59.

110. Helman, "Zionism," 101.

111. Letter from Arthur Wauchope to Dr. Chaim Arlosoroff, 25 January 1932, Joseph Yekutieli Maccabi Archive (Ramat Gan, Israel), 2-1-9 and 2-1-22.

112. Collins, "Jews, Antisemitism, and Sports," 142.

113. Helman, "Zionism," 97–98; Helman, "Sport on the Sabbath," 48.

114. As Anat Helman describes, these exchanges were not always positive. Helman, "Zionism," 97–98.

115. Helman, "Sport on the Sabbath," 49–50.

116. *Ha'aretz*, 1 April 1932, 2; *Ha'aretz*, 21 March 1932, 2; *Ha'aretz*, 30 March 1932, 2; *Do'ar ha-Yom*, 4 April 1932; *Davar*, 1 April 1932, 5. See also *Report*, National Archives (Washington, DC), 13 April 1932, 867, no. 9111/76, in the Joseph Yekutieli Maccabi Archive (Ramat Gan, Israel), 2-1-22.

117. *Do'ar ha-Yom*, 4 April 1932; *Davar*, 1 April 1932, 5.

118. *Ha'aretz*, 21 March 1932, 2.

119. *Davar*, 1 December 1931.

120. *Davar*, 9 December 1931.

121. *Davar*, 9 December 1931.

122. *Do'ar ha-Yom*, 3 December 1931, 2.

123. *Do'ar ha-Yom*, 3 December 1931, 2.

124. *Davar*, 15 December 1931.

Chapter 3

1. Inaugurated in February 1930, Mugrabi Hall was Tel Aviv's primary cultural center. It was a multipurpose theater where High Holiday services had been held the previous month, and it was the first building to house a cinema and a theater in one complex.

2. *Ha-Boker*, 5 November 1937.

3. Theoretical material for this chapter and Chapter 4 is drawn from works such as Franco, *Dancing Modernism*; Kealiinohomoku, "An Anthropologist Looks at Ballet"; Shay, *Choreographic Politics*; and Spencer, *Society and the Dance*. Dance history concepts and comparisons with other societies are also drawn from studies such as Conner, *Spreading the Gospel*; Daly, *Done into Dance*; Daniel, *Dance and Social Change*; Graff, *Stepping Left*; Kraut, *Choreographing the Folk*; Manning, *Ecstasy and the Demon*; Ross, *Moving Lessons*; and Savigliano, *Tango*.

4. *Ohel* means "tent" and "implies the opposite of the luxurious European theaters." Hirshberg, *Music*, 60.

5. Eshel, *Lirkod im ha-halom*, 11–19. See also Eshel, "Concert Dance in Israel."

6. *Do'ar ha-Yom*, 11 November 1926.

7. *Do'ar ha-Yom*, 11 November 1926.

8. *Do'ar ha-Yom*, 11 November 1926.

9. Ornstein, "Development."

10. For a discussion of Jewish cultural developments in Weimar Germany, see Brenner, *Renaissance of Jewish Culture*.

11. Initially begun in France and Italy, the center of ballet moved to Russia in the late nineteenth century and gained international prominence in the early twentieth century through the efforts of Serge Diaghilev and his company, the Ballet Russes.

12. For an additional discussion on *Ausdruckstanz*, see S. J. Cohen, "Modern Dance and Ausdruckstanz"; and Toepfer, *Empire of Ecstasy*.

13. The song competition was announced in the *Palestine Post Weekend Supplement* and in *Ha'aretz*. It was held by the Mailamm Jewish Musical Association of New York. Manuscripts of songs were to be sent to Hebrew University, Jerusalem. *Palestine Post*, 22 October 1937; *Ha'aretz*, October 1937.

14. The Eretz Israeli Song Competition, held on November 23, 1937, was hosted by the Armon Theatrical Agency and had the same structure as the National Dance Competition, including the awarding of three prizes.

15. In July 1935 the first International Folk Dance Festival and Conference was held in London. This was the first gathering of its kind, and it included live performances as well as discussions, which were documented in the *Journal of the English Folk Dance and Song Society*. This conference, which included dancers from several European countries, grappled with issues of dance and national culture. Similarly, Germany held two Dancers' Congresses in May 1927 and June 1928, respectively, to examine the place of German dance in the theater. The third Dancers' Congress, held in Munich in 1930, was the first International Modern Dance Congress. In addition, at the Olympic Games held in Berlin in 1936, there was both an International Dance Competition and a German Dance Festival. It is also interesting to note that the Academy Awards began in the United States in 1928. See Partsch-Bergsohn, *Modern Dance*, 40–45, 59–63; Koegler, "In the Shadow"; and *Journal of the English Folk Dance and Song Society* v. 2 (1935).

16. For additional information on Gertrud Kraus, see G. Manor, *Haye ha-mahol*; and Ingber, "The Gamin Speaks." For a further discussion of expressionist dancers in the Yishuv in this era, see Friedhaber, "Pioneers of Expressionism." For additional relevant visual images of several of the dancers, see Aldor, *Ve-eich roked gamal*; Ingber, *Seeing Israeli and Jewish Dance*; Himmelreich and Silver-Brody, *Alfons Himelraikh*; Oren and Raz, *Zoltan Kluger*; and Silver-Brody, *Mood and Movement*.

17. Berlin writer and lawyer Sammy Gronemann first visited Palestine in 1929 and immigrated in 1936. His impressions of the country are described in Schlör, *Tel Aviv*, 98–99.

18. The names of all the members of the supervising committee are as follows: the chair and playwright Sammy Gronemann (lawyer); the poet Leah Goldberg (*Davar*); M. Gais (*Yiddish Rondsho*); the journalist J. Wolman (for a newspaper from outside Palestine); Dr. Saul Tchernichovsky (poet); Sh. Samt (*Ha'aretz*); the journalist Uri Kesari (*Teshah ba'Erev*); Batya Krofnik (visitor); S. Shapira (*Haboker*); and Dr. Rosenfeld (*Ha-Brit Ha'Ivrit Ha'Olamut*). This information is taken from the program cover for the competition. It is unclear how this particular group of people were chosen to be on the supervising committee and how the committee functioned in the competition.

19. There were about 150,000 residents in Tel Aviv in 1937.

20. According to the program of the competition, the first-prize winner received a shield. In a personal interview, though, as well as in her book, Yardena Cohen claimed that she won a sculpture, which she left on the bus with the Egged driver because it was too heavy for her to carry home. According to an article in *Ha'aretz*, the Municipality intended to have the shield rotate among the first-prize winners for three years, indicating that they assumed there would be subsequent annual dance competitions. It remains unclear why there were no further contests in the years to follow. See *Ha'aretz*, 19 October 1937.

21. *Ha-Boker*, 21 October 1937. The *Palestine Post* also lists the votes, with a slight discrepancy from *Ha-Boker*. They list Cohen receiving 178 votes, Nikova 171 votes, and the Ornstein Sisters 151 votes. See *Palestine Post*, 25 October 1937.

22. Yardena Cohen was the sixth generation to live in the country on her father's side; her mother was born in Russia and immigrated with the immigration wave known as the second aliyah.

23. Nikova worked with the Palestine Opera from 1925 to 1928.

24. The audience was described as being so enthusiastic about the dancing that they "went so far as to demand dances in operas which did not call for them." Blumenfeld, "Dance Pioneering," 17, 56–57.

25. Eshel, *Lirkod im ha-halom*, 15.

26. In the program of the National Dance Competition, the *Mirror* piece was titled *In Front of the Mirror*. I refer to it as *The Mirror* because it came to be known by that name. The title of the piece *Shevet Achim Gam Yachad* stems from Psalm 133:1. For an important and detailed discussion of the Ornstein Sisters and their works, see Aldor, *Ve-eich roked gamal*.

27. Eshel, *Lirkod im ha-halom*, 15. Elsa Dublon was also active in the folk dance movement and stated that she created the well-known folk dance *Mayim, Mayim*, discussed in Chapter 4. The origins of *Mayim, Mayim* have been debated. For a detailed discussion on the matter, see Ingber, "Shorashim," in her *Seeing Israeli and Jewish Dance*, 166n19.

28. See, for instance, D. Manor, "Orientalism"; and Peleg, *Orientalism*.

29. In the 1940s Cohen brought her ideas about biblical dances to the kibbutzim, where she choreographed and organized holiday pageants. See Ingber, "The Priestesses"; and Ingber, "Shorashim."

30. Eshel, *Lirkod im ha-halom*, 18.

31. *Haboker*, 15 October 1937.

32. For an important discussion of the use of the imagined Orient in Hebrew literature, see Peleg, *Orientalism*.

33. Kalmar and Penslar, "Introduction," xix.

34. Yardena Cohen, interview by author, Haifa, Israel, 2 August 1998.

35. Y. Cohen, *Hatof vehayam*, 46.

36. Yardena Cohen, personal statement, Dance Library of Israel (Tel Aviv, Israel). To view a photograph of Yardena Cohen with Ovadia Mizrahi in the 1950s, see Spiegel, "Cultural Production in Tel Aviv," 75.

37. Y. Cohen, *Hatof vehayam*, 53.

38. With the large immigration from Germany came a growth of the local piano market in Palestine. In the 1930s especially, owning a piano became a "status symbol and a culture symbol." Hirshberg, *Music*, 113–17.

39. Throughout her life, Cohen worked with Arabs, seeking to bring peace through dance,

teaching Muslim, Christian, Druse, and Jewish students together in her studio. See Ingber, "The Priestesses," 457.

40. Yardena Cohen, interview by author, Haifa, Israel, 2 August 1998. In my translations from the original Hebrew, I define the term *mizrah* as either "East" or "Orient" interchangeably.

41. Jehoash Hirshberg describes Cohen's conflicted relationship with her musicians. See Hirshberg, *Music*, 201.

42. Y. Cohen, *Hatof vehayam*, 51.

43. Y. Cohen, *Hatof vehayam*, 53.

44. For an analysis of the connection between Wigman's work and German nationalism, see Manning, *Ecstasy and the Demon*. For a documentary with excerpts from Wigman's choreography, see Snyder and Macdonald, *Mary Wigman*.

45. See also Spiegel, "Cultural Formulation." I wish to thank Janice Ross for her discussions with me on this section.

46. In her book Cohen describes the process of acquiring her costumes for the competition. The dresses she wore were from an Arab woman. Y. Cohen, *Hatof vehayam*, 51–52.

47. Erdman, "Dance Discourses," 288.

48. Erdman, "Dance Discourses," 288.

49. Erdman, "Dance Discourses," 288.

50. Program of the Competition, Dance Library of Israel (Tel Aviv, Israel).

51. Yardena Cohen, interview by author, Haifa, Israel, 2 August 1998.

52. Isadora Duncan was evidently a well-known figure in the life of the Yishuv because her autobiography was translated into Hebrew by Abraham Shlonsky in 1929. In addition, segments of Duncan's autobiography were published in the literary weekly *Ketuvim*, beginning in November 1928.

53. For further information on Isadora Duncan, see her autobiography, *My Life*; Ann Daly's study, *Done into Dance*; and Vertinsky, "Isadora Goes to Europe."

54. *The Day* (New York), 30 September 1928.

55. *Palestine Bulletin*, 15 March 1928.

56. Blumenfeld, "Dance Pioneering," 57.

57. For a further discussion of Nikova's Yemenite Company, see Elron, "Lirkod ivrit."

58. Interestingly, Nikova's ethnographic work in Palestine took place at the same time as Katherine Dunham was studying Haiti in search of the first true African dance.

59. Kalmar and Penslar, "Introduction"; D. Manor, "Orientalism."

60. *Ha-Boker*, 15 October 1937.

61. *Ha-Boker*, 15 October 1937.

62. Rina Nikova, "Introductory Remarks" in Performance Bill of the Vaudeville Theater, England, 12 September 1938, Dance Library of Israel (Tel Aviv, Israel).

63. *Ha-Boker*, 11 November 1937.

64. I viewed a version of this dance on video, *The Art of Natan Axelrod, 1937*, Israeli Film

Archive at the Dance Library of Israel (Tel Aviv, Israel). A copy of this video is also housed at the Steven Spielberg Jewish Film Archive, Axelrod no. 14, Carmel newsreel 109, VTAX14. For further information on Axelrod's newsreels, see Luterman and Tryster, *Israel Newsreel Collection*.

65. Program bills of Rina Nikova's performances, Dance Library of Israel (Tel Aviv, Israel).

66. This song was later given Hebrew words. Eshel, *Lirkod im ha-halom*, 18.

67. Eshel, *Lirkod im ha-halom*, 18. This dance, titled *B'nei Hanevi'im*, could be translated as "Children of the Prophets." I have selected the translation "The Prophet's Sons" because that was what Rina Nikova called the piece in English on subsequent performance programs.

68. For instance, see the photograph in Eshel, *Lirkod im ha-halom*, 19.

69. Although other events or shows had programs featuring Hebrew and English, because this was the period of the British Mandate, this competition had only a Hebrew program, which indicates that it was intended for an exclusively Hebrew audience.

70. This critic signs his articles Sh. Shriah. It appears that his full name was Shriah Shapiro. He wrote arts criticism in the *Palestine Bulletin* and the Hebrew press. He became a close friend of Yardena Cohen. I refer to him in my text by his printed name, Shriah.

71. *Ha-Boker*, 15 October 1937.

72. *Ha-Boker*, 15 October 1937.

73. *Ha-Boker*, 15 October 1937.

74. *Omer*, 29 October 1937.

75. *Omer*, 29 October 1937.

76. *Palestine Post*, 19 November 1937.

77. *Ha-Boker*, 5 November 1937.

78. *Tesha ba-Erev*, 11 November 1937, 13. In this final sentence, Kesari makes use of a pun on the word *kol*, which means both "voice" and "vote." I have translated it here as "voice," but it has a double meaning.

79. *Omer*, 29 October 1937.

80. *Ha-Boker*, 15 October 1937.

81. *Ha-Boker*, 15 October 1937.

82. *Ha-Boker*, 15 October 1937.

83. *Palestine Post*, 19 November 1937.

84. *Omer*, 29 October 1937.

85. *Ha-Boker*, 5 November 1937.

86. *Ha'aretz*, 27 October 1937.

87. For more information on the dancer Argentina, see Bennahum, *Antonia Mercé*.

88. *Omer*, 29 October 1937.

89. *Ha-Boker*, 5 November 1937.

90. *Tesha ba-Erev*, 11 November 1937, 13.

91. For an important discussion of the representation of Jewish Palestine at the World's Fair in New York in 1939–1940, see Kirshenblatt-Gimblett, "Performing the State."

92. The ways in which Nikova's and Cohen's dances were interpreted and reviewed in Europe are intriguing. They are beyond the scope of this chapter but should be the subject of further study.

93. *Omer*, 29 October 1937.

94. *Ha'aretz*, 27 October 1937.

95. *Ha'aretz*, 27 October 1937.

96. *Ha'aretz*, 27 October 1937.

97. *Ha'aretz*, 27 October 1937.

98. *Omer*, 29 October 1937. In 1994 Yardena Cohen, well-known for her broadly penned handwritten letters, wrote a note in which she addressed Goldberg's criticisms. In this note Cohen states that, in the years that followed, she and Leah Goldberg became friends and Goldberg became her best critic. Only back then, according to Cohen, Goldberg did not know what Cohen's background was, how many generations her family had been in Palestine, and how she had grown up under the same sun as the Arabs. In Cohen's view Goldberg came to deeply understand these matters in later years. See Yardena Cohen, handwritten note, 12 December 1994, Dance Library of Israel (Tel Aviv, Israel).

99. *Ha-Boker*, 5 November 1937.

100. *Ha'aretz*, 27 October 1937.

101. *Ha'aretz*, 27 October 1937.

102. *Ha-Boker*, 5 November 1937.

103. *Palestine Post*, 19 November 1937.

Chapter 4

1. Kibbutz Dalia was a Shomer Ha-Tzair kibbutz established in 1939.

2. The Histadrut (General Federation of Labourers in the Land of Israel) was founded in 1920, with important social and cultural functions besides being a labour union. The Cultural Division of the Histadrut was established in 1931.

3. In addition, in April 1945 Gurit Kadman organized the first leadership course for folk dance leaders and teachers at the Kibbutz Teachers' Seminar in Tel Aviv. See Hermon, "Development of Folkdance," 113–14. See also Gurit Kadman, interview by Ayalah Dan-Caspi, 11 February 1981.

4. After statehood Kadman was also prominent in the field that became known as ethnic dance. For her biography, see Friedhaber, *Gurit kadman*.

5. Kadman, *Am roked*, 8.

6. A few Arab debkas were also featured. In addition, for the second festival in 1931,

Kadman included *Hora Agadati*, which had been created in the Yishuv. See Ingber, "Vilified or Glorified? Views of the Jewish Body," 40–41.

7. Friedhaber, "First Folk Dance Festival"; Friedhaber, "Mi-ben shemen"; Ingber, "Vilified or Glorified? Views of the Jewish Body."

8. Ashkenazi, *Sipur maholot ha'am b'daliah*, 26, 73–76. See also Laban, *A Life for Dance*.

9. Ayalah Goren-Kadman, interview by author, New York, 1 August 2005.

10. Ashkenazi, *Sipur maholot ha'am b'daliah*, 74.

11. Friedhaber, "First Folk Dance Festival"; Friedhaber, "Mi-ben shemen"; Ingber, "Vilified or Glorified? Views of the Jewish Body"; and Kadman, *Am roked*. Gurit Kadman later reflected that it was fortuitous that she had declined to organize the dance component for the choir festival because during the rehearsal, the stage broke with 1,000 people standing on it. Although they held the festival regardless, they would not have been able to dance on a broken stage. See Gurit Kadman, interview by Ayalah Dan-Caspi, 11 February 1981.

12. Friedhaber, *Hava netze b'meholot*, 32. See also Ingber, "Vilified or Glorified? Views of the Jewish Body"; and Kadman, *Am roked*.

13. See Ashkenazi, *Sipur maholot ha'am b'daliah*.

14. *Mishmar*, 31 May 1944, 2.

15. Kadman, *Am roked*, 11.

16. *Palestine Post*, 17 July 1944, 3.

17. Ingber, "Shorashim," 8.

18. *Palestine Post*, 17 July 1944, 3. The superb nature of the natural amphitheater was also commented on in the press reports of the 1947 festival. See *Ha-Olam ha-Zeh*, 26 June 1947, 9; *Ha'aretz*, 27 June 1947, 9; *Davar*, 3 July 1947; and *Davar*, 27 June 1947, 4.

19. It is not clear which of the Ornstein dancers (Margalit, Shoshana, or Yehudit) attended.

20. The composers included Girosov, Paul Ben-Chaim, Nahum Nardi, and Yizhar. *Davar*, 25 July 1944. It was also noted in the press—and viewed as a shame—that the Ben Shemen students were not able to attend the festival because of illness. See, for instance, *Mishmar*, 23 July 1944.

21. Friedhaber, "First Folk Dance Festival," 29–33.

22. See Kadman, *Am roked*.

23. For further discussions of some of these dancers, see, for instance, Ingber, "Shorashim"; Friedhaber, "Development of Folk Dance"; Friedhaber, *Hava netze b'meholot*; Goren, *Sadot lavshu mahol*; G. Manor, *Haye ha-mahol*; Roginsky, "Orientalism"; and Sharett, *Kuma eha*.

24. Friedhaber, *Hava netze b'meholot*, 29 and 39. The piece called *Hallel* is not documented in the program of the festival.

25. Friedhaber, *Hava netze b'meholot*, 34.

26. Program of the Dalia Festival, 1944. For a fuller discussion of the dances on the program, see Ashkenazi, *Sipur maholot ha'am b'daliah*; Y. Cohen, *Hatof vehamahol*; Friedhaber, *Hava netze b'meholot*; Ingber, "Shorashim" and "Vilified or Glorified? Views of the Jewish Body";

and Kadman, *Am roked.* The press also noted that couples dances were popular at the festival in 1944, an aspect that is beyond the scope of this chapter but should be the topic of further study. See, for instance, *Mishmar*, 23 July 1944.

27. Newspaper accounts range from 20,000 to 30,000 people.

28. *Ha-Olam ha-Zeh*, 26 June 1947, 9.

29. *Palestine Post*, 22 June 1947, 3.

30. *Yedi'ot Aharonot*, 22 June 1947; *Ha-Boker*, 22 June 1947, 4.

31. Gurit Kadman, quoted in Ingber, "Shorashim," 9–10. To view some film footage from the 1947 Dalia Festival, see Kfir and Rubin's documentary *I Was There in Color.*

32. The Karmiel Dance Festival, the successor to the Dalia Festivals, also includes the tradition of staying up through the night. For a further discussion of the development of Dalia traditions and their relationship to Karmiel, see Spiegel, "New Israeli Rituals."

33. Gurit Kadman, interview by Ayalah Dan-Caspi, 11 February 1981.

34. *Mishmar*, 3 July 1947, 2.

35. *Davar*, 22 June 1947, 1; *Kol ha-Am*, 6 July 1947. Members of the U.N. praised the Arab participation.

36. *Mishmar*, 23 July 1944.

37. *Davar*, 27 June 1947, 4.

38. *Mishmar*, 23 July 1944.

39. Kraus's *Davka* was received with "thunderous applause." *Palestine Post*, 17 July 1944, 3.

40. *Palestine Post*, 17 July 1944, 3.

41. *Davar*, 27 June 1947, 4.

42. *Kol ha-Am*, 6 July 1947.

43. *Davar*, 27 June 1947, 4.

44. *Ha'aretz*, 27 June 1947, 9.

45. *Mishmar*, 3 July 1947, 2.

46. *Mishmar*, 4 July 1947, 5.

47. *Palestine Post*, 22 June 1947, 3.

48. *Mishmar*, 23 July 1944.

49. *Palestine Post*, 22 June 1947, 3.

50. *Ha'aretz*, 27 June 1947, 9.

51. *Palestine Post*, 22 June 1947, 3.

52. *Ha-Olam ha-Zeh*, 26 June 1947, 9.

53. *Mishmar*, 23 July 1944. Regarding the relationship between Jews and dance throughout history, see, for instance, Friedhaber, "Dance in the Jewish-Mediterranean Communities"; Friedhaber, "Bibliographic Sources"; and Ingber, *Seeing Israeli and Jewish Dance.*

54. Program of the Dalia Festival, 1947.

55. *Bulletin of the Cultural Division of the Histadrut*, August 1947, Lavon Institute (Tel Aviv, Israel).

56. *Bulletin of the Cultural Division of the Histadrut,* August 1947.

57. Both of these minor holidays (Lag b'Omer and Tu b'Av) are characterized by rejoicing, music, and dance.

58. *Bulletin of the Cultural Center of the Histadrut,* August 1947.

59. *Davar,* 1947 (no specific date), Dalia Archives (Kibbutz Dalia, Israel).

60. *Mishmar,* 29 June 1947, 2.

61. Friedhaber, *Hava netze b'meholot,* 45; Kadman, *Am roked,* 14; Sachar, *History of Israel,* 265; Segev, *One Palestine,* 475–76. For a powerful portrait of life in the Yishuv in this era, especially in the 1940s, see Oz, *Tale of Love and Darkness.*

62. Notes of committees in the *Bulletin of the Cultural Division of the Histadrut,* 1946–1947.

63. *Mishmar,* 23 July 1944.

64. *Davar,* 21 July 1944.

65. *Bulletin of the Cultural Division of the Histadrut,* August 1947.

66. *Yedi'ot Aharonot, La-Isha,* 25 June 1947.

67. For an important study of the debka in Jewish Israeli and Palestinian Arab society, see Kaschl, *Dance and Authenticity.*

68. For a discussion of the Jewish Yemenite tradition in Israeli dance, see Bahat-Ratzon, *Beregel yehefa.* For a discussion of dances considered "ethnic" in Israeli dance, see Kadman, *Rikude edot.*

69. *Mishmar,* 23 July 1944.

70. *Mishmar,* 26 July 1944.

71. Benari's opinion was disputed and, in fact, the Arab debka did become an integral part of the emerging Israeli folk dances.

72. *Bulletin of the Cultural Division of the Histadrut,* August 1947.

73. Although these conversations reflect a range of views about the suitability of Yemenite dance for the newly emerging Israeli form, its influence was present from the inception of the folk dance movement and played a strong role throughout its development.

74. Avraham Levinsohn and Chaim Freedman, directors of the cultural and educational center of the Histadrut, were against holding the festival at that time. Although they later became supporters of the festival and of the burgeoning folk dance movement, they tried to persuade Kadman to delay the event in 1944. See Friedhaber, *Hava netze b'meholot,* 37, 40. Regarding Avraham Levinsohn, see also Ingber, "Vilified or Glorified? Views of the Jewish Body." The folk dancer and folk dance choreographer Zev Chavatzelet wrote an article in 1945 addressing the issue of dancing during this period. *Mishmar,* 22 July 1945.

75. Gurit Kadman, quoted in Ingber, "Shorashim," 8.

76. Kadman, *Am roked,* 12. Zvi Friedhaber notes that this line of A. D. Gordon's was influenced by the words of poet Mordechai Warshavsky. Friedhaber, *Hava netze b'meholot,* 37.

77. Ingber, "Vilified or Glorified? Views of the Jewish Body."

78. *Mishmar,* 19 July 1944, 2.

79. *Ha'aretz*, 22 June 1947, 1.

80. *Yedi'ot Aharonot*, 27 June 1947, 2.

81. *Yedi'ot Aharonot*, 27 June 1947, 2.

82. *Yedi'ot Aharonot*, 27 June 1947, 2.

83. Gurit Kadman, quoted in Ingber, "Shorashim," 10; Kadman, *Am roked*, 16–17.

84. See, for instance, Baumel, "In Everlasting Memory"; Ben-Amos and Bet-El, "Holocaust Day"; Brog, "Victim and Victors"; Ofer, "Commemorating the Holocaust"; and Young, *Texture of Memory*.

85. In the summer of 1947, just after the second Dalia Festival, folk dancers from the Yishuv toured the European Displaced Persons camps. In contrast to the frail European Jewish bodies, the Eretz Israeli folk dancers projected an image of strength and freedom. See Ingber, "Vilified or Glorified? Views of the Jewish Body."

86. *Or ha-Yom*, 27 June 1947, Dalia Archive (Kibbutz Dalia, Israel).

87. *Davar*, 27 June 1947, 4.

88. *Or ha-Yom*, 27 June 1947, Dalia Archive (Kibbutz Dalia, Israel).

89. Gathering together was a key feature in creating public culture in European Jewish society as well. In his study of Jewish public culture in the late Russian Empire, Jeffrey Veidlinger discusses the power of the audience and of gathering a society together in the creation of public culture. Veidlinger, *Jewish Public Culture*.

90. *Mishmar*, 4 July 1947, 5.

91. *Ha'aretz*, 27 June 1947, 4.

92. *Davar*, 27 June 1947, 4.

93. *Ha'aretz*, 22 June 1947, 1.

94. *Yedi'ot Aharonot*, 22 June 1947.

95. *Ha'aretz*, 27 June 1947.

96. *Devar ha-Shavu'ah*, 26 June 1947, 13.

97. *Bulletin of the Cultural Division of the Histadrut*, August 1947.

98. *Ha-Olam ha-Zeh*, 26 June 1947, 9.

99. Although the 1944 Dalia Festival also took place on the Sabbath, there was no religious protest or unrest over this event, most likely because it was a smaller festival and did not take place during a period of discussions about the future of religion in the emerging state.

100. *Ha-zofeh*, 22 June 1947. For a further discussion of Mizrahi, see Kolatt, "Religion."

101. *Ha-zofeh*, 20 June 1947.

102. *Ha-Boker*, 23 June 1947.

103. *Ha-Boker*, 23 June 1947.

104. Yitzhak Greenboim is also known as Yitzhak Gruenbaum. After the establishment of the state, he became the first minister of the interior.

105. *Ha-zofeh*, 24 June 1947, 1.

106. *Ha-Mashkif*, 23 June 1947.

107. *Bulletin of the Cultural Division of the Histadrut*, August 1947.

108. *Ha'aretz*, 25 June 1947, 2; *Ha-Boker*, 27 June 1947; *Ha-Mashkif*, 23 June 1947.

109. *Ha-zofeh*, 23 June 1947.

110. *Ha-zofeh*, 23 June 1947.

111. *Ha-zofeh*, 23 June 1947.

112. *Ha-zofeh*, 23 June 1947, 2.

113. *Ha-zofeh*, 24 June 1947. The Torah portion that week was *Zot Chukat Hatorah* (Numbers 9:1–22:1).

114. *Ha-zofeh*, 29 June 1947.

115. *Ha-zofeh*, 23 June 1947, 1.

116. *Ha-zofeh*, 23 June 1947.

117. *Ha-zofeh*, 23 June 1947, 2.

118. *Ha-zofeh*, 24 June 1947, 2.

119. The Hebrew daily *Mishmar* had only one article about the religious protest. The Hebrew daily *Yedi'ot Aharonot* did not cover the religious dispute.

120. *Davar*, 27 June 1947, 4.

121. Ya'akov Uri was one of the founders of Moshav Nahalal, the first moshav (cooperative agricultural settlement) established in the Jezreel Valley. After the establishment of the state, Uri became a member of the Knesset, the Israeli parliament, from 1951 to 1955.

122. *Bulletin of the Cultural Division of the Histadrut*, August 1947.

123. *Davar*, 27 June 1947, 4.

124. *Bulletin of the Cultural Division of the Histadrut*, August 1947.

125. *Bulletin of the Cultural Division of the Histadrut*, August 1947.

126. *Davar*, 27 June 1947, 4.

127. *Bulletin of the Cultural Division of the Histadrut*, August 1947.

128. *Bulletin of the Cultural Division of the Histadrut*, August 1947.

129. *Ha'aretz*, 4 July 1947. This concept was also discussed by a writer in *Ha'aretz*, 26 June 1947.

130. *Ha-Boker*, 4 July 1947.

131. *Ha'aretz*, 4 July 1947, 8.

132. Kolatt, "Religion," 295.

Conclusion

1. For a greater discussion of the role of the Masada myth in Israeli society, see Zerubavel, *Recovered Roots*. For a discussion of the oath-taking ceremony, see pp. 130–31 in that book.

2. See, for instance, Azaryahu, "McIsrael"; O. Almog, "Globalization of Israel"; Eisenstadt,

Transformation of Israeli Society; Ezrahi, "Globalization"; and Rebhun and Waxman, *Jews in Israel.*

3. Lomsky-Feder and Ben-Ari, *Military and Militarism*, 302.

4. Katriel, *Communal Webs*, 5.

5. Katriel, *Communal Webs*, 29.

6. See, for instance, Ben-Rafael, "Mizrahi and Russian Challenges"; Dahan-Kalev, "You're So Pretty"; Shohat, "Mizrahim in Israel"; and Smooha, "Jewish Ethnicity in Israel."

7. Dominguez, *People as Subject*, 103.

8. For a further discussion of Sara Levi-Tanai and the development of the Inbal Dance Company, see Roginsky, "Orientalism."

9. For a more extensive discussion of Zehava Ben, see Horowitz, *Mediterranean Israeli Music*. For a further examination of music in contemporary Israel, see Regev and Seroussi, *Popular Music.*

10. T. Mayer, "From Zero to Hero," 111.

11. See Herzog, "Homefront and Battlefront"; and Lomsky-Feder and Ben-Ari, *Military and Militarism*, 310. See also Ochs, *Security and Suspicion.*

12. Lomsky-Feder and Gabi Zohar, quoted in Lomsky-Feder and Ben-Ari, *Military and Militarism*, 303.

13. "Some 400 Israelis are killed on the road every year, and the latest research by the European Transport Safety Council has shown that Israel ranks eighth out of 30 in the number of road accident deaths per million residents." Reuters Blog, 12 November 2009. http://blogs.reuters.com/axismundi/2009/11/12/zakas-other-work/ (accessed November 22, 2010).

14. Katriel, *Communal Webs*, 42–43. See also Katriel, *Talking Straight.*

15. O. Almog, *The Sabra*, 145.

16. *Los Angeles Times*, 3 May 2008. For a further discussion of contemporary dance in Israel, see, for instance, Aldor, "Borders of Contemporary Israeli Dance."

17. Melman, *New Israelis*, 216.

18. Melman, *New Israelis*, 146.

19. The organization Women of the Wall, established in 1988, has been challenging the ultra-Orthodox hegemony of the Western Wall plaza, seeking the right for women to pray as a group, read from the Torah, and don tallit at the Western Wall. For a greater discussion about the disputes with El Al, see N. Efron, *Real Jews.*

20. *New York Times*, 1 May 1998.

21. *New York Times*, 5 May 1998.

22. *New York Times*, 5 May 1998.

23. *New York Times*, 24 October 1999.

24. *New York Times*, 21 July 1998.

25. *Ynet*, 26 June 2008.

26. *Washington Post*, 11 July 2008.

27. *Washington Post*, 11 July 2008.

28. *Washington Post*, 11 July 2008.

29. For a further discussion of these holidays, see for instance, Handelman and Katz, "State Ceremonies of Israel"; and Young, "When a Day Remembers."

30. *New York Times*, 24 October 1999.

31. *Los Angeles Times*, 3 May 2008.

Bibliography

Archival and Library Collections

Central Zionist Archives, Jerusalem
Dalia Archive, Kibbutz Dalia, Israel
Dance Library of Israel, Tel Aviv
Diaspora Research Institute of Tel Aviv University, Ramat Aviv, Israel
Eliasaf Robinson Collection, Department of Special Collections and University Archives,
    Stanford University, Stanford, California
Institute for Jewish Festivals and Holidays, Kibbutz Beit Hashita, Israel
Israeli Documentation Center for the Performing Arts, Tel Aviv University, Ramat Aviv, Israel
Jerusalem Municipality Archives, Jerusalem
Jewish National and University Library, Jerusalem
Joseph Yekutieli Maccabi Archive, Ramat Gan, Israel
Judaica Collection, Harvard College Library, Cambridge, Massachusetts
Lavon Institute, Tel Aviv
Museum of the History of Tel Aviv and Jaffa, Tel Aviv
Personal Collection of Zila Agadati, Tel Aviv
Rubin Museum, Tel Aviv
Steven Spielberg Jewish Film Archive, Jerusalem
Tel Aviv–Jaffa Municipality Archives, Tel Aviv
Wingate Institute for Physical Education and Sport, Netanya, Israel

Yad Tabenkin Archives, Ramat Efal, Israel

Interviews by Author

Agadati, Zila. 19 April 1999, Tel Aviv, Israel.
Bertonov, Devorah. 9 August 1998, Holon, Israel.
Cohen, Yardena. 2 August 1998, Haifa, Israel.
Goldman, Vera. 4 August 1998, Tel Aviv, Israel.
Goren-Kadman, Ayalah. 13 July 1998 and 8 April 1999, Jerusalem, Israel; and 1 August 2005, New York.
Har-Zion, Yehuda. 26 July 1998, Ramat Efal, Israel.
Kasten, Hilda. 4 May 1999, Tel Aviv, Israel.
Levi-Tanai, Sara. 26 April 1999, Tel Aviv, Israel.
Nadav, Raḥel. 11 May 1999, Tel Aviv, Israel.
Starostiniatsky, Akiva. 3 July 2000, Kibbutz Dalia, Israel.

Additional Interviews

Kadman, Gurit, interview by Ayalah Dan-Caspi, Oral History Archives of the Lavon Institute, 11 February 1981.

Newspapers and Periodicals

Davar, daily newspaper. Tel Aviv, 1925–present. Hebrew.
Devar ha-Shavu'a, weekly newspaper. Tel Aviv, 1946–present. Hebrew.
Do'ar ha-Yom, daily newspaper. Jerusalem, 1919–1936. Hebrew.
Ha'aretz, daily newspaper. Tel Aviv, 1919–present. Hebrew.
Ha-Boker, daily newspaper. Tel Aviv, 1935–1966. Hebrew.
Ha-Mashkif, daily newspaper. Tel Aviv, 1938–1948. Hebrew.
Ha-Olam ha-Zeh, weekly magazine. Jerusalem, Tel Aviv, 1947–present. Hebrew.
Hazit ha-Am, biweekly and later weekly magazine. Jerusalem, 1932–1934. Hebrew.
Ha-zofeh, daily newspaper. Jerusalem, Tel Aviv, 1937–present. Hebrew.
Jüdische Rundschau, weekly newspaper. Berlin, 1896–1938. German.
Karnenu, Hebrew quarterly. Jerusalem, 1924–1963. Hebrew.
Ketuvim, literary weekly. Tel Aviv, 1926–1933. Hebrew.
Kol ha-Am, daily and later weekly periodical. Tel Aviv, 1947–present. Hebrew.

Kol-noa, fortnightly magazine. Tel Aviv, 1931–1935. Hebrew.

Mishmar, daily newspaper. Tel Aviv, 1943–present (known as *Al ha-Mishmar* beginning in 1948). Hebrew.

Omer, weekly supplement of *Davar*. Tel Aviv, 1936–1942. Hebrew.

Palestine Bulletin. See *Palestine Post*.

Palestine Post, daily newspaper. Jerusalem, 1933–1948 (replaced the *Palestine Bulletin* in 1933; known as the *Jerusalem Post* since 1948). English.

Tesha ba-Erev, weekly magazine. Jerusalem, Tel Aviv, 1937–1947 (known as *Ha-olam ha-Zeh* since 1947). Hebrew.

Yedi'ot Aharonot, daily newspaper. Tel Aviv, 1939–present. Hebrew.

Films and Videos

Agadati, Baruch, producer. *The First Maccabiah*. Film (Palestine, 1932). Steven Spielberg Jewish Film Archive.

———, director. *Zot hi ha'aretz*. Film (Palestine, 1935). Steven Spielberg Jewish Film Archive.

Axelrod, Natan, director. Carmel Newsreels (Palestine, 1935–1941). Steven Spielberg Jewish Film Archive.

Bergstein, Leah. Videos. Dance Library of Israel, H-360, H-378.

Bloome, A. J., director. *My People's Dream* (U.S.A., 1934). Steven Spielberg Jewish Film Archive.

Cohen, Yardena. Videos. Dance Library of Israel, H-723, H-323.

Galeser, Yosef, director. *Fruehling in Palastina*. Film (Germany, 1928). Steven Spielberg Jewish Film Archive.

Gross, Yaakov, director and producer. *Agadah B'holot* (Legend in the Dunes). Film (Israel, 2009). Steven Spielberg Jewish Film Archive.

Gross, Yaakov. *Yaakov Ben Dov: avi seret ha'ivri* (Ya'akov Ben Dov: Father of the Hebrew Film). Videotape. Jerusalem, Israel: Steven Spielberg Jewish Film Archive, 1989.

Halachmi, Chaim, director. *Vayehi bimei*. Film (Palestine, 1932). Steven Spielberg Jewish Film Archive.

Ideal Travel Talks: Palestine 1934. Film (1934). Steven Spielberg Jewish Film Archive.

Israel's House of Wisdom. Film (1944). Steven Spielberg Jewish Film Archive.

Kadman, Gurit. Documentary and videos. Dance Library of Israel, H-138, H-317.

Kfir, Avishai, director and producer, and Itzhak Rubin, producer. *I Was There in Color*. Documentary film (2009).

"Kookie." In *The Art of Natan Axelrod, 1937*. Film (1937). Dance Library of Israel, H-228.

Kraus, Gertrud. Videos. Dance Library of Israel, H-65, H-181.

Leman, Juda, director. *The Land of Promise*. Film (U.S.A., 1935). Steven Spielberg Jewish Film Archive.

Lerski, Helmar, director. *Awodah*. Film (Hungary, 1935). Steven Spielberg Jewish Film Archive.

Look Homeward Wanderers. Film (1947). Steven Spielberg Jewish Film Archive.

Palestinska Kronika. Film (Poland, 1930). Steven Spielberg Jewish Film Archive.

Schweig, Shmuel. *The Day Came*. Film (Israel, 1950). Steven Spielberg Jewish Film Archive.

Shalit, Lionel. "Film Clips of the First Maccabiah Games." Joseph Yekutieli Maccabi Archive, 228, Video 29.

Simmenauer, Felix. *Die Fragmenter der drei Makkabi Filme: Makkabaer, Antwerpen 1930, Die Erste Makkabiah 1932*. Film (1989). Joseph Yekutieli Maccabi Archive, Video 428.

Snyder, Allegra Fuller, and Annette Macdonald. *Mary Wigman, 1886–1973: "When the Fire Dances Between the Two Poles."* Videotape. Pennington, NJ: Princeton Book Co., 1991.

Tryster, Hillel. *Agadati: Screen of an Artist*. Videotape. Jerusalem: Steven Spielberg Jewish Film Archive, 1997.

Wynn, George, director. *Springtime in the Holy Land*. Film (Great Britain, 1930). Steven Spielberg Jewish Film Archive.

Books, Journal Articles, and Other Sources

Agadati: arba panim (Agadati: Four Faces). Tel Aviv: Rubin Museum, 1985.

Aldor, Gaby. "The Borders of Contemporary Israeli Dance: Invisible Unless in Final Pain." *Dance Research Journal* 35 (2003): 81–97.

——— . *Ve-eich roked gamal* (And How Does a Camel Dance). Tel Aviv: Resling, 2011.

Almog, Oz. "The Globalization of Israel: Transformation." In Anita Shapira, ed., *Israeli Identity in Transition*, 233–56. Westport, CT: Praeger, 2004.

——— . *The Sabra: The Creation of the New Jew*, trans. Haim Watzman. Berkeley: University of California Press, 2000.

Almog, Shmuel. *Zionism and History: The Rise of a New Jewish Consciousness*. New York: St. Martin's Press, 1987.

Almog, Shmuel, Jehuda Reinharz, and Anita Shapira, eds. *Zionism and Religion*. Hanover, NH: University Press of New England, 1998.

Alouf, Jehoshua. "The Beginning of Physical Education and Sport in Modern Israel." In Uriel Simri, ed., *International Seminar on the History of Physical Education and Sport*, 3–6. Netanya, Israel: Wingate Institute for Physical Education and Sport, 1968.

Alter, Robert. *The Invention of Hebrew Prose: Modern Fiction and the Language of Realism*. Seattle: University of Washington Press, 1988.

Anderson, Benedict. *Imagined Communities: Reflections on the Origin and Spread of Nationalism*. London: Verso, 1991.

Arbel, Rachel, ed. *Blue and White in Color: Visual Images of Zionism, 1897–1947*. Tel Aviv: Beth Hatefusoth: Nahum Goldmann Museum of the Jewish Diaspora, 1997.

Aronis, Carolin. "Balconies of Tel Aviv: Cultural History and Urban Politics." In Maoz Azaryahu and S. Ilan Troen, eds., *Tel Aviv, The First Century: Visions, Designs, Actualities*, 348–72. Bloomington: Indiana University Press, 2011.

Aronoff, Myron J. "Myths, Symbols, and Rituals of the Emerging State." In Laurence J. Silberstein, ed., *New Perspectives on Israeli History: The Early Years of the State*, 175–92. New York: New York University Press, 1991.

Aryeh-Sapir, Nili. *Itsuvam shel tarbut ve-chinukh ironiyim: sipure tzekhesim ve-chagigot be-Tel-Aviv bi-shenoteha ha-rishonot* (The Formation of Urban Culture and Education: Stories of and About Ceremonies and Celebrations in Tel Aviv in Its First Years). Tel Aviv: Tel Aviv University, 2006.

———. "Karnaval betel aviv: purim ba'ir ha'ivrit harishonah" (Carnival in Tel Aviv: Purim in the First Hebrew City). *Mechkarei Yerushalayim Befolklor Yehudi* 22 (2003): 99–121.

———. "Tahalukhat ha'or: chanukah kechag leumi betel aviv bashanim 1909–1936" (The Parade of Light: Chanukah as a National Holiday in Tel Aviv, 1909–1936). *Cathedra* 103 (2002): 131–50.

Aryeh-Sapir, Nili, and Michal Held. "'Vatilbash Malkhut': 'malkat ester' shel karnaval purim betel aviv; sipur ishi ve'iguno beheksher tarbuti" (Queen Esther of the Tel Aviv Purim Carnival: A Personal Narrative in Its Cultural Context). *Masekhet* 8 (2008): 97–115.

Ashkenazi, Ruth. *Sipur maholot ha'am b'daliah* (The Story of the Folk Dances at Dalia). Haifa: Tamar, 1992.

Avineri, Shlomo. *The Making of Modern Zionism: The Intellectual Origins of the Jewish State*. New York: Basic Books, 1981.

Avi-Shulamit, A. "Purim b'eretz yisrael" (Purim in the Land of Israel). *Karnenu* (January 1931): 36.

———. "Yemei ha-purim b'eretz yisrael" (The Days of Purim in the Land of Israel). *Karnenu* (February 1932): 36.

Azaryahu, Maoz. "McIsrael: On the 'Americanization' of Israel." *Israel Studies* 5.1 (2000): 41–64.

———. *Tel Aviv: Mythography of a City*. Syracuse, NY: Syracuse University Press, 2007.

———. "Tel-Aviv's Birthdays: Anniversary Celebrations of the First Hebrew City, 1929–1959." *Israel Studies* 14 (2009): 1–20.

Azaryahu, Maoz, and S. Ilan Troen, eds. *Tel Aviv, the First Century: Visions, Designs, Actualities*. Bloomington: Indiana University Press, 2011.

Bahat-Ratzon, Naomi, ed. *Beregel yehefa: masoret yehude teman be-mehol be-yisrael* (Barefooted: Jewish-Yemenite Tradition in Israeli Dance). Tel Aviv: Amutat "Eeleh ve-tamar," 1999.

Baldwin, P. M. "Liberalism, Nationalism, and Degeneration: The Case of Max Nordau." *Central European History* 13 (1980): 99–120.

Band, Arnold J. *Nostalgia and Nightmare: A Study in the Fiction of S. Y. Agnon*. Berkeley: University of California Press, 1968.

Banner, Lois. *American Beauty.* New York: Knopf, 1983.

Bartal, Israel. "The Ingathering of Traditions: Zionism's Anthology Projects." *Prooftexts* 17 (January 1997): 88–91.

Bashan, Refa'el. *Yesh li reayon* (Selected and New Interviews). Tel Aviv: Am Oved, 1965.

Baumel, Judith Tydor. " 'In Everlasting Memory': Individual and Communal Holocaust Commemoration in Israel." *Israel Affairs* 1 (1995): 146–70.

Ben-Amos, Avner, and Ilana Bet-El. "Holocaust Day and Memorial Day in Israeli Schools: Ceremonies, Education, and History." *Israel Studies* 4 (1999): 258–84.

Ben-David, Orit. "Tiyul (Hike) as an Act of Consecration of Space." In Eyal Ben-Ari and Yoram Bilu, eds., *Space and Place in Contemporary Israeli Discourse and Experience*, 129–45. Albany: State University of New York Press, 1997.

Bennahum, Ninotchka Devorah. *Antonia Mercé, "La Argentina."* Hanover, NH: University Press of New England, 1999.

Ben-Rafael, Eliezer. "Mizrahi and Russian Challenges to Israel's Dominant Culture: Divergences and Convergences." *Israel Studies* 12 (2007): 68–91.

Ben-Yishai, A. Z. In *Moreh Derech: The Second Maccabiah.* Joseph Yekutieli Maccabi Archive. Hebrew.

Berkowitz, Michael. *Western Jewry and the Zionist Project, 1914–1933.* Cambridge, UK: Cambridge University Press, 1997.

———. *Zionist Culture and West European Jewry Before the First World War.* Cambridge, UK: Cambridge University Press, 1993.

Bernstein, Deborah. *Pioneers and Homemakers: Jewish Women in Pre-State Israel.* Albany: State University of New York Press, 1992.

Biale, David. *Eros and the Jews: From Biblical Israel to Contemporary America.* New York: Basic Books, 1992.

Blumenfeld, Leon. "Dance Pioneering in the Palestine." *Dance Magazine* (March 1929).

Bohlman, Philip V. *The World Centre for Jewish Music in Palestine, 1936–1940.* New York: Oxford University Press, 1992.

Borut, Jacob. "Jews in German Sports During the Weimar Republic." In Michael Brenner and Gideon Reuveni, eds., *Emancipation Through Muscles: Jews and Sports in Europe*, 77–92. Lincoln: University of Nebraska Press, 2006.

Boyarin, Daniel. *Unheroic Conduct: The Rise of Heterosexuality and the Invention of the Jewish Man.* Berkeley: University of California Press, 1997.

Brenner, Michael. *The Renaissance of Jewish Culture in Weimar Germany.* New Haven, CT: Yale University Press, 1996.

Brenner, Michael, and Gideon Reuveni, eds. *Emancipation Through Muscles: Jews and Sports in Europe.* Lincoln: University of Nebraska Press, 2006.

Brinker, Menahem. *Ad ha-simtah ha-teveryanit: ma'amar al sipur u-ma-hashavah bi-yetsirat brener* (Narrative Art and Social Thought in Y. H. Brenner's Work). Tel Aviv: Am Oved, 1990.

Brodsky, Adriana Mariel. "The Contours of Identity: Sephardic Jews and the Construction of Jewish Community in Argentina, 1880 to the Present." Ph.D. diss., Duke University, 2004.

Brog, Mooli. "Victim and Victors: Holocaust and Military Commemoration in Israeli Collective Memory." *Israel Studies* 8 (fall 2003): 65–99.

Bunzl, John. "Hakoah Vienna: Reflections on a Legend." In Michael Brenner and Gideon Reuveni, eds., *Emancipation through Muscles: Jews and Sports in Europe*, 106–118. Lincoln: University of Nebraska Press, 2006.

Butler, Judith. *Gender Trouble: Feminism and the Subversion of Identity.* New York: Routledge, 1999.

———. "Performative Acts and Gender Constitution: An Essay in Phenomenology and Feminist Theory." In Sue-Ellen Case, ed., *Performing Feminisms: Feminist Critical Theory and Theatre*, 270–82. Baltimore: Johns Hopkins University Press, 1990.

Carmiel, Batia. *Bate ha-kafe shel tel-aviv: 1920–1980* (Tel Aviv's Coffeehouses, 1920–1980). Tel Aviv: Eretz Israel Museum, 2007.

———. *Korbman: Tsalam tel-avivi aher, 1919–1936* (Korbman: A Different Kind of Tel Aviv Photographer, 1919–1936). Tel Aviv: Eretz Israel Museum, 2004.

———. *Tel Aviv be-tahposet ve-kheter: hagigot purim ba-shanim 1912–1935* (Tel Aviv in Costume and Crown: Purim Celebrations in Tel Aviv, 1912–1935). Tel Aviv: Eretz Israel Museum, 1999.

Cohen, Colleen Ballerino, Richard Wilk, and Beverly Stoeltje, eds. *Beauty Queens on the Global Stage: Gender, Contests, and Power.* New York: Routledge, 1996.

Cohen, Mortimer J. "Tel Aviv: The City of Purim." In Philip Goodman, ed., *The Purim Anthology*, 73–82. Philadelphia: Jewish Publication Society of America, 1949.

Cohen, Selma Jeanne. "Modern Dance and *Ausdruckstanz*: A Comparison of Aesthetics." In Gunhild Oberzaucher-Schuller, ed., *Ausdruckstanz: Eine mitteleuropäische Bewegung der ersten Hälfte des 20. Jahrhunderts*, 161–65. Wilhelmshaven, Germany: Florian Noetzel Verlag, 1992.

Cohen, Yardena. *Hatof vehamahol* (The Drum and the Dance). Tel Aviv: Sifriyat Poalim, 1963.

———. *Hatof vehayam* (The Drum and the Sea). Tel Aviv: Sifriyat Poalim, 1976.

Collins, Tony. "Jews, Antisemitism, and Sports in Britain, 1900–1939." In Michael Brenner and Gideon Reuveni, eds., *Emancipation Through Muscles: Jews and Sports in Europe*, 142–55. Lincoln: University of Nebraska Press, 2006.

Conner, Lynne. *Spreading the Gospel of the Modern Dance: Newspaper Dance Criticism in the United States, 1850–1934.* Pittsburgh: University of Pittsburgh Press, 1997.

Dahan-Kalev, Henriette. "You're So Pretty—You Don't Look Moroccan." *Israel Studies* 6 (2001): 1–14.

Daly, Ann. *Done into Dance: Isadora Duncan in America.* Bloomington: Indiana University Press, 1995.

Daniel, Yvonne. *Dance and Social Change in Contemporary Cuba.* Bloomington: Indiana University Press, 1995.

De Grazia, Victoria. *How Fascism Ruled Women: Italy, 1922–1945*. Berkeley: University of California Press, 1992.

Deslandes, Paul R. "The Male Body, Beauty, and Aesthetics in Modern British Culture." *History Compass* 8 (2010): 1191–1208.

Divine, Donna Robinson. *Exiled in the Homeland: Zionism and the Return to Mandate Palestine*. Austin: University of Texas Press, 2009.

Dominguez, Virginia R. *People as Subject, People as Object*. Madison: University of Wisconsin Press, 1989.

Donner, Batia. *To Live with the Dream: An Exhibition at the Tel Aviv Museum of Art*. Tel Aviv: Dvir, 1989.

Druyan, Nitza. *Be-ein marvad kesamim: olei teiman be-eretz yisrae'el 1881–1914* (Without a Magic Carpet: Yemenite Immigration to Palestine, 1881–1914). Jerusalem: Mekhon Ben-Tsevi, 1981.

Duncan, Isadora. *My Life*. Garden City, NY: Garden City Publishing, 1927.

Efron, John M. *Defenders of the Race: Jewish Doctors and Race Science in Fin-de-Siecle Europe*. New Haven, CT: Yale University Press, 1994.

——— . *Medicine and the German Jews: A History*. New Haven, CT: Yale University Press, 2001.

Efron, Noah J. *Real Jews: Secular Versus Ultra-Orthodox—The Struggle for Jewish Identity in Israel*. New York: Basic Books, 2003.

Eisen, George. "The Maccabiah Games: A History of the Jewish Olympics." Ph.D. diss., University of Maryland, 1979.

——— . "Zionism, Nationalism, and the Emergence of the Jüdische Turnershaft." *Leo Baeck Institute Yearbook* 28 (1983): 247–62.

Eisenstadt, S. N. *The Transformation of Israeli Society: An Essay in Interpretation*. London: Weidenfield & Nicolson, 1985.

Elron, Sari. "Lirkod ivrit: ha'ivriut biyitziratan shel rina nikova ulehakatah hateymanit" (Dancing Hebrew: Hebrew Characteristics in the Dances of Rina Nikova and Her Yemenite Group). In Henia Rottenberg and Dina Roginsky, eds., *Rav-koliyut vesiach: machol beyisrael* (Dance Discourse in Israel), 155–86. Tel Aviv: Resling, 2009.

Engelstein, Laura. *The Keys to Happiness: Sex and the Search for Modernity in Fin-de-Siecle Russia*. Ithaca, NY: Cornell University Press, 1992.

Erdman, Joan L. "Dance Discourses: Rethinking the History of the 'Oriental Dance.'" In Gay Morris, ed., *Moving Words*, 288–305. London: Routledge, 1996.

Eshel, Ruth. "Concert Dance in Israel." *Dance Research Journal* 35 (2003): 61–80.

——— . *Lirkod im ha-halom: reshit ha-mahol ha-omanuti be-erets yisrael 1920–1964* (Dancing with the Dream: The Development of Artistic Dance in Israel, 1920–1964). Tel Aviv: Dance Library of Israel, 1991.

Even-Zohar, Itamar. "The Emergence of a Native Hebrew Culture in Palestine: 1882–1948." In Jehuda Reinharz and Anita Shapira, eds., *Essential Papers on Zionism*, 727–44. New York: New York University Press, 1996.

Ezrahi, Yaron. "Globalization and Its Impact on Israel." In Alan Dowty, ed., *Critical Issues in Israeli Society*, 151–65. Santa Barbara, CA: Praeger, 2004.

Feldestein, Ariel L. "Filming the Homeland: Cinema in Eretz Israel and the Zionist Movement." In Miri Talmon and Yaron Peleg, eds., *Israeli Cinema: Identities in Motion*, 3–15. Austin: University of Texas Press, 2011.

First Maccabiah Song Book. 1932. Hebrew.

Franco, Mark. *Dancing Modernism, Performing Politics.* Bloomington: Indiana University Press, 1995.

Friedhaber, Zvi. "Bibliographic Sources in Research of Dance Among the Jews." *Israel Dance* (1986): 31–34.

———. "The Dance in the Jewish-Mediterranean Communities Since the Expulsion from Spain Until the Beginning of the 19th Century." Ph.D. diss., Hebrew University, Jerusalem, 1986.

———. "The Development of Folk Dance in Israel." *Israel Dance* (1987–1988): 33–39.

———. "The First Folk Dance Festival at Dalia in 1944." *Israel Dance Annual* (1985): 29–33.

———. *Gurit kadman: em vekala* (Gurit Kadman: Mother and Bride). Haifa: Haifa Press, 1989.

———. *Hava netze b'meholot: lekorot rikudei am b'yisrael* (Let's Go Dancing: History of Folk Dance in Israel). Tel Aviv: Mercaz Letarbut u-le'hinuh, Histadrut, 1994.

———. "Mi-ben shemen ad lekenes ha-meholot ha-rishon bekibbutz dalia b'shnat 1944" (From Ben Shemen to the First Dance Festival at Kibbutz Dalia, 1944). *Rokdim* 13 (1992): 12–15.

———. "Pioneers of Expressionism." *Israeli Dance Annual* (April 1995): 50–53.

Fuchs, Esther, ed., *Israeli Women's Studies: A Reader.* New Brunswick, NJ: Rutgers University Press, 2005.

Gai, Carmit. *Hanna rovina* (Hanna Rovina). Tel Aviv: Am Oved, 1995.

Geldern, James Von. *Bolshevik Festivals, 1917–1920.* Berkeley: University of California Press, 1993.

Gellner, Ernest. *Nations and Nationalism.* Ithaca, NY: Cornell University Press, 1983.

Gertz, Nurith. *Myths in Israeli Culture: Captives of a Dream.* London: Valentine Mitchell, 2000.

———. *Sifrut ve-ideologyah be-erets-yisrael bi-shenot ha-sheloshim* (Literature and Ideology in Eretz Israel During the 1930s). Tel Aviv: Ha-Universitah Ha-Petuhah, 1988.

Gillerman, Sharon. "Strongman Siegmund Breitbart and Interpretations of the Jewish Body." In Michael Brenner and Gideon Reuveni, eds., *Emancipation through Muscles: Jews and Sports in Europe*, 62–76. Lincoln: University of Nebraska Press, 2006.

Gilman, Sander L. *Difference and Pathology: Stereotypes of Sexuality, Race, and Madness.* Ithaca, NY: Cornell University Press, 1985.

———. *The Jew's Body.* New York: Routledge, 1991.

———. "Salome, Syphilis, Sarah Bernhardt and the Modern Jewess." In Linda Nochlin and Tamar Garb, eds., *The Jew in the Text: Modernity and the Construction of Identity*, 97–120. London: Thames & Hudson, 1995.

———. *The Visibility of the Jew in the Diaspora: Body Imagery and Its Cultural Context.* Syracuse, NY: Syracuse University, 1992.

Gluzman, Michael. *Ha-guf ha-tsiyoni: le'umiyut, migdar u-miniyut ba-sifrut ha-ivrit ha-hadasha* (The Zionist Body: Nationalism, Gender, and Sexuality in Modern Hebrew Literature). Tel Aviv: Hakibbutz Hameuchad, 2007.

Goodman, Philip, ed. *The Purim Anthology.* Philadelphia: Jewish Publication Society, 1949.

Goren, Yoram. *Sadot lavshu mahol* (Fields Dressed in Dance). Ramat-Yohanan, Israel: Hotsaat Kibuts Ramat-Yohanan, 1983.

Gorny, Yosef. *Zionism and the Arabs, 1882–1948: A Study of Ideology.* New York: Oxford University Press, 1987.

Graff, Ellen. *Stepping Left: Dance and Politics in New York City, 1928–1942.* Durham, NC: Duke University Press, 1997.

Greenblatt, Edith Lilian. "Recreational Israeli Dance as a Modern Participatory Art Form: A Computer-Aided Study of Rikudai am-yisraeli, 1987." M.A. thesis, University of California, Los Angeles, 1993.

Guilat, Yael. "The Yemeni Ideal in Israeli Arts and Culture." *Israel Studies* 6 (fall 2001): 26–53.

Guttmann, Allen. "Berlin 1936: The Most Controversial Olympics." In Alan Tomlinson and Christopher Young, eds., *National Identity and Global Sports Events: Culture, Politics, and Spectacle in the Olympics and the Football World Cup*, 65–82. Albany: State University of New York Press, 2006.

Halperin, Hagit, and Galiyah Sagiv, eds. *Me-agvaniyah ad simfonyah: ha-shira ha-kalah shel avraham shlonski uparodyot al shirato* (Muse to Amuse: The Light Verse of Abraham Shlonsky). Tel Aviv: Sifriyat Poalim, 1997.

Halpern, Ben, and Jehuda Reinharz. *Zionism and the Creation of a New Society.* Hanover: University Press of New England, 2000.

Handelman, Don, and Elihu Katz. "State Ceremonies of Israel: Remembrance Day and Independence Day." In Shlomo Deshen, Charles S. Liebman, and Moshe Shokeid, eds., *Israeli Judaism*, 75–85. New Brunswick, NJ: Transaction, 1995.

Harris, Monford. "Purim: The Celebration of Dis-Order." *Judaism* 26 (spring 1977): 161–70.

Hart, Mitchell. *The Healthy Jew: The Symbiosis of Judaism and Modern Medicine.* New York: Cambridge University Press, 2007.

Helman, Anat. "'Even the Dogs in the Streets Bark in Hebrew': National Ideology and Everyday Culture in Tel Aviv." *Jewish Quarterly Review* 92.3–4 (2002): 359–82.

——— . *Or ve-yam hikifuha: tarbut tel avivit bi-tekufat ha-mandat* (Urban Culture in 1920s and 1930s Tel Aviv). Haifa: Hotsa'at Ha-sefarim shel Universitat Haifa, 2007.

——— . "Sport on the Sabbath: Controversy in 1920s and 1930s Jewish Palestine." *International Journal of the History of Sport* 25 (January 2008): 41–64.

——— . "Two Urban Celebrations in Jewish Palestine." *Journal of Urban History* 32 (March 2006): 380–403.

——— . "Was There Anything Particularly Jewish About 'The First Hebrew City'?" In Barbara

Kirshenblatt-Gimblett and Jonathan Karp, eds., *The Art of Being Jewish in Modern Times*, 116–27. Philadelphia: University of Pennsylvania Press, 2008.

———. *Young Tel Aviv: A Tale of Two Cities*. Waltham, MA: Brandeis University Press, 2010.

———. "Zionism, Politics, Hedonism: Sports in Interwar Tel Aviv." In Jack Kugelmass, ed., *Jews, Sports, and the Rites of Citizenship*, 95–113. Urbana: University of Illinois Press, 2007.

Hermon, Shalom. "The Development of Folkdance in Modern Israel: From the Beginnings to the Establishment of the State of Israel (1882–1948)." In Uriel Simri, ed., *Physical Education and Sport in Jewish History and Culture: Proceedings of an International Seminar*, 109–14. Netanya, Israel: Wingate Institute for Physical Education and Sport, 1981.

Hertzberg, Arthur. *The Zionist Idea*. Philadelphia: Jewish Publication Society, 1997.

Herzog, Hanna. "Homefront and Battlefront: The Status of Jewish and Palestinian Women in Israel." In Esther Fuchs, ed., *Israeli Women's Studies: A Reader*, 208–31. New Brunswick, NJ: Rutgers University Press, 2005.

Hever, Hannan. "'Our Poetry Is Like an Orange Grove': Anthologies of Hebrew Poetry in Erets Israel." *Prooftexts* 17 (January 1997): 199–225.

———. *Paytanim u-viryonim: tsemihat ha-shir ha-politi ha-ivri be erets-yisrael* (Poets and Zealots: Rise of Political Hebrew Poetry in Eretz Israel). Jerusalem: Mosad Bialik, 1994.

Himmelreich, Alfons, and Vivienne Silver-Brody. *Alfons Himelraikh: tsalam al ha-gag* (Alfons Himmelreich: Photographer on the Roof). Tel Hai: Open Museum of Photography, 2005.

Hirschfeld, Ariel. "Locus and Language: Hebrew Culture in Israel, 1890–1990." In David Biale, ed., *Cultures of the Jews*, v. 3, *Modern Encounters*, 289–340. New York: Schocken, 2002.

Hirshberg, Jehoash. *Music in the Jewish Community of Palestine, 1880–1948*. Oxford, UK: Clarendon, 1995.

Hoberman, John [M.]. "'How Fiercely That Gentile Rides!': Jews, Horses, and Equestrian Style." In Jack Kugelmass, ed., *Jews, Sports, and the Rites of Citizenship*, 31–50. Urbana: University of Illinois Press, 2007.

———. *Sport and Political Ideology*. Austin: University of Texas Press, 1984.

Hobsbawm, Eric J. *Nations and Nationalism Since 1780: Programme, Myth, Reality*. Cambridge, UK: Cambridge University Press, 1990.

Hobsbawm, Eric, and Terence Ranger, eds. *The Invention of Tradition*. Cambridge, UK: Cambridge University Press, 1983.

Horowitz, Amy. *Mediterranean Israeli Music and the Politics of the Aesthetic*. Detroit: Wayne State University Press, 2010.

Ingber, Judith Brin. "The Gamin Speaks: Conversations with Gertrud Kraus." *Dance Magazine* 50 (March 1976): 45–50.

———. "The Priestesses." *Dance Chronicle* 18 (1995): 453–65.

———, ed. *Seeing Israeli and Jewish Dance*. Detroit: Wayne State University Press, 2011.

———. "Shorashim: The Roots of Israeli Folk Dance." *Dance Perspectives* 59 (autumn 1974):

1–59. Reprinted in Judith Brin Ingber, ed., *Seeing Israeli and Jewish Dance*, 99–169 (Detroit: Wayne State University Press, 2011).

———. "Vilified or Glorified? Nazi Versus Zionist Views of the Jewish Body in 1947." In Judith Brin Ingber, ed., *Seeing Israeli and Jewish Dance*, 251–277. Detroit: Wayne State University Press, 2011.

———. "Vilified or Glorified? Views of the Jewish Body in 1947." *Jewish Folklore and Ethnology Review* 20 (2000): 39–58.

Jacobs, Jack. "The Politics of Jewish Sports Movements in Interwar Poland." In Michael Brenner and Gideon Reuveni, eds., *Emancipation through Muscles: Jews and Sports in Europe*, 93–105. Lincoln: University of Nebraska Press, 2006.

Jordan, Ruth. *Daughter of the Waves: Memories of Growing Up in Pre-War Palestine.* New York: Taplinger, 1982.

Journal of the English Folk Dance and Song Society. London: Cecil Sharp House, 1935.

Kadimah: Ha-Mizrah be-omanut Yisrael (To the East: Orientalism in the Arts in Israel). Jerusalem: Israel Museum, 1998.

Kadman, Gurit. *Am roked* (Dancing Nation). Tel Aviv: Schocken, 1969.

———. *Rikude edot be-yisra'el* (Dances of the Ethnic Communities of Israel). Givatayim, Israel: Massada Press, 1982.

Kalmar, Ivan Davidson, and Derek J. Penslar, eds. *Orientalism and the Jews.* Waltham, MA: Brandeis University Press, 2005.

———. "Orientalism and the Jews: An Introduction." In Ivan Davidson Kalmar and Derek J. Penslar, eds., *Orientalism and the Jews*, xiii–xl. Waltham, MA: Brandeis University Press, 2005.

Kaschl, Elke. "Beyond Israel to New York: How to Perform 'Community' Under the Impact of Globalization." In Judith Brin Ingber, ed., *Seeing Israeli and Jewish Dance*, 329–53. Detroit: Wayne State University Press, 2011.

———. *Dance and Authenticity in Israel and Palestine: Performing the Nation.* Leiden: Brill, 2003.

Katriel, Tamar. *Communal Webs: Communication and Culture in Contemporary Israel.* Albany: State University of New York Press, 1991.

———. *From Soul Talks to Talk Radio in Israeli Culture.* Detroit: Wayne State University Press, 2004.

———. *Talking Straight: Dugri Speech in Israeli Sabra Culture.* New York: Cambridge University Press, 1986.

———. "Trips and Hiking as Secular Rituals in Israeli Culture." *Jewish Folklore and Ethnology Review* 17 (1995): 6–13.

Kaufman, Haim. "'Hapoel' b'tekufat ha-mandat, 1923–1936" (Hapoel in the Mandate Period, 1923–1936). Ph.D. diss., University of Haifa, 1993.

———. "Jewish Sports in the Diaspora, Yishuv, and Israel: Between Nationalism and Politics." *Israel Studies* 10.2 (2005): 147–67.

——— . "Yesoda shel 'hitagdut hasport hapoel.'" *Katedrah* (June 1996): 122–49.

Kealiinohomoku, Joann. "An Anthropologist Looks at Ballet as a Form of Ethnic Dance." In Roger Copeland and Marshall Cohen, eds., *What is Dance?* 533–50. Oxford, UK: Oxford University Press, 1983.

Kesari, Uri. "Mi-esther ad esther." *Kol-noa* (21 March 1932), 6–7.

Kirshenblatt-Gimblett, Barbara. "Performance Studies." In Henry Bial, ed., *The Performance Studies Reader*, 43–56. New York: Routledge, 2007.

——— . "Performing the State: The Jewish Palestine Pavilion at the New York World's Fair, 1939/1940." In Barbara Kirshenblatt-Gimblett and Jonathan Karp, eds., *The Art of Being Jewish in Modern Times*, 98–115. Philadelphia: University of Pennsylvania Press, 2008.

Koegler, Horst. "In the Shadow of the Swastika: Dance in Germany, 1927–1936." *Dance Perspectives* 57 (spring 1974): 3–48.

Kolatt, Israel. "Religion, Society, and State in the National Home Period." In Shmuel Almog, Jehuda Reinharz, and Anita Shapira, eds., *Zionism and Religion*, 273–301. Hanover, NH: University Press of New England, 1998.

Kraut, Anthea. *Choreographing the Folk: The Dance Stagings of Zora Neale Hurston.* Minneapolis: University of Minnesota Press, 2008.

Kressel, Getzel. *Leksikon ha-sifrut ha-ivrit ba-dorot ha-aharonim* (Encyclopedia of Modern Hebrew Literature), v. 2. Merhavyah, Israel: Sifriyat Poalim, 1967.

——— . *Toldot ha-itonut ha-ivrit be-erets yisrael* (History of the Hebrew Press in Palestine). Jerusalem: Zionist Library, 1964.

Krüger, Arnd, and William Murray, eds. *The Nazi Olympics: Sport, Politics, and Appeasement in the 1930s.* Urbana: University of Illinois Press, 2003.

Krüger, Michael. "Body Culture and Nation Building: The History of Gymnastics in Germany in the Period of Its Foundation as a Nation-State." *International Journal of the History of Sport* 13 (December 1996): 409–17.

Kugelmass, Jack, ed. *Jews, Sports, and the Rites of Citizenship.* Urbana: University of Illinois Press, 2007.

Kunda, Sigal Davidi, and Robert Oxman. "The Flight of the Camel: The Levant Fair of 1934 and the Creation of a Situated Modernism." In Haim Yacobi, ed., *Constructing a Sense of Place: Architecture and the Zionist Discourse*, 52–75. Burlington, VT: Ashgate, 2004.

Laban, Rudolf. *A Life for Dance.* London: MacDonald & Evans, 1975.

Ladd, Tony, and James A. Mathiesen. *Muscular Christianity: Evangelical Protestants and the Development of American Sport.* Grand Rapids, MI: Baker, 1999.

Large, David Clay. *Nazi Games: The Olympics of 1936.* New York: Norton, 2007.

Levine, Lawrence W. *Highbrow/Lowbrow: The Emergence of Cultural Hierarchy in America.* Cambridge, MA: Harvard University Press, 1988.

LeVine, Mark. *Overthrowing Geography: Jaffa, Tel Aviv, and the Struggle for Palestine, 1880 1948.* Berkeley: University of California Press, 2005.

Liebman, Charles S., and Eliezer Don-Yehiya. *Civil Religion in Israel.* Berkeley: University of California Press, 1983.

Lissak, Moshe, and Zohar Shavit, eds. *Toldot ha-yishuv ha-yehudi be-erets yisrael me-az ha-aliyah ha-rishonah* (The History of the Jewish Community in Eretz-Israel Since 1882). Jerusalem: Bialik Institute, 1998.

Lomsky-Feder, Edna, and Eyal Ben-Ari, eds. *The Military and Militarism in Israeli Society.* Albany: State University of New York Press, 1999.

Luterman, Wendy, and Hillel Tryster, eds. *Israel Newsreel Collection*, v. 1, *1932–1956.* Jerusalem: Steven Spielberg Jewish Film Archive, 1992.

Mann, Barbara E. *A Place in History: Modernism, Tel Aviv, and the Creation of Jewish Urban Space.* Stanford, CA: Stanford University Press, 2006.

Manning, Susan. *Ecstasy and the Demon: Feminism and Nationalism in the Dances of Mary Wigman.* Berkeley: University of California Press, 1993.

Manor, Dalia. *Art in Zion: The Genesis of Modern National Art in Jewish Palestine.* London: Routledge Curzon, 2005.

———. "Orientalism and Jewish National Art: The Case of Bezalel." In Ivan Davidson Kalmar and Derek J. Penslar, eds., *Orientalism and the Jews*, 142–61. Waltham, MA: Brandeis University Press, 2005.

Manor, Giora, ed. *Agadati: haluts ha-mahol ha-hadash be erets yisrael* (Agadati: Pioneer of the Modern Dance in Israel). Tel Aviv: Dance Library of Israel, 1986.

———. *Haye ha-mahol shel gertrud kraus* (The Life and Dance of Gertrud Kraus). Tel Aviv: Hakibbutz Hameuchad, 1978.

Marmorstein, Emile. *Heaven at Bay: The Jewish Kulturkamp in the Holy Land.* London: Oxford University Press, 1969.

Mayer, Paul Yogi. "Equality—Egality: Jews and Sport in Germany." *Leo Baeck Institute Yearbook* 25 (1980): 221–41.

Mayer, Tamar. "From Zero to Hero: Masculinity in Jewish Nationalism." In Esther Fuchs, ed., *Israeli Women's Studies: A Reader*, 97–117. New Brunswick, NJ: Rutgers University Press, 2005.

Meah b'tnuah (One Hundred Years of Movement). Netanya, Israel: Wingate Institute for Physical Education and Sport, 1998.

Melman, Yossi. *The New Israelis.* New York: Birch Lane Press, 1992.

Miron, Dan. *Bodedim be-moadam: li-deyoknah shel ha-republikah ha-sifruti ha-ivrit bi-tehilat ha me-ah ha-esrim* (When Loners Come Together: Hebrew Literature in the Early Twentieth Century). Tel Aviv: Am Oved, 1987.

Mosse, George L. *Confronting the Nation: Jewish and Western Nationalism.* Hanover, NH: University Press of New England, 2000.

———. *The Image of Man: The Creation of Modern Masculinity.* New York: Oxford University Press, 1996.

——— . *The Nationalization of the Masses: Political Symbolism and Mass Movements in Germany from the Napoleonic Wars Through the Third Reich.* Ithaca, NY: Cornell University Press, 1991.

Naor, Mordechay. *Tel aviv be-reshitah 1909–1934* (The Beginning of Tel Aviv, 1909–1934). Jerusalem: Yad Yitzhak Ben Tzvi Institute, 1984.

Neusner, Jacob. *History and Torah.* London: Vallentine, Mitchell, 1965.

Norwood, Stephen H. "'American Jewish Muscle': Forging a New Masculinity in the Streets and in the Ring, 1890–1940." *Modern Judaism* 29 (2009): 167–93.

Nye, Robert A. *Masculinity and Male Codes of Honor in Modern France.* New York: Oxford University Press, 1993.

Ochs, Juliana. *Security and Suspicion: An Ethnography of Everyday Life in Israel.* Philadelphia: University of Pennsylvania Press, 2011.

Ofer, Dalia. "Commemorating the Holocaust During the First Decade of Israel." *Jewish Social Studies* 6 (winter 2000): 24–55.

——— . "Fifty Years After: The Yishuv, Zionism, and the Holocaust, 1933–1948." In Yisrael Gutman and Avital Saf, eds., *Major Changes Within the Jewish People in the Wake of the Holocaust,* 463–95. Jerusalem: Yad Vashem, 1996.

Ofrat, Gideon. *One Hundred Years of Art in Israel.* Boulder, CO: Westview Press, 1998.

Oren, Ruth, and Guy Raz. *Zoltan Kluger, Tsalam Rashi, 1933–1958* (Zoltan Kluger, Chief Photographer, 1933–1958). Tel Aviv and Jerusalem: Eretz Israel Museum and Yad Izhak Ben-Zvi, 2008.

Ornstein, Margalit. "Development of the Art of Movement." *Ketuvim* (1929).

Oz, Amos. *A Tale of Love and Darkness.* New York: Harcourt, 2003.

Ozouf, Mona. *Festivals and the French Revolution.* Cambridge, MA: Harvard University Press, 1991.

Pamphlet of Agadati's Traditional Masquerade Balls. Purim 1929. Jewish National and University Library (Jerusalem, Israel). Hebrew.

Partsch-Bergsohn, Isa. *Modern Dance in Germany and the United States.* Philadelphia: Harwood Academic, 1994.

Peleg, Yaron. *Orientalism and the Hebrew Imagination.* Ithaca, NY: Cornell University Press, 2005.

Penslar, Derek J. "Broadcast Orientalism: Representations of Mizrahi Jewry in Israeli Radio, 1948–1967." In Ivan Davidson Kalmar and Derek J. Penslar, eds., *Orientalism and the Jews,* 182–200. Waltham, MA: Brandeis University Press, 2005.

——— . *Israel in History: The Jewish State in Comparative Perspective.* London: Routledge, 2007.

——— . "Transmitting Jewish Culture: Radio in Israel." *Jewish Social Studies* 10.1 (2003): 1–29.

——— . *Zionism and Technocracy: The Engineering of Jewish Settlement in Palestine, 1870–1918.* Bloomington: Indiana University Press, 1991.

Petrone, Karen. *Life Has Become More Joyous, Comrades: Celebrations in the Time of Stalin.* Bloomington: Indiana University Press, 2000.

Pieterse, Jan Nederveen. "Aesthetics of Power: Time and Body Politics." *Third Text* 22 (spring 1993): 33–42.

Piterberg, Gabriel. "Domestic Orientalism: The Representation of 'Oriental' Jews in Zionist/Israeli Historiography." *British Journal of Middle Eastern Studies* 23 (1996): 125–45.

Pomrock, Zvi Abraham. *Chelouche: ha-telavivi ha-rishon* (Chelouche: The First Tel-Avivian). Jerusalem: Carmel, 2007.

Porat, Dina. *The Blue and Yellow Stars of David: The Zionist Leadership in Palestine and the Holocaust, 1939–1945.* Cambridge, MA: Harvard University Press, 1990.

Portnoy, Eddy. "Move Over Miss Polonia." *Guilt and Pleasure* 2 (spring 2006): 113–19.

Presner, Todd. *Muscle Judaism: The Jewish Body and the Politics of Regeneration.* New York: Routledge, 2007.

Program Booklet for Agadati's Traditional Masquerade Balls. Purim 1930. Jewish National and University Library (Jerusalem, Israel). Hebrew.

Programme for Purim. Jerusalem: Head Office of the Jewish National Fund, c. 1930. Central Zionist Archives (Jerusalem, Israel), 15223.

Putney, Clifford. *Muscular Christianity: Manhood and Sports in Protestant America, 1880–1920.* Cambridge, MA: Harvard University Press, 2001.

Ratzaby, Shalom. "The Polemic About the 'Negation of the Diaspora' in the 1930s and Its Roots." *Journal of Israeli History* 16 (1995): 19–38.

Raz-Krakotzkin, Amnon. "The Zionist Return to the West and the Mizrahi Jewish Perspective." In Ivan Davidson Kalmar and Derek J. Penslar, eds. *Orientalism and the Jews*, 162–81. Waltham, MA: Brandeis University Press, 2005.

Rebhun, Uzi, and Chaim Waxman, eds. *Jews in Israel: Contemporary Social and Cultural Patterns.* Waltham, MA: Brandeis University Press, 2004.

Regev, Motti, and Edwin Seroussi. *Popular Music and National Culture in Israel.* Berkeley: University of California Press, 2004.

Reinharz, Jehuda, and Anita Shapira, eds. *Essential Papers on Zionism.* New York: New York University Press, 1996.

Reiss, Steven A. "Tough Jews: The Jewish American Boxing Experience, 1890–1950." In Steven A. Reiss, ed., *Sports and the American Jew*, 60–104. Syracuse, NY: Syracuse University Press, 1998.

Reuveni, Gideon. "Sports and Militarization in Jewish Society." In Michael Brenner and Gideon Reuveni, eds., *Emancipation Through Muscles: Jews and Sports in Europe*, 44–61. Lincoln: University of Nebraska Press, 2006.

Riley, Denise. *Am I That Name? Feminism and the Category of "Women" in History.* Minneapolis: University of Minnesota Press, 1988.

Rinott, Moshe. "Religion and Education: The Cultural Question and the Zionist Movement, 1897–1913." *Studies in Zionism* 5 (spring 1984): 1–17.

Roberts, Mary Louise. *Civilization Without Sexes: Reconstructing Gender in Postwar France, 1917-1927.* Chicago: University of Chicago Press, 1994.

Rodrigue, Aron. *Images of Sephardi and Eastern Jewries in Transition: The Teachers of the Alliance Israélite Universelle, 1860-1939.* Seattle: University of Washington Press, 1993.

Roginsky, Dina. "The Israeli Folk Dance Movement: Structural Changes and Cultural Meanings." In Judith Brin Ingber, ed., *Seeing Israeli and Jewish Dance,* 315-27. Detroit: Wayne State University Press, 2011.

———. "Orientalism, the Body, and Cultural Politics in Israel: Sara Levi Tanai and the Inbal Dance Theater." *Nashim* 11 (spring 2006): 164-97.

Rokem, Freddie. "Ha-dybbuk be-erets yisrael: hateatron, habikoret, ve-hitgavshuta shel ha-tarbut ha-ivrit" (The Reception of *The Dybbuk* in Palestine: Theatre, Criticism, and the Emergence of Hebrew Culture). *Katedrah* 20 (July 1981): 183-202.

———. "Hebrew Theater from 1889 to 1948." In Linda Ben-Zvi, ed., *Theater in Israel,* 51-84. Ann Arbor: University of Michigan Press, 1996.

Roshwald, Aviel. *The Endurance of Nationalism: Ancient Roots and Modern Dilemmas.* New York: Cambridge University Press, 2006.

Ross, Janice. *Moving Lessons: Margaret H. Doubler and the Beginning of Dance in American Education.* Madison: University of Wisconsin Press, 2000.

Sachar, Howard M. *A History of Israel: From the Rise of Zionism to Our Time.* New York: Knopf, 2007.

Said, Edward. *Orientalism.* New York: Vintage, 1978.

Saposnik, Arieh Bruce. *Becoming Hebrew: The Creation of a Jewish National Culture in Ottoman Palestine.* Oxford, UK: Oxford University Press, 2008.

Savigliano, Marta E. *Tango and the Political Economy of Passion.* Boulder, CO: Westview Press, 1995.

Schlör, Joachim. *Tel Aviv: From Dream to City.* London: Reaktion Books, 1999.

Schmidt, Gilya Gerda. *The Art and Artists of the Fifth Zionist Congress, 1901.* Syracuse, NY: Syracuse University Press, 2003.

Schoeps, Julius H. "Modern Heirs of the Maccabees: The Beginning of the Vienna Kadimah, 1882-1897." *Leo Baeck Institute Yearbook* 27 (1982): 155-70.

Schweid, Eliezer. "The Rejection of the Diaspora in Zionist Thought: Two Approaches." *Studies in Zionism* 5 (spring 1984): 43-70.

Scott, Joan Wallach. *Gender and the Politics of History.* New York: Columbia University Press, 1988.

Sefer hamaccabiah. Tel Aviv: Maccabi World Union, 1935. Hebrew.

Segev, Tom. *One Palestine, Complete: Jews and Arabs Under the British Mandate.* New York: Henry Holt, 2000.

———. *The Seventh Million: The Israelis and the Holocaust.* New York: Hill & Wang 1994.

Sered, Susan Starr. *What Makes Women Sick? Maternity, Modesty, and Militarism in Israeli Society.* Hanover, NH: University Press of New England, 2000.

Shaffer, Marguerite S., ed. *Public Culture: Diversity, Democracy, and Community in the United States.* Philadelphia: University of Pennsylvania Press, 2008.

Shafir, Gershon. *Land, Labor, and the Origins of the Palestinian Conflict, 1882–1914.* New York: Cambridge University Press, 1989.

Shahar, Natan. "The Eretz Israeli Song and the Jewish National Fund." In Ezra Mendelsohn, ed., *Studies in Contemporary Jewry 9*, 78–91. New York: Oxford University Press, 1993.

Shaked, Gershon. *Panim aherot bi-yetsirato shel shai agnon* (Agnon: A Writer with a Thousand Faces). Tel Aviv: Hakibbutz Hameuchad, 1989.

Shapira, Anita. *Land and Power: The Zionist Resort to Force, 1881–1948.* New York: Oxford University Press, 1992.

——— . "The Origins of the Myth of the 'New Jew': The Zionist Variety." In Jonathan Frankel, ed., *Studies in Contemporary Jewry 13*, 253–68. New York: Oxford University Press, 1997.

Sharett, Rena. *Kuma eha* (Arise, Brother). Tel Aviv: Tel Aviv Press, 1988.

Sharnopolsky, S. *Guide to Palestine: Palestine Land of Health Resorts—Moreh-derekh le-eretz yisrael.* Tel Aviv: Hashachar, 1936. Eliasaf Robinson Collection, Stanford University.

Shavit, Yaakov, Yaakov Goldshtain, and Hayim Beer, eds. *Leksikon ha-ishim shel erets-yisrael, 1799–1948* (Dictionary of Personalities in Eretz Israel, 1799–1948). Tel Aviv: Am Oved, 1983.

Shavit, Yaakov, and Shoshana Sitton. *Staging and Stagers in Modern Jewish Palestine: Creation of Festive Lore in a New Culture, 1882–1948.* Detroit: Wayne State University Press, 2004.

Shavit, Zohar. *Ha-hayim ha-sifrutiyim be-erets yisrael, 1910–1933* (Literary Life in Eretz Israel, 1910–1933). Tel Aviv: Hakibbutz Hameuchad, 1982.

Shay, Anthony. *Choreographic Politics: State Folk Dance Companies, Representation, and Power.* Middletown, CT: Wesleyan University Press, 2002.

Sherman, Atara. "Physical Education in the United States and Eretz-Israel, a Comparative Study: 1881–1932." In Uriel Simri, ed., *Comparative Physical Education and Sport: Proceedings of an International Seminar*, 198–209. Netanya, Israel: Wingate Institute for Physical Education and Sport, 1979.

Shoham, Hizky. "'A Huge National Assemblage': Tel Aviv as a Pilgrimage Site in Purim Celebrations (1920–1935)." *Journal of Israeli History* 28 (March 2009): 1–20.

——— . "Purim Celebrations in Tel Aviv, 1908–1936: A Renewed Study of Symbols, Tradition, and Public Sphere in Popular Zionist Culture" (Hebrew). Ph.D. diss., Bar-Ilan University, Ramat Gan, Israel, 2006.

Shohat, Ella. "The Invention of the Mizrahim." *Journal of Palestine Studies* 29 (fall 1999): 5–20.

——— . "Mizrahim in Israel: Zionism from the Standpoint of Its Jewish Victims." *Social Text* 19/20 (fall 1988): 1–35.

Silver-Brody, Vivienne. *Documenters of the Dream: Pioneer Jewish Photographers in the Land of Israel: 1890–1933.* Jerusalem: Magnes Press, 1998.

——. *"Mood and Movement": Alfons Himmelreich's Dance Photographs, 1936–1961.* Ramat Gan, Israel: Museum of Israeli Art, 1987.

Simri, Uriel. *Ha-hinuh ha-gufani ve ha-sport b'eretz yisrael bashanim 1917–1927* (Physical Education and Sport in Eretz Israel, 1917–1927). Netanya, Israel: Wingate Institute for Physical Education and Sport, 1971.

Simri, Uriel, and Meir Benayahu. *Ha-hinuh ha-gufani ve ha-sport b'eretz yisrael lifnei milhemet ha-olam ha-rishona* (Physical Education and Sports in Eretz Israel Before World War I). Netanya, Israel: Wingate Institute for Physical Education and Sport, 1969.

Smooha, Sammy. "Jewish Ethnicity in Israel: Symbolic or Real." In Uzi Rebhun and Chaim Waxman, eds., *Jews in Israel: Contemporary Social and Cultural Patterns,* 47–80. Waltham, MA: Brandeis University Press, 2003.

Sobel, Zvi, and Benjamin Beit-Hallahmi. "Introduction." In Zvi Sobel and Benjamin Beit-Hallahmi, eds., *Tradition, Innovation, Conflict: Jewishness and Judaism in Contemporary Israel,* 1–22. Albany: State University of New York Press, 1991.

Söder, Hans-Peter. "A Tale of Dr. Jekyll and Mr. Hyde? Max Nordau and the Problem of Degeneracy." In Rudolf Käser and Vera Pohland, eds., *Disease and Medicine in Modern German Cultures,* 56–70. Ithaca, NY: Cornell University Press, 1990.

Spencer, Paul. *Society and the Dance.* Cambridge, UK: Cambridge University Press, 1985.

Spiegel, Nina S. "Constructing the City of Tel Aviv: Urban Space, Physical Culture, and the Natural and Built Environment." *Rethinking History: The Journal of Theory and Practice* 16, no. 4 (2012): 497–516.

——. "Cultural Formulation in Eretz Israel: The National Dance Competition of 1937." *Jewish Folklore and Ethnology Review* 20 (2000): 24–38.

——. "Cultural Production in Tel Aviv: Yardena Cohen and the National Dance Competition of 1937." In Judith Brin Ingber, ed., *Seeing Israeli and Jewish Dance,* 71–87. Detroit: Wayne State University Press, 2011.

——. "New Israeli Rituals: Inventing a Folk Dance Tradition." In Simon J. Bronner, ed., *Jewish Cultural Studies 3,* 392–418. Oxford, UK: Littman Library of Jewish Civilization, 2011.

——. "Sporting a Nation: The Origins of Athleticism in Modern Israel." In Leonard J. Greenspoon, ed., *Jews in the Gym: Judaism, Sports, and Athletics,* 189–96. West Lafayette, IN: Purdue University Press, 2012.

Stanislawski, Michael. *Zionism and the Fin de Siècle: Cosmopolitanism and Nationalism from Nordau to Jabotinsky.* Berkeley: University of California Press, 2001.

Stein, Kenneth W. *The Land Question in Palestine, 1917–1939.* Chapel Hill: University of North Carolina Press, 1984.

Stern, Bat-Sheva Margalit. "Who's the Fairest of Them All? Women, Womanhood, and Ethnicity in Zionist Eretz Israel." *Nashim: A Journal of Jewish Women's Studies and Gender Issues* 11 (2006): 142–63.

Taylor, Matthew. "Round the London Ring: Boxing, Class, and Community in Interwar London." *London Journal* 34 (July 2009): 139–62.

Toepfer, Karl. *Empire of Ecstasy: Nudity and Movement in German Body Culture, 1910–1935.* Berkeley: University of California Press, 1997.

Troen, S. Ilan. *Imagining Zion: Dreams, Designs, and Realities in a Century of Jewish Settlement.* New Haven, CT: Yale University Press, 2003.

Tryster, Hillel. *Israel Before Israel: Silent Cinema in the Holy Land.* Bloomington: Indiana University Press, 1995.

———. "'The Land of Promise' (1935): A Case Study in Zionist Film Propaganda." *Historical Journal of Film, Radio, and Television* 15 (1995): 187–217.

Veidlinger, Jeffrey. *Jewish Public Culture in the Late Russian Empire.* Bloomington: Indiana University Press, 2009.

Vertinsky, Patricia. "Isadora Goes to Europe as the 'Muse of Modernism': Modern Dance, Gender, and the Active Female Body." *Journal of Sport History* 37 (spring 2010): 19–39.

Walkowitz, Daniel J., and Lisa Maya Knauer, eds. *Contested Histories in Public Space: Memory, Race, and Nation.* Durham, NC: Duke University Press, 2009.

Wedemeyer, Bernd. "Body-Building or Man in the Making: Aspects of the German Bodybuilding Movement in the Kaiserreich and Weimar Republic." *International Journal of the History of Sport* 11 (December 1994): 472–84.

Wein, Chaim. *The Maccabiah Games in Eretz Israel.* Israel: Maccabi World Union and Wingate Institute for Physical Education and Sport, 1983.

Weiss, Meira. *The Chosen Body: The Politics of the Body in Israeli Society.* Stanford, CA: Stanford University Press, 2002.

Wu, Judy Tzu-Chun. "'Loveliest Daughter of Our Ancient Cathay!': Representations of Ethnic and Gender Identity in the Miss Chinatown U.S.A. Beauty Pageant." *Journal of Social History* 31 (fall 1997): 5–31.

"*Yahadut ha-sheririm*": *Yehudim be'olam ha-sport* (Jews in the World of Sports). Tel Aviv: Bet ha-tefutsot 'al shem Nahum Goldman, 1985.

Yahav, Dan. "'Hapoel'-'Maccabi': maavak ideologi-politi bishnot ha-esrim ve-ha-sheloshim" ("'Hapoel'-'Maccabi': Ideological Political Struggle in the 1920s and 1930s"). *Mifne* 7 (December 1994): 44–47.

Yoffe, A. B., ed. *Esrim ha-shanim ha-rishonot: sifrut ve-omanut be-tel aviv ha-ketanah, 1909–1929* (The First Twenty Years: Literature and Arts in Tel-Aviv, 1909–1929). Tel Aviv: Keren Tel Aviv le-sifrut ule-omanut ve-Hotsaat ha-Kibuts ha-meuhad, 1980.

Young, James E. *The Texture of Memory: Holocaust Memorials and Meaning.* New Haven, CT: Yale University Press, 1994.

———. "When a Day Remembers: A Performative History of Yom Hashoah." *History and Memory* 2 (winter 1990): 54–75.

Zakim, Eric. "The Case of the Missing Representation: Abstraction, Orientalism, and the

1929 Wailing Wall Riots in Palestine." In Eliyana R. Adler and Sheila E. Jelen, eds., *Jewish Literature and History: An Interdisciplinary Conversation*, 177–206. Bethesda: University Press of Maryland, 2008.

———. *To Build and Be Built: Landscapes, Literature, and the Construction of Israeli Identity.* Philadelphia: University of Pennsylvania Press, 2006.

Zeira, Moti. *Keru'im anu: zikhatah shel ha-hityashvut ha-ovedet bi-shenot ha-eshrim el ha-tarbut ha-yehudit* (Rural Collective Settlement and Jewish Culture in Eretz Israel during the 1920s). Jerusalem: Yad Yitzhak Ben Zvi, 2002.

Zerubavel, Yael. *Recovered Roots: Collective Memory and the Making of Israeli National Tradition.* Chicago: University of Chicago Press, 1995.

Zipperstein, Steven J. *Elusive Prophet: Ahad Ha'am and the Origins of Zionism.* Berkeley: University of California Press, 1993.

Zweiniger-Bargielowska, Ina. "Building a British Superman: Physical Culture in Interwar Britain." *Journal of Contemporary History* 41 (October 2006): 595–610.

.

Index

Page numbers in italics refer to illustrations

Abramov, Dinah, 199n63
Adloyada. See Purim, in Tel Aviv
aesthetic of defiance, 19–20, 21; and
   contemporary Israeli culture, 180–81; and
   Dalia Folk Dance Festivals, 135, 154–58, 176;
   and Maccabiah Games, 58, 81–83, 176; and
   Queen Esther competitions, 44–45, 55
aesthetic of fusion, 15–17, 20; and
   contemporary Israeli culture, 178–79; and
   Israeli folk dance, 152–54, 172; and National
   Dance Competition, 107, 108–15, 128–31,
   176; and Queen Esther competitions,
   40–44, 55, 176
aesthetic of togetherness, 17–18, 20, 83–85;
   Dalia Folk Dance Festivals, 161–62;
   Maccabiah Games, 83–85
aesthetic of toughness, 8–11, 20, 191n49; and
   contemporary Israeli culture, 179–80; and
   Dalia Folk Dance Festivals, 158–60, 176;
   image of, *10*; and Jewish body, 8–11, 158–59;
   and Maccabiah Games, 75–80, 176
Agadati: galas, 27, 35, 196n16
Agadati, Baruch (Baruch Kaushanski), 30, 49,
   99, 138, 196n14, 197n23; and cancellation

of Queen Esther competition, 45, 51–54;
carnival balls, 27, 35, 198n37; *Hora
Agadati,* Dalia Festival, 1947, 150; *Kan*
(Here), 196n16; manifestos in name of
Esther, 52–54; masquerade gala of 1931,
203n123; selection of Queen in 1931,
53–54; and symbol of lions carrying
tablets, 28
Aga Film, 203n117
Agudat Yisrael, 173
Ahad Ha'am (Asher Ginsburg), 4, 12, 72, 101
Aharonson, Shlomo Hacohen, 47
Ahasuerus, 22
Ahdut Ha'avoda, 194n88
Aisenstein, Bathia, 199n63
al-Jama'a, 93
Alliance Israèlite Universelle (AIU), 190n37
Almog, Oz, 19–20
Aloni, Menahem, 145
Alouf, Yehoshua, 68
The Ambassador, 185
Amitai, Mordechai, 155
Amos, Dan B., 151
Anaphaza (Ohad Naharin), Batsheva Dance
   Company, *183*–84
Ansky, S., 116

anti-Semitism: and athletics, 72–73; rise of in Europe, 73, 81; stereotyped image of Jewish body, 9, 75–76

Arab dance: considered to be low culture, 125; debate about incorporation into Israeli folk dance, 152–54; debka, 139, 143, 153, 196n16, 215n6, 218n71; ethnography used to describe, 125–26; viewed as connected to land, 153

Arab riots of 1929, 19, 44, 55, 72, 81, 176

Arazi, Shlomo, 67

Argentina (Spanish dancer), 126

Arlosoroff, Chaim, 12, 92

Armon Theatrical Agency, Tel Aviv, 103

Armored Corps, 177

arts institutions, 15–16

Ashkenazim, 23, 110, 172, 178

athletics: and anti-Semitism, 72–73; connection to nationalism in Europe, 72; as way of transforming Jewish people, 73. *See also* Maccabiah athletes; Maccabiah Games, first

At the Well (Yemenite Ballet Company), *118–19*, 125

Ausdruckstanz. See German dance expressionism

Austria, 18, 68, 72, 136, 206n44

Avi-Shulamit, A., 42, 55–56

Avizohar, Y., 46

Balfour, Lord, 12

ballet, 101–2, 104, 114, 118–19, 127, 129, 146, 180; biblical, 116

Ballet Russes, 210n11

Bar Kokba revolt, 60–61

Bartal, Israel, 192n62

Batsheva Dance Company, 7; performance for Israel's fiftieth anniversary, 181–83

belly dancing, 110

Ben, Zehava, 179

Benari (Brodsky), Nahum, 151, 153, 161, 164, 168–69

Ben-Avi, Itamar, 61–62, 88

Ben Baruch, Shalom, 80, 81

Ben-Gurion, David, 1, 194n88; condemned Dalia Festival on Sabbath, 163–64; status quo agreement, 181

Benjamin (Rabbi). *See* Hatalmi, Yehoshua (Rabbi Benjamin)

Ben Shemen (youth village), 136

Ben-Yehuda, Eliezer, 61

Ben-Yishai, Ze'ev, 49, 52, 66; "Eulogy for Queen Esther," 50–51

Bergstein, Lea, 138, 150

Berkovitz, Y. D., 26

Berlin, Meir, 166

Berlin Maccabi club, 207n68

Bertonov, Devorah, 138, 152–53

The Beseda (Czech dance), on pergola stage, Dalia Festival, 1944, *141*

Betar (Revisionist sports organization), 68, 86

Bezalel School of Arts and Crafts (now Bezalel Academy of Art), 15, 27, 28, 99

bikkurim (Hag Ha-Bikkurim), 14, 137, 151. *See also* Shavuot

Black Sabbath, 152

Bloch, Zev, 169–70

Blumenfeld, Leon, 116

Blumenfeld, Rachel, 53, *54*, 203n118

Bodenweiser, Gertrud, 104

Borrer, A. (pseud.), 49–50

boxing, Jews in Europe and U.S., 73

Brainin, David, *105*

Brenner, Michael, 73

Brenner, Yosef Haim, 12

British Mandate, 1–2; curfew for Dalia Folk Dance Festival, 1947, 140, 143; development of football under, 92–93; expansion of Tel Aviv during, 17–18; opposition to second Maccabiah Games, 92, 96; support of first Maccabiah Games, 58, 66, 92–93, 96. *See also* Yishuv

Bukharan Queen Esther, 201n88

Butler, Judith, 9

Cain and Abel (Ornstein Sisters), 102, 105, 107

Calatrava, Santiago, 183

camels, 27, 43, 198n40

Carmiel, Batia, 28, 198n42

celebration versus sorrow dichotomy. *See* aesthetic of defiance

Chancellor, John, 66

Chelouche, Aharon, 30, *31*

Chelouche, Avraham, 30

Chelouche, Riquetta, 30, 32, 40

Chelouche, Ya'akov, 30

Chelouche, Yosef Eliyahu, 30

Chords Bridge, Jerusalem (Bridge of Springs), 177; inauguration of in 2008, 177, 183–84

Choreographers Association, 6–7

Cohen, Colleen Ballerino, 29

Cohen, Idan, 185

Cohen, Mortimer J., 40, 42

Cohen, Yardena, 102, 104, 107–15, 125–31, 138, 145, 150, 212n22, 212n39; and aesthetic of fusion, 115, 130, 131; critics' assessments of her work, 125–31; *The Dance of Ovadia,* Dalia Festival, 1947, 150; East-West dichotomy, 107, 109–15; and Goldberg, 215n98; *Hallel,* 138; influenced by German dance expressionism, 111–12; *The Mourner: A Woman Whose Art Is to Lament,* 107, *108,* 115; schooled in European rehearsal model, 110–11; and Sephardic musicians, 109–11, 115; *The Sorceress: A Magician and Fortune Teller in Biblical Times and Today,* 107, 111–*12, 113,* 115; *A Village Dance: Debka,* 102, 115; *The Wedding Dance: How Does One Dance Before the Bride,* 112, *114,* 115

Collins, Tony, 92

concert dance. *See* theatrical dance

Council for the Sabbath, 164

Courbertin, Pierre de, 59

Crowning of the People's Muse (French folk festival), 27

Cultural Division, Histadrut, 133, 141, 151, 153, 154, 161, 164

Cymbal, Tova, 150

Dalia Folk Dance Festivals, 4, 7, 133–73; aesthetic of defiance, 135, 154–58, 176; aesthetic of togetherness, 161–62; aesthetic of toughness, 158–60, 176; collective singing of "Hatikvah," 161; encompassed major tensions of Yishuv, 134; goal of fostering national folk dance, 7, 134, 172; held after establishment of state,

7, 133; ideals of socialist Zionism, 135, 158–59; issue of participation of concert dancers, 145–46, 172; occurred during and after World War II and Holocaust, 135; and production of folk culture, 12; and question of folk dance performance, 147; Sabbath controversy (*See* Sabbath controversy, Dalia Folk Dance Festival); spread to Diaspora, 7; women and men dancing together, 158. *See also* Dalia Folk Dance Festival, 1944; Dalia Folk Dance Festival, 1947

Dalia Folk Dance Festival, 1944: *The Beseda* (Czech dance), on pergola stage, *141;* dancing during, *159; Davka* (Gertrud Kraus), 155; held on the Sabbath, 135, 219n99; initiated and organized by Gurit Kadman, 136–38; *Megillat Rut* (Story of Ruth), pageant of, 137, 138, *139, 140;* nicknamed *davka* event, 155; program, 138–40; *Shir Ha-shirim* (The Song of Songs), 139

Dalia Folk Dance Festival, 1947, 140–44; Arab participants, *142,* 143–44; British-imposed curfew, 140, 143; crowds at, 141–43; *Dance of the Well, 149;* extensive press coverage, 141; folk and holiday dances, 150–51; folk dance group performing at, *160;* folk dancers in vineyard of Kibbutz Dalia, *160;* and Gurit Kadman, 141–43; *Mayim, Mayim* (dance), 150; schedule change, 151–52; *Vayehi Or* (And There Was Light), *157,* 158

Damari, Saadia, 139

Dana International, 185

dance companies, in contemporary Israel, 6

Dance Magazine, 116

Dance of Esau (Tehilla Rössler), 102

The Dance of Ovadia (Yardena Cohen), Dalia Festival, 1947, 150

Dance of the Guards (Yemenite Ballet Company), 117–18

Dance of the Well, Dalia Festival, 1947, *149*

Davar, 15, 46, 51, 65, 93, 144, 168, 202n105

davka, 19–20, 97, 156, 159

The Day Came, 187n1

debka, 102, 115, 139, 143, 196n16, 215n6, 218n71

Debka (Yardena Cohen; Yemenite Ballet
Company), 102, 118
Diaghilev, Serge, 210n11
Diaspora Jews: anti-Semitic image of bodies
of, 9, 75–76; Orientalized in Yishuv, 16;
prominence in athletics in interwar period,
73
Dizengoff, Meir, 66; and cancellation of
Purim carnival procession in 1929, 45;
contribution to building of Maccabiah
stadium, 205n33; and Maccabiah Games,
68, 69, 70; reception of Queen Esther in
Agadati's 1931 revival, 53, *54*
Do'ar ha-Yom, 30, 51, 61, 64, 82, 90, 93, 100,
199n49
Dublon, Elsa, 102, 212n27
dugri, 180
Duncan, Isadora, 115, 213n52

East-West dichotomy, 18; and contemporary
Israeli culture, 178–79; and folk dance,
152–54, 175; and Jewish beauty, 40–44, 55,
175; and theatrical dance, 107, 175; Western
European Jewish attitudes toward North
African and Middle Eastern Jews, 190n37
educational system, focus on *yedi'at ha'aretz*
(knowledge of the land), 17
Ehrenkranz, Yehuda, 158
El Al, 181
Elbaz, Andre, 178
Elitzur, 75
Erdman, Joan L., 114
Eretz Israel, 187n2
Eretz Israeli dance. *See* theatrical dance
Eretz Israeli Song Competition, 102, 210n13,
211n14
Eretz Israeli songs, 67
Eretz Israeli Sports Federation, 205n22
Erleigh, Lady, 69
Esther, Queen, biblical story of, 5, 21, 22
Europe: association with high culture, 99,
124–25; carnivals, 27, 196n19; connection
of athletics to nationalism, 72; and
degenerating Jewish life in Diaspora, 16;
folk dances, 140; interwar emphasis on
physical culture, 11; nationalism, 13, 14; rise

of anti-Semitism in, 73, 81
Eurovision contest, 185

festival of choirs, 136–37
festival of the vineyards, 14
Fichman, Y., 26
fifth aliyah, 18
Fifth Zionist Congress, Basel, 187n6
film, achievements in, 16
Fishman (Maimon), Rabbi Yehuda Leib, 163,
164
flower wars, 23, 198n38
folk arts, 16
folk dance, Israeli, 102, 133, 189n23; and
aesthetic of fusion, 152–54, 172; and
aesthetic of toughness, 158–60; attempts to
re-create biblical dances, 148–50; Bible and
Jewish holidays as sources of inspiration,
135, 147–48, 150; dancers' tour of European
Displaced Persons camps, 219n85; dances
performed at closing performance,
Dalia Festival, 1947, 150; development of
"Hebrew-style" dance, 148; distinctions
between folk and concert dance, 131, 145;
East-West dichotomy, 152–54; efforts to
distinguish from theatrical dance, 98; and
high-low cultural dichotomy, 135, 144–47,
172; and labor Zionist values, 135; and
old-new dichotomy, 147–52; paradox of
creating, 144–47, 172; as performance, 147;
set structure and designated music, 145;
viewed as form of resistance, 155–56. *See
also* Dalia Folk Dance Festivals
football, development in Palestine in 1920s by
British, 92–93
fourth aliyah, 18
Freedman, Chaim, 218n74
Friedman, Yehezkel, 64
funerals, public, 12

galut, 2, 16
Gamzu, Haim, 149
German dance expressionism (*Ausdruckstanz*),
101–2, 111–12
German gymnastics movement, 9, 72
German Physical Culture Movement, 9

Germany, immigration of Jews from, 18
gibush, 178
Gitai, Amos, 184–85
golah, 2
Goldberg, Leah: and Dalia Folk Dance Festival, 144, 148, 150, 152–54; and National Dance Competition, 104, 121, 122–23, 124, 126, 127, 129
Gordon, A. D., 17, 155, 194n88, 218n76
Gordon, Judah Leib: "Awake, My People," 76, 79
Grazovsky, Y., 26
Greenboim, Yitzhak, 163–64, 219n104
Gronemann, Sammy, 103–4, 211n17
Gutmann, Nahum, 196n9
Gutman (Piltz), Ilza, 137

Ha'am, Ahad, 4, 12, 72, 101
Ha'aretz, 15, 30, 37, 38, 90, 93; articles discussing connection between Olympics and Maccabiah Games, 60; initiation of literature section, 99; views about Dalia Festivals in, 146, 156, 161, 167; views about Queen Esther competition in, 41–42, 46–48, 199n49
Habima (The Stage), 15, 67
Haboker, 107, 116, 121, 167
Hadassah, 63
Haganah, 152
Haggadah, 193n70, 200n70
Hag Ha-Bikkurim. *See* Shavuot
Ha-goren (Rivka Sturman), 139, 196n16
Haitztadion (The Stadium), 76, 77
Hakoah, Vienna, 73
Halachmi, Chaim, 196n12
Halevi, Moshe, 197n23
Hallel (Yardena Cohen), 138
halutza (female pioneer), 38, *39*
Haman, 22, 51, 53
Hameiri, Avigdor, 49, 67, 81, 87–88, 202n107; "Hymn for the Maccabees," 76, 79–80
Hanukkah, 13
Hapoel, 36, 74–75; boycott of Maccabiah Games, 85–89, 95, 175
Hapoel Hamizrahi (the Mizrahi Worker), 163
Hapoel Hatzair, 50, 194n88

Harris, Monford, 22
Ha-Shadchan [The Matchmaker] (Elsa Dublon), 102
Hasidic dance, 152–53, 161–62
Hatalmi, Yehoshua (Rabbi Benjamin), 81–82
"Hatikvah," 70, 71, 72, 161, 178, 187n6, 206n52
Hazit ha-Am, 82
Ha-zofeh, 162, 163, 165
Hebrew aesthetics, and societal tensions, 7–20
Hebrew language: modernization of, 11, 15; one of three official languages of Palestine in 1922, 15
Hebrew literature, movement of center from Europe to Palestine, 15
Hebrew press and radio, 15
Hebrew University, 12, 15
Hefker, 40, *41,* 43
Herzl, Theodor, 3, 192n59; *Altneuland,* 11–12, 109
Herzliya Gymnasium, Tel Aviv, 68, 72, 90
Herzog, Yitzhak HaLevi, 165–66
Hey Harmonika (Rivka Sturman), Dalia Festival, 1947, 150
high-low cultural dichotomy, 18; and folk dance, 135, 144–47, 172; and National Dance Competition, 98–99, 125–28
Histadrut (General Federation of Labourers in the Land of Israel), 74–75, 215n2; Cultural Division, 133, 141, 151, 153, 154, 161, 164
Hitler, Adolph, 18, 19, 140
H.L.H. (journalist), 65, 89, 94–95
Hobsbawn, Eric, 11
Hoffman, Yaniv, 183
holiday dances, Dalia Festival, 1947, 150
holidays and festivals: celebrating the Yishuv, 12; emphasizing outdoors and agriculture, 13–14; and the kibbutzim, 14–136; new ways of celebrating, 13–14; in Ottoman period, 12. *See also specific holidays and festivals*
Holm, Hanya, 106
Holocaust, 19; folk dance festivals during and after, 135, 155
Holocaust Martyrs and Heroes Remembrance Day (Yom Hashoah Ve-Hagevurah), 184

Holocaust memorial ceremony, 1947 Dalia
Festival, *157*, 158
Hora Agadati (Baruch Agadati), Dalia Festival,
1947, 150, 215n6
hora dancing: in celebration of establishment
of state of Israel, 1–2; at Dalia Festival,
1947, 150; linked to tourism in Palestine, 7;
and Maccabiah Games, 67–68; and Purim
festivals, 23, 196n16
Hora (Tehilla Rössler), National Dance
Competition, 102
Huberman, Bronislav, 15
"Hymn of Purim," 28

Idelsohn, Abraham Zvi (Ben-Yehuda), 15
Imber, Naftali Herz, 206n52
Inbal Dance Company, 7, 178–79
Independence Day holiday. *See* Yom
Ha'atzmaut
India, 19
Institute of Jewish Song (Institute of Jewish
Music), 15
Inter-Kibbutz Music Committee, 133, 136
internal Orientalism: applied to Arab
and Eastern European Jews, 16, 153; in
Ashkenazic society, 40–43; in theatrical
dance, 107, 109–15, 116, 117
International Folk Dance Festival and
Conference, 1935, 211n15
Israel, State of: establishment of, 1; lack of
recognition of diversity of subcultures
in early years, 178; Independence Day
celebrations, 1
Israeli culture, contemporary: absence of
civil marriage and divorce, 181; aesthetic
of defiance, 180–81; aesthetic of fusion,
178–79; aesthetic of toughness, 179–80;
aggressive driving, dancing, and speech,
180, 221n13; as culture of debate, 184–85;
debate over Sabbath observance in public
sphere, 181; East-West dichotomy, 178–79;
embodied public culture, 184–85; "ethos of
the warrior," 179; intertwined with politics,
185; old-new dichotomy, 177; religious-
secular dichotomy, 181–84; socialist-
bourgeois dichotomy, 177–78; tensions and

aesthetics in, 176–84
Israeli folk dance. *See* folk dance, Israeli
Israeli Folk Dance Committee, 133
Israel Prize, 136

jazz cafes, 18
Jepthah's Daughter (Yehudit Ornstein and
Studio), National Dance Competition, 105,
107
Jewish Agency, 163, 173
Jewish-Arab relations, and Maccabiah Games,
93–95
Jewish beauty: East-West dichotomy, 40–44;
lack of ideal, 36–37; and nationalism, 29–36
Jewish body: and aesthetic of toughness, 8–11,
158–59; anti-Semitic image of European
Jewish body, 9, 75–76; goal of cultivation of
in Yishuv, 59, 72, 76–80; "new," 158. *See also*
muscle Jewry
Jewish gymnastic associations, 9
Jewish National Fund (JNF), 22, 27, 45, 196n14,
197n23; and Dalia Sabbath controversy,
164; Poster, 1930s, *10*
Jewish sports associations, in Europe, 73
Jewish summer camps, U.S.: "Dalia Dance
evenings," 7
Jooss, Kurt, 102
Jordan, Ruth, 8, 20, 95, 115

Kadman, Gurit (Gert Kaufmann), 133, 135, 147,
153, 188n17, 215n6, 216n11; aim to establish
community of dancers, 161; decision to
convene dance festival during Holocaust,
155, 218n74; first leadership course for
folk dance leaders at Kibbutz Teachers'
Seminar, 215n3; and goal of Dalia Festivals,
147; and hora dancing at Dalia Festival,
1947, 150; incorporation of Holocaust
remembrance into 1947 festival, *157*,
158; initiation and organization of Dalia
Festivals, 136–39; prominence in ethnic
dance field, 215n4; role in 1947 Dalia
Festival, 141–43
Kalmar, Ivan, 16, 107
Kan (Here), 196n16
Karmiel Dance Festival, 7, 180, 181, 185, 189n24,

217n32; 2008, 178

Karni, Y., 26, 67

Katriel, Tamar, 177

Kerobez, 42, 200n79

Kesari, Uri, 122, 127, 156–58; "Mi-Esther ad Esther" (from Esther to Esther), 30–36, 37, 120

Ketuvim, 50, 101

Kibbutz Dalia, 7, 133, 215n1; Shavuot Festival, 133, 137; view of, 1947, *134. See also* Dalia Folk Dance Festivals

Kibbutz Ein Harod, 133, 137, 139; *halutzot* working in the field, *39*

Kibbutz Ein Hashofet, 137; Shavuot pageant, 138

kibbutzim: best-known institution of socialist Zionism, 5, 17; festivals and holiday pageants, 14, 136; and myth of gender equality, 5; weakening of, 177

Kibbutz Ramat Hashofet, 137, 139

Kibbutz Tel Yosef, 139

Kipnis, Hanna, 67

Kirshenblatt-Gimblett, Barbara, 190n30

Kisch, Frederick H., 70

Klampt, Jutta, 106

Kol-noa, 30, 31

Kook, Rabbi Abraham Isaac, 9, 11, 45, 46

Koplewitz, Lilian Milwitzki, 205n24

krakoviaks, 139, 196n16

Kraus, Gertrud: *Davka*, 155; involvement in Dalia Festivals, 136, 138, 145, 146–47; and National Dance Competition, 102, 122; in *Night, 123*

Krofnik, Batya, 125–30, 211n18

Laban, Rudolf von, 102, 104, 136

Laban technique, 106

labor Zionism: and concert dance, 101; emphasis on worker, 17; father of, 155; and folk dancing, 135, 158–59; political dominance, 17, 194n88; and transformative potential of the land, 17, 64, 135, 137, 158–59. *See also* socialist Zionism

Lag b'Omer, 151, 152, 218n57

land: and differences between socialist and urban Zionists, 65; and folk dancing, 135,

150, 153, 158–59; and outdoor festivals, 14; transformative potential of, 17, 64, 135, 137, 158–59; *yedi'at ha'aretz* (knowledge of the land), 17

The Land of Promise (film), 193n79

League of Nations, 1

Lederman, Yaffa, 34, 36–37

Lelewer, Herman, 70

Le-Tzion, Rishon, 139

Levant Fair, Tel Aviv, 58, 204n4

Levensohn, Lotta, 26

Levi, Eliza Vizer, 102

Levin, Dania, 102, 106

Levinska, Miriam, 37, *41*, 43

Levinski, Yom-Tov, 151

Levinsohn, Avraham, 148–49, 161, 218n74

Levi-Tanai, Sara, 138, 139, 179

Lieberman, Tzvi, 36–37, 38

low culture: definition in theatrical dance, 99. *See also* high-low cultural dichotomy

Lubin, Arye, 197n23

Lufban, Yitzhak (pseud. A. Borrer), 49–50

Lupolianski, Uri, 183

Maccabees, 60–63, 72, 75, 204n9; "Hymn for the Maccabees," 76; as Maccabiah athletes were called, 80–84, 96

Maccabeus, Judas, 207n67

Maccabiah athletes: contrast to feminized image of Diaspora Jewish body, 9, 75–76; emphasis on blonde hair, 76; images of in posters, pamphlets, and advertisements, 76, *78*

Maccabiah Games, contemporary, 6

Maccabiah Games, first, 4, 7, 57–96; and aesthetic of defiance, 81–83, 176; and aesthetic of togetherness, 83–85; and aesthetic of toughness, 75–80, 176; Arab boycott of, 93–95; British support and participation, 58, 66, 92–93, 96; and conflict between socialist and urban Zionists, 59; connection with militarization, 80–81; construction of stadium, 66–*67*; and display of city of Tel Aviv, 65–67; and display of Jewish strength, 57; flag of, 70; grand march of

Maccabiah Games (*continued*)
national teams, 68, *69–70,* 206n44; and integration of culture and physical space of Tel Aviv, 66–67; interplay of Zionism and other nationalisms, 57, 68–69; and Jewish history and symbolism, 59–63; and major tensions of Yishuv culture, *58;* mass calisthenics, 3–85, 95, 208n79; modeled after modern Olympics, 57; official poster of, 76–79; opening and closing of, 68–72, *69, 70, 71;* organized in conjunction with Diaspora Jews, 57; parade, 68, *69;* politics of participation, 85–95; and promotion of Hebrew language and culture, 60, 67–68; and promotion of Jewish immigration, 63–65; rabbinic approval and support for, 89–92; religious-secular tensions, 89–92; selection of name, 61–63; socialist-bourgeois tensions, 85–89, 175; transformation of European event, 12, 58
Maccabiah Games, second, 96, 204n1, 205n25; British opposition to, 92, 96
Maccabi movement, 57, 73, 74, 95; and sports and militarization, 80–81
Maccabi World Union, 68, 70, 74–75, 82–83, 207n68; and negotiations about Hapoel's participation in games, 68, 85–88
Mahol Ha-goren, 139
mahol omanuti (artistic dance). *See* theatrical dance
Mailamm Jewish Musical Association of New York, 210n13
Many, Zemira, 199n63
Mapai, 163, 194n88
Marshall, Barak, 178, 179
Masada, 177
May Day, dance for, 150
Mayer, Tamar, 179
Mayim, Mayim (dance), 139, 150, 212n27
mazurka, 196n16
Mea Shearim, Jerusalem, 48
Megillat Rut (Story of Ruth), pageant of, Dalia Festival, 1944, 137, 138, *139, 140*
Mehola Dance Company, performance for dedication of Chords Bridge, 181, 183–84
Melchett, Lord, 69

Melman, Yossi, 180–81
Memorial Day. *See* Yom Hazikaron
menorah, 28, *33,* 177, 198n44
Meyuhas, Yosef, 34
Meyuhas-Polani, Chana, 28, 30, *34–36, 35,* 37, 40, 76, 199n63
The Mirror (Ornstein Sisters), National Dance Competition, 105, *106,* 212n26
Mishmar, 155
Mishmar li'Yeladim (Guard for Children), 155
Miss Israel contest, contemporary, 6
Mitzvah Dance (Dania Levin and Studio), National Dance Competition, 102
Mizrahi, Ovadia, 109
Mizrahim, 16, 99, 178, 190n37, 194n83
Mizrahi party, 162–63, *163,* 168–69
Mosse, George, 3, 13
The Mourner: A Woman Whose Art Is to Lament (Yardena Cohen), 107, *108,* 115
movement choirs, 136
Mugrabi Hall, Tel Aviv, 6, 67, 97, *98,* 103, 202n103, 210n1
muscle Jewry, 3, 8–9, 72–75; discourse of connected to German ideologies, 9; and goal of rebuilding of Jewish body, 72; image of, *10;* tied to national goals, 76–80
muscular Christianity movement, U.S., 11
Muskeljudentum. See muscle Jewry

N. (*Davar* journalist), 65, 93–94
Nadav, Rahel, *118,* 139, 170
Nadivi, Yehuda, 23
Naharin, Ohad, 182
Naiman, Y. M., 144, 145–46, 159, 161
Nardi, Nahum, 67
National Committee (Va'ad Leumi), 163
National Dance Competition, 4, 7, 97–131; aesthetic of fusion, 107, *108*–15, 128–31, 176; and central tensions of Yishuv, 97; critical challenges of structure and concept of event, 122–25; critics' judgment of public's choice of winners, 121–22; critics' ratings of dancing, 125–28; dances based on biblical themes, 107; distinctions between high and low art, 6, 12, 98–99; East-West dichotomy, 178; goal of finding authentic

Hebrew dance, 6, 97–98, 107; old-new dichotomy, 97–99; prize given to winner, 104, 211n20; socialist-bourgeois dichotomy, 120–25; spectators as judges, 120–21, 131; supervising committee, 211n18

Neve Tzedek neighborhood, Jaffa, 30, 42

"new" Jew: and folk dancing, 7, 158–59; and image of Palestine, 42; as new Hebrew, 12; and new Jewish physique, 3, 11, 32, 76, 175, 176

Nikova, Rina, 99, 102, 104, 127, 128, 139; critics' assessments of her work, 125, 127–28, 130; distinction between high and low art, 117; East-West dichotomy, 107, 116–20, 131; at Palestine Opera, *105; The Prophet's Sons,* 107, 118, *119*–20; *At the Well,* 118–19, 125

Noa (Ahinoam Nini), 179

Nordau, Max, 8–9, 72, 75, 85, 95, 208n72

Nosa, Sh., 161

Ohel-Shem Hall, Tel Aviv, 67, 102

Ohel Theater, 15, 99

old-new dichotomy, 11–15; and contemporary Israeli culture, 177; and folk dance, 147–52; and Maccabiah Games, 58, 59–63; and National Dance Competition, 97–99

Olmert, Ehud, 183

Orientalism, 194 n82. *See also* internal Orientalism

Ornstein, Margalit, 99, 101, 102, 104, 106, 138, 148

Ornstein Sisters (Shoshana and Yehudit), 104–5, 130; *Cain and Abel,* 102, 107; *Jepthah's Daughter* (Yehudit Ornstein and Studio), 105, 107; *The Mirror,* 105, *106,* 212n26; *Shevet Achim Gam Yachad* (Brothers Dwell Together) (Shoshana Ornstein and Studio), 105, 107; *Valor* (Shoshana Ornstein and Studio), 102, 105; *Waves,* 102, *103,* 105

Orthodox community, 13, 192n58; attack on Purim celebrations, 203n123; challenge of folk dances to traditional norms of, 135; disagreement with innovations of secular Zionists, 13, 14, 55, 192n59; increasingly greater role in public arena, 181; opposition to new Hebrew culture, 166–67; resolution

of religious issue in favor of Queen Esther competition in 1928, 47–48; and Sabbath controversy of 1947 Dalia Festival, 162–72; sports organization, 75; support for Maccabiah Games if religious observances were followed, 89–92; view of Queen Esther competition as abomination of Judaism, 45–49. *See also* ultra-Orthodox Jews

Orthodox Hebrew Community Council of Jaffa and Tel Aviv, 90–91

Orthodox rabbinate of Palestine, 45. *See also* Orthodox community

Oved, Margalit, 179

pageants, on the kibbutzim, 14, 136

Palestine: under British Mandate (*See* British Mandate); under Ottoman rule, 1, 12. *See also* Yishuv

Palestine Broadcasting Service, 15

Palestine Bulletin, 60, 66, 73, 75, 83–84

Palestine Opera, 15, 99, 104

Palestine Orchestra, 15, 102

Palestine Pavilion, Paris Exhibition, 1938, 127

Palestine Post, 121, 131, 138, 141, 148, 149–50

Palestine Singing Ballet. *See* Yemenite Ballet Company

Palestinian Arabs: and defense implications of Maccabiah Games, 81; participation in Dalia Folk Dance Festival, 1947, *142,* 143–44; political conflict with Jews, 19; protest of Maccabiah Games, 93–95; riots of 1929, 19, 44, 55, 72, 81, 176

Palucca, Gret, 102, 104, 105, 109

Passover fair, Rehovot, 12

Penslar, Derek, 16, 107

performance studies, 8

Pesach (Passover), 14

Pieterse, Jan Nederveen, 11, 191n49

Piltz, Ilza Gutman. *See* Gutman (Piltz), Ilza

Piltz, Shimon, 143, 146–47

Pines, Yehiel Michael, 34

Poland, immigration of Jews from in 1920s, 18

polkas, 139, 196n16

Presner, Todd, 9

professional dance. *See* theatrical dance

The Prophet's Sons (Rina Nikova and Yemenite Ballet Company), 107, 118, *119–20*

Purim: debate over transformation of and appropriate way to celebrate, 44, 55–56; as holiday of inversions, 22; in traditional Judaism, 22; Zionist transformation of, 5, 12, 13, 22–26

Purim, in Tel Aviv, 4, 58, 60; Adloyada Purim Parade, 5, 23, *24, 25*, 26, 61; adoption of street names to reflect Scroll of Esther, 26, 197n26; cancellation of parade in 1929, 45, 55, 176; central to Yishuv life, 5; contest to select new title for carnival, 26; costume balls, 5, 23, 27, 198n37; cultivation of joy, 25–26; dancing in the streets, 23; influence of European carnival practices, 23, 25; promotion of tourism, 5, 23; question of who had authority to change, 55–56. *See also* Queen Esther competitions

Queen Esther competitions, 4, 5, 7, 21–56; absence of image of *halutza*, 38; and aesthetic of defiance, 19–20, 21, 44–45, 55; and aesthetic of fusion, 5–6, 40–44, 55; canceled after 1930, 21–22, 45, 55; delegation of queen's reign, 28–29; election gala, 27, 199n67; incorporation of old and new, 27–29; Jewish symbolism of gifts given to queens, 28; longer lasting in Diaspora than in Palestine, 6, 201n95; and major cultural tensions of Yishuv, 21–22, 55; often held on Tu b'Shevat, 198n34; program for masquerade ball during Purim, 1929, *35*; socialist versus bourgeois views of, 38–40, 55; Tel Aviv municipal ceremony for, 27–28; tensions over appropriate role of Judaism in Yishuv, 44–54; and woman as nation, 21, 28, 29–36; women's bodies out of bounds of contest, 29–30

Queen Esther competitions, advocates of, 49–51; final effort to revive tradition in 1931, 53–54; response of Agadati to termination, 51–54; use of exaggerated language to defend, 50–51; view of as consistent with Jewish tradition and practice, 28, 49, 50

Queen Esther competitions, opposition to, 21–22, 46–49; use of exaggerated language and biblical references to oppose, 46; viewed as affront to socialist Zionism, 38–40; viewed as inconsistent with Jewish life, 46–47; viewed by religious leaders as abomination of Judaism, 47–49

Rabin, Yitzhak, 184

Rabinovitz, Alexander Ziskind, 46, 202n96

Rava, 26

Ravina, Menashe, 197n23

religious-secular dichotomy, 13–15, 19–20; in contemporary Israeli culture, 181–84; and Dalia Folk Dance Festivals, 162–72, 176; at early Zionist Congresses, 192n59; and Maccabiah Games, 89–92; and Queen Esther competitions, 21–22, 46–54, 176

Remez, David, 163

Reuben, Reuben, 197n23

Reuveni, Gideon, 80–81

Rikud Habe'er, 139

Rishon Le-Tzion, 74

Rivlin, Avraham, 84–85

Rokeach, Israel, 66

romantic nationalism, 136, 158

rondo, 196n16

Rosenfeld, Alexander, 205n33

Rosh Hashanah, 13

Rössler, Tehilla, 102, 105–6, 129–30

Russian festivals, 3

Sabbath controversy, Dalia Folk Dance Festival, 1947, 162–72; creation of fissure between secular and religious communities, 171–72; non-Orthodox response, 167–70; Orthodox protest, 165–67; prevalence of Orthodox view at 1951 Dalia Festival, 171–72

sabra, 179, 180

Said, Edward, 194n82

salon dancing, 18

Samburski, Menachem, 94

Sanhedrin, 62

Saposnik, Arieh B., 12, 187n3

Schatz, Boris, 15

Schweig, Shmuel, 187n1
Schweiger, Yitzhak: "Dayenu be 'esther hamalka'" (Enough of "Queen Esther"), 38–39
second intifada, 181
Second Zionist Congress, Basel, 8
secular Zionism. *See* socialist Zionism
Sefer hamaccabiah, 209n105
Seminar Hakibbutzim, 136, 137
Sephardim, 16, 178, 194n83
Shacharit le-yeladim, 26
Shankar, Uday, 108–9
Shapira, Yeshayahu, 136
Shavuot, 14; *bikkurim,* 14, 137, 151; and folk dancing festivals, 133, 137, 138–39, 150
sheep-shearing festival, 14
Sheinfeld, Niv, 180
sherele, 139
Shevet Achim Gam Yachad (Brothers Dwell Together) (Shoshana Ornstein and Studio), National Dance Competition, 105, 107
Shifman, Yaakov, 197n23
Shir Ha-shirim (The Song of Songs), Dalia Folk Dance Festival, 1944, 139
Shlonsky, Abraham, 158, 197n30
Shriah (journalist), 121, 122, 123–24, 125, 126–27, 129–30, 150, 162, 214n70
Shulchan Aruch, 48
Shushan, 22
Shwartz, Baruch, 170
Silman, K. (Kadish Yehuda), 61, 62
Simchat Beit Hasho'eva ceremony, 150
Sixth Zionist Congress, Basel, 187n6
socialist-bourgeois dichotomy, 175; and contemporary Israeli culture, 177–78; and Maccabiah Games, 58–59, 85–89; and National Dance Competition, 120–25; and Queen Esther competitions, 38–40, 55
socialist Zionism, 13; call for society without status and rank, 18; competing strains of, 188n14; and Dalia Folk Dance Festivals, 135, 158–59; discontent with Queen Esther competitions, 38–40, 55; emphasis on agricultural labor, 17, 65; emphasis on collective, 17; emphasis on outdoor festivals, 13–14; ideals of equality, sharing,

and unity, 18, 158; invention of new ways of celebrating holidays, 13–14; and the kibbutz, 5; political dominance of in Mandate era, 17; romantic images of the rural, 18; shift in hierarchy of traditional Jewish holiday calendar, 13; shift of power away from God to strength of Jewish people, 13; transformation of Purim, 5, 12, 13, 22–26; use of *bourgeois* in derogatory manner, 18; yielding of authority to rabbinic leaders, 14–15. *See also* socialist-bourgeois dichotomy
Sokolow, Nahum, 11–12, 67
Song of Fate (Mary Wigman), 111–12, *113*
The Sorceress: A Magician and Fortune Teller in Biblical Times and Today (Yardena Cohen), 107, 111–*12*, *113*, 115
sound films, 16
sports: in Europe, 74; and militarization, 80–81; in Yishuv, 73 (*See also* Maccabiah Games; Maccabi World Union)
Star of David, 28, 76, *79*
Stoeltje, Beverly, 29
Sturman, Rivka, 138, 139, 150; *Ha-goren,* 138, 196n16; *Hey Harmonika,* 150
Suez Canal, 19
Sukkot (Festival of Booths), 14, 150
Suzanne Dellal Center for Dance and Theater, Tel Aviv, 7
Szold, Henrietta, 63, 80

tango, 18
Tarfon, Rabbi, 50, 51, 203n112
Tchelebi-Lazar, Sarah, 199n63
tcherkessia, 139, 196n16
Tcherkov, Lilia, 28, 30, *31*
Tchernichovsky, Saul, 104, 119
Technion University, 15
Tel Aviv: anniversaries of in 1929 and 1934, 12; art museum, 15; cultural and economic center of Yishuv during Mandate period, 5; division of public and private space by 1920s, 45; expansion of, 17–18; movement of visual arts center from Jerusalem to, 15; naming of, 11–12; postcard promoting city as center of Hebrew culture, *58*;

Tel Aviv (*continued*)
preparations to host first Maccabiah Games, 65–69, 205n23; use of Maccabiah Games to present positive image of the Yishuv, 64
Tel Hai, 12
Tenai, Shlomo, 156
Ten Commandments, 28
theatrical dance: aim to connect to Middle East, 100; artistic process, 107–20; creating, 99–106; defined, 97; efforts to develop authentic Hebrew style, 107; efforts to distinguish from folk dance, 98; goals of originality and authenticity, 97–99; influenced by European dance, 100–101. *See also* National Dance Competition
Tordis, Elinor, 104
Toscanini, Arturo, 15
Trumpeldor, Yosef, 12
Tryster, Hillel, 193n79
Tsabari, Tsipora, 28, 32–34, *33*, 40–43, *41*, 44, 47–48, 153, 200n78, 202n102
Tu b'Av, 150, 151, 218n57
Tu b'Shevat (Arbor Day), 14, 150
Turnen (German gymnastic movement), 9, 72

ultra-Orthodox Jews, 192n58; exemption from army service, 181; protest against performance of Batsheva Dance Company, 182–83; protest against performance of Mehola dance troupe, 183–84; sermon against selection of Queen Esther, 48–49
U.N. Special Committee on Palestine (UNSCOP), 140, 141
urban Zionism, 17, 18, 38, 55, 59, 65, 120, 131. *See also* socialist-bourgeois dichotomy
Uri, Ya'akov, 151, 168, 169, 200n121
Ussishkin, Menahem, 46, 47, 202n99
Uziel, Ben-Zion Meir Hai, 47, 69, 89–90, 165, 209n105

Valor (Shoshana Ornstein and Studio), 102, 105
Vayehi Or (And There Was Light), Dalia Folk Dance Festival, 1947, *157*, 158
A Village Dance: Debka (Yardena Cohen), National Dance Competition, 115

visual arts, movement of center of from Jerusalem to Tel Aviv after 1929, 15

waltz, 18
Wandervogel youth association, 136
Wauchope, Arthur, 69, 70, 92
Waves (Ornstein Sisters), National Dance Competition, 102, *103*, 105
The Wedding Dance (Yardena Cohen), National Dance Competition, 112, *114*, 115
Wein, Chaim, 64, 205n22
Western Wall, Jerusalem, 177; Orthodox delineation of how Jews are permitted to pray at, 181, 221n19
Wigman, Mary, 102, 105–6, 109, 111–12; *Song of Fate*, 111–12, *113*
Wilk, Richard, 29
Women of the Wall, 221n19

Yair, A., 86
Yarkon River, 66
yedi'at ha'aretz (knowledge of the land), 17
Yedid, Eliyahu, 109
Yedidya, Ben Tzion, 100–101, 121
Yedi'ot Aharonot, 156, 161
Yedioth Tel Aviv (Tel Aviv News), 49
Yekutieli, Yosef, 59, 60, 61, 63, 74, 81, 90, 204n9
Yemenite Ballet Company, 102, 104, 116–17, 153; and Dalia Folk Dance Festivals, 145; *Dance of the Guards*, 117–18; *Debka*, 118; *The Prophet's Sons*, 107, 118, *119*–20; *At the Well*, *118*–19, 125
Yemenite dance, 152–53, 218n73
Yemenite Jews: both belittled and viewed as authentic, 16; participation in 1928 Purim parade, 43; pride in selection of Tsipora Tsabari as Queen Esther, 41–43; selection of Yemenite queen in subsequent years, 43–44, 201n88
Yishuv: building of embodied public culture, 1–3, 175–84; connecting to Middle East (*See* East-West dichotomy); debate over propriety of holding celebrations during difficult times (*See* aesthetic of defiance); development of football in 1920s by British, 92–93; export of festivals to

Jewish Diaspora, 4; and Hebrew cultural aesthetics, 4–20; ideal of unity, 18, 158; ideology and daily life, 8; interrelationship between city and kibbutz, 5; inventing of traditions, 3, 11–15; negotiation of shared meaning, 3; new cultural developments, 15–17; political conflict between Jews and Arabs, 19

Yom Ha'atzmaut (Independence Day), 1, 180–81, 184

Yom Hazikaron (Memorial Day), 177, 180–81, 184

Yom Kippur (Day of Atonement), 13, 29

Yom Tel Hai (Tel Hai Day), 12

Zefira, Bracha, 67

Zeresh (wife of Haman), 51

Zerubavel, Yael, 60

Zionism: and concept of transformation, 3; embraced both new and old aspects of culture, 11; rhetoric and concepts, 64. *See also* Labor Zionism; socialist Zionism; urban Zionism

Zionist congresses in Europe, 3; Fifth Zionist Congress, Basel, 187n6; religious-secular dichotomy, 192n59; Second Zionist Congress, Basel, 8; Sixth Zionist Congress, Basel, 187n6

Zionist Executive, 45

Zionist youth movements, Germany. *See* Wandervogel youth association

Zot hi ha'aretz (This Is the Land) (film), 27, 193n79

About the Author

Nina S. Spiegel is the Rabbi Joshua Stampfer Associate Professor of Israel Studies at Portland State University. She holds a PhD in history from Stanford University, and her articles have appeared in publications such as *Jewish Cultural Studies, Jewish Folklore and Ethnology Review,* and *Rethinking History: The Journal of Theory and Practice.* She has also served on the board of directors of the Congress on Research in Dance.

CPSIA information can be obtained
at www.ICGtesting.com
Printed in the USA
FSHW022105241121
86393FS